The Manufactured Home
Buyer's Handbook

The Manufactured Home Buyer's Handbook

Wes Johnson

McFarland & Company, Inc., Publishers

Jefferson, North Carolina, and London

LIBRARY OF CONGRESS CATALOGUING-IN-PUBLICATION DATA

Johnson, Wes, 1960–
    The manufactured home buyer's handbook / Wes Johnson.
      p.   cm.
    Includes index.

    ISBN 0-7864-2209-2 (softcover : 50# alkaline paper)

    1. House buying — United States.   2. Prefabricated houses —
United States.   I. Title.
    HD255.J59   2005
    643'.12 — dc22   2005012765

British Library cataloguing data are available

On the cover: sample floorplan *(detail);* modular home
(courtesy Manufactured Housing Institute)

Manufactured in the United States of America

McFarland & Company, Inc., Publishers
  Box 611, Jefferson, North Carolina 28640
  www.mcfarlandpub.com

To my wife, Amy

Acknowledgments

First and foremost, I want to thank my soulmate, Amy, for teaching me the true meaning of love and teaching my heart to sing. Who knew that angels rode motorcycles? Thanks to my mother who, despite her own tribulations in life, found time to encourage and support me in times when I needed it most. I'd like to thank my best friend, John Catoe; John always offered intelligence when the world seemed bereft of it, humor when nothing else would suffice, and most of all steadfast friendship through many years. I'd also like to thank Randy and Mac — they could not have been closer brothers had we shared the same blood — and my uncle, Don. The latter three may be lost to this earth but they will always live on in the hearts of those who loved them. Finally, I'm grateful for the grace of God — who for some reason saw fit to keep me alive despite my best efforts to the contrary — for allowing me to slowly learn from my mistakes and my misfortunes, for granting me some modicum of intelligence, or when that intelligence failed me for providing me with some measure of providence. Oddly enough, the latter often came just when it was least expected and often came in the guise of one of the aforementioned persons. What are we but words and dreams, and what is the meaning of life if not our relationships with others? So for this book (my words) and the next (my dream) and all the exceptional people who have made my life abundant and meaningful (unfortunately there are so many that space prohibits my mentioning them), I'm grateful and blessed.

Table of Contents

Preface

Perhaps few earthly possessions are seen in the same light as manufactured homes. There is a level of misunderstanding and stigma regarding them which the manufactured housing industry in no small way has brought upon itself. I had a very close friend who for years literally refused to come to my home. The reason? Because of financial considerations, I lived in a single-wide mobile home in the country at the time. Although it was fairly modern and roomy given that I lived there alone, it made my friend experience abysmal discomfort because it reminded her of growing up in a "trailer." The very act of walking inside was traumatic for her — it brought back memories of how other people made her feel because she had once lived in one. Does that seem ridiculous? Look at the portrayals of "trailer park trash" in society and on television. It's one of the last stereotypes that people feel free to fling about in our politically correct society.

This image has resulted in part from the years of substandard housing that many manufacturers produced. I've seen and heard just about every complaint around: people literally falling through cheap floors, windows and doors that will never completely shut, constant water leaks (and the resulting damage), homes burning down to ashes in five minutes because of inferior wiring, homes being ripped apart during storms.... Fortunately, quality has improved prodigiously because of newer Department of Housing and Urban Development (HUD) standards for manufactured housing. Now, flooring often features a 25 year warranty and is not as prone to water damage as it once was. Studies have also shown that modern manufactured houses are *less* likely to catch on fire than their site-built counterparts. During a recent hurricane in Florida (Charley), manufactured homes built after 1994 showed remarkable wind resistance, while older ones were often torn to shreds. There are still many quality issues that potential buyers need to be aware of, however, and this book will help you find those problems and have them fixed properly so that your family's health and pocketbook remain intact. Most consumers still report at least one major problem with their manufactured home, and often there are defects that consumers don't know about because they don't know what to look for — or because the damage is hidden inside their walls, their ceiling cavities, or underneath their homes. With this book as a guide, consumers can avoid trouble before it occurs or remedy it to their satisfaction after the fact.

The manufactured housing industry also inadvertently feeds a negative stereotype of itself because of the tactics its salespeople employ. Take every trick a used car salesperson ever had and then multiply the total exponentially — that should give you an approximate understanding of what goes on at the dealer lots which are strewn across the country by the thousands. Dealerships foster a culture in which whatever makes the sale is encouraged, and outright lying is the norm. *The Manufactured Home Buyer's Handbook* gives you a good idea of the tactics the potential home buyer may face, and it gives the consumer counter responses to keep from being at a disadvantage. Readers will learn how to fight fire with fire, getting the homes they really want without paying thousands of extra dollars for inflated options or bogus fees. The current reality is that buyers turn to manufactured housing for economic reasons, but they often get "soaked," paying far too much for the home and the setup. Then they are sometimes swindled again by being verbally assured of one thing when the fine print of a lengthy contract states otherwise. Many trusting customers end up paying just as much as site-built owners do. The moral is that what seems like a bargain isn't always a bargain.

Manufactured home consumers have also traditionally been charged far too much for insurance and loan interest. The insurance problem remains difficult to totally overcome, but in the area of financing, options are often now available that allow careful shoppers to secure truly competitive loan rates. This important subject is covered in detail because the average manufactured home buyer can save literally tens of thousands of dollars by choosing and managing the loan wisely. Methods for shaving years off your mortgage will be discussed, along with the loans to avoid. "Dealership financing" has resulted in record levels of repossessed homes, and you don't want to be another statistic in this category.

This book also focuses heavily on energy efficiency. "Mobile homes" used to be notorious for wasting heating and cooling energy, but now there are a lot of energy efficient options to select from in many cases. This goes hand in hand with saving the consumer money, but it's also important for the country as a whole in these economic and resource-depleted times. In fact, our nation could save $134 billion in the next 15 years alone if all residential windows were replaced with Energy Star models! Energy efficiency may cost a little more initially, but in the long run it's a win-win proposition for everyone. In general, options are often overlooked in regard to manufactured homes. Many people don't realize that to a large degree you can custom order your home with the construction features you want. For as little as a few hundred or a few thousand dollars, you can make your manufactured home a much more gratifying place to live — a place that truly fits your lifestyle.

There is yet one more important emphasis this book offers that has typically been missing in the treatment of the subject by other authors— the *setup* of the manufactured homes. Even if a new manufactured home arrives in excellent shape, mistakes in the foundation and setup can spell premature doom for it. Settling, water damage, and more can literally destroy your home — and in most cases they *won't be covered under warranty*. Dealers, as a rule, brag about their setup people being the "best in the business." The truth is, there is a wide spectrum of setup workers from the very good to the very, very bad. The only way to guarantee a good setup is for consumers to know what to look for and verify it's done right themselves.

As you can see from the preceding discussion, times have changed greatly for the manufactured housing industry in recent years. For the most part, the changes should be welcomed by the families who live in such homes or those who are shopping for a manufactured home. Manufactured housing, even in the worst of times, thrived because it was a needed economical alternative for many people. Now, as the quality and list of available options have grown, these homes are increasingly being considered and purchased by many families who could easily finance site-built homes. If you can get a comparable home for a fraction of the cost, why not?

There are still many potential pitfalls for manufactured home buyers, but you can get a good deal on a great home if you are careful and take charge of the process. Here are the most effective strategies I've found and the crucial knowledge about the industry you need to take control. Hopefully, *The Manufactured Home Buyer's Handbook* will also serve as a modest impetus to help bring about change in this industry. The final chapter is addressed to legislators as well as consumers because this is a business sector that needs to be overhauled in many respects. As the book points out, those government agencies that are supposed to be protecting manufactured homeowners are failing miserably. There are millions of residents who live in these homes, and millions more will. At the current overall rate of growth, in the near future over 25 percent of voters will live in manufactured housing. More consumers need to use their voices and their votes to change the system. The book's conclusion describes several changes that would be a tremendous boon to manufactured home buyers and a giant step toward erasing the negative stereotype associated with these homes and the industry at large.

In effect, *The Manufactured Home Buyer's Handbook* is a tale about two aspects of the same story: an industry which has struggled mightily with quality and respectability, yet one which still holds out the promise of providing "dream homes" to housing consumers. To those who would charge that this book is too negative, I respond that it is the product of a great deal of research and of having lived through the process of buying and setting up a manufactured home myself. It serves the purpose of allowing home buyers to actually realize their dreams without the accompanying nightmares which have followed the sales of many manufactured homes.

Introduction

With the average cost of a new home in the United States reaching $250,000 in 2003 (Consumer Reports, "*Housewrecked*," (*http://www.con-sumerreports.org/*), there are a lot of people who simply cannot afford the payments that come along with the American dream. Prices are also continuing to rise vigorously in most markets, buoyed on burgeoning increases in home sales. According to the National Association of Realtors, in the past year alone home prices increased an average of 7 percent, while many areas registered double-digit gains. (The Northeast saw costs soar 16.7 percent.) Home prices were predicted to rise again over 5 percent in 2003. However, many home buyers have found an alternative that they can afford — manufactured housing. Built in manufacturing facilities around the country and then delivered to dealerships which can now be found everywhere as well, these homes often provide a cost-efficient solution for people on a budget. The cost per square foot is dramatically lower than for site-built homes (usually in the range of 33 percent and up to 50 percent less for basic models), so you can afford a much larger home for your money if you need space. Even if your budget isn't constrained, the many tens of thousands of dollars you can save does represent an attractive alternative for many consumers.

Approximately 10 percent of United States citizens now live in manufactured housing according to bankrate.com, and that number is rising. Many regions boast higher numbers — in South Carolina, for instance, the 2000 U.S. census data indicates 20 percent of all homes are manufactured. Roughly 20 percent of new homes sold in the United States in 2002 were built in factories and then shipped out to dealerships. Despite the manufactured housing industry having been in what they describe as a "correction mode" (which might more accurately be termed a serious "slump" to the casual observer; the industry shipped fewer homes in 2002 than any other year since 1963), one of the largest manufacturers, Champion

5

Enterprises, Inc., which has 39 manufacturing plants and hundreds of retail outlets across the country, estimated the industry as a whole would still sell over 200,000 homes in 2002 alone. That's down from 348,000 homes in 1999. Clayton Homes, Inc., is another large company in the industry. While it only has 20 manufacturing facilities, it has even more company-owned and independent retailers than Champion. Even though Clayton's sales fell off by about 50 percent in 2001/2002 (from over 30,000 units in fiscal year 2000), they still sold about 20,000 homes in 2002 and have been able to remain profitable through the industry's contraction mode according to the *Los Angeles Times'* Jesus Sanchez. Most companies are also beginning to see the light at the end of the tunnel—customer traffic and sales are starting to pick up. Current trends in manufactured housing financing and the prevailing low interest rates are likely to spur this trend along at a faster pace. For the first time, the major banks are offering traditional mortgages for manufactured homes at competitive rates. Furthermore, interest rates for 30 year fixed mortgages as of February 2005 are still hovering near their lowest point in 45 to 50 years (although the Federal Reserve has been raising interest rates for the last few quarters, mortgage rates have actually fallen so far in 2005 after climbing somewhat in 2004). Surplus factory capacity and a flourish of repossessed homes have also combined to suppress prices. The bottom line is that right now, you can get an exceptionally nice home for a very affordable price. More and more Americans are finding themselves considering — and buying — these homes once again. The economic climate is perfect for manufactured housing to soar back to its heyday, when over one in three of new homes sold were manufactured units. For evidence of this upward trend, look no further than the fact that the financial guru Warren Buffet decided to purchase Clayton Homes, Inc., in April 2003 (according to the *Los Angeles Times*) for $1.7 billion as well as finance troubled Oakwood Homes Corporation. If Warren Buffet thinks the manufactured home industry is a good investment, that's a pretty reliable indicator of future growth. The big three companies in the industry were Champion, Fleetwood, and Clayton in that order. Recently, and no doubt due to Mr. Buffet's interests in troubled Oakwood (Oakwood ranked fourth in sales), Clayton Homes acquired Oakwood and leap-frogged to the number one position. For an enlightening and entertaining account of the takeover of Clayton's Tennessee empire, read Jennifer Reingold's article "The Ballad of Clayton Homes," *Fast Company*, Issue 78, January 2004, page 76. You can find it online at *www.fastcompany.com/magazine/78/claytonhomes.html*.

The financial attractiveness of manufactured housing is actually how this book came about, albeit on a somewhat lesser scale than the one Mr.

Buffet was envisioning. My wife and I needed a housing solution, and payments in the $500 to $600 dollar range looked a lot better than the $1,000 plus category. We found, however, that there are other costs involved in dealing with the manufactured housing industry, some of which are truly daunting. We thought of ourselves as educated consumers, and we researched and did our homework for over a year before we finally decided on and purchased a home. It was a beautiful 2,400 square foot floor plan, all for under $100,000. Make no mistake, there are some attractive and well-built manufactured homes out there. Just ask Governor Mike Huckabee of Arkansas—who moved into a triple-wide "mobile mansion" donated to the state by Champion Enterprises, Inc., for 18 months while his "other" mansion was being renovated. By all accounts (including First Lady Janet Huckabee's, who gave media tours of it), the $110,000 home was an outstanding residence. In fact, the first lady of Arkansas graciously consented to provide a quote for this book: "Our stay in a manufactured home was nothing short of wonderful. It was a perfect solution for a very unique and difficult situation. We wouldn't hesitate to stay in a manufactured home again." The truth is, *most* people who choose to live in manufactured housing end up largely satisfied with their decision to purchase one. (Over 80 percent are satisfied, as we'll see in the chapter "Final Analysis.")

One thing any useful book about manufactured housing should do is address some faulty preconceptions. Some people think that most manufactured homes are small and cramped, that they are mostly found in warmer climates, or that most inhabitants are retirees or single-parent families on a budget. None of these impressions are necessarily true. Since we're at the beginning of our journey, and since you're most likely wondering if a manufactured home might be a good fit for you, let's look at the actual demographics. Most of these figures are culled from the Manufactured Housing Institute's production numbers and from Foremost Insurance Company data (2002), which is derived from routinely conducted surveys in this market. Of industry home shipments, 80 percent are now multisection units, which can be quite roomy. The largest manufactured home markets are found in Texas, Florida, California, and North Carolina (in that order). What may be more surprising is that even in an industry slump, demand is up in such states as Connecticut, Alaska, California, and Washington. States like Pennsylvania, Michigan, and Ohio all have hundreds of thousands of households living in manufactured homes. Over half of owners of manufactured homes are currently married (56 percent) and employed full time (55 percent). The average household size is 2.3 people. While the median income for such homeowners is approximately $29,000, a substantial minority (17 percent) make over $50,000 a year. (Eleven percent have a net worth of over $250,000 and 4 percent have a net worth over $500,000). Almost as many executives and professionals live in manufactured homes as laborers, and 47 percent have some college education; 29 percent of owners of manufactured homes see their home as a relatively temporary residence (planning to live there less than five years), but 57 percent plan to always live there. If there is a trend here, it's that more than ever before, manufactured home owners are a reflection of society as a whole. There is no stereotype that adequately fits this group of consumers. A very diverse array of people in many different regions have decided that manufactured housing makes sense for them.

So we see that the economic equation has enticed a wide variety of consumers in various regions and that many of these customers have no regrets. If the story ended there, you wouldn't need this book. There remain a sizable number of customers who were turned off or taken in by the customary sales process. Unfortunately, we also found we had many lessons yet to learn *after* we signed our 30-year contract. That's a terrible time for new surprises, especially bad ones. Many of those satisfied customers mentioned previously still had at least one major problem with their new home, and many had more than one (*Consumer Reports*, 1998). Numerous other customers who reported being content with their new homes have serious problems lurking in the interior structure of which they are unaware simply because they didn't know what to look for or because they weren't present when the home was set up. So we wanted to warn other consumers and help them avoid the pitfalls we found. Unless you are a VIP, you probably won't have your home donated to you, and you may need some help dealing with what can be some genuinely difficult issues before the sale, during negotiations, throughout the setup, and after you've moved in.

Last year, we spoke with the president of one of the major manufacturers to complain about how his dealerships had misrepresented their products. We had written him a letter, and he personally called us to say he was "very embarrassed" about what happened to us while we were shopping for a home. He told us it was a "shame" that the salespeople were the way they were, but that was the state of the "industry as a whole." (The consummate salesman, however, he turned this around into a pitch by saying they were going to make it up to us with a "special" interest rate he wrangled just for us if we would give his company another try. The "special rate" turned out to be 9.9 percent, the exact deal everyone who walked in off the street was getting at that time. It was also 3 percent higher than the current bank rate for the same loan.) The president also offered us what he promised would be a very attractive price (and it was), but then the company made up for it by attempting to charge us almost $20,000 just to "set up" the new home. (We declined his not-so-generous offer.) In essence, it was business as usual, and none of them are about to change their ways. We searched scores of dealerships from a half dozen different manufacturers, and the routine looked similar. If you go this route, and many people almost have to if they want a new home, be aware that you are swimming with sharks, and they think you are their next meal. They don't care about you or your needs— their one goal is to make as much money as possible. They will use every trick and tool at their disposal. The good news is that you can get out alive if you are extremely careful, and you might even be able to own that "dream home" you were promised for payments you can live with, too.

You will have to be your own guardian, however. Many customers think the local building inspector will catch any problems or are convinced by a dealer they are fully protected by a guarantee. The local building inspector in most cases only checks a few basic setup elements like piers, underpinning, where the electrical power meets the home, and where the plumbing enters the earth. You have to be concerned with much more. Furthermore, manufactured homes are governed by HUD (the Department of Housing and Urban Development) and federal law. As we were told by our local HUD office, "Good luck getting anyone down from Washington." (The exception here is a subset of manufactured homes referred to as "modular" homes. These are more expensive factory-built homes which are constructed to local building code standards. Modular homes ship when they are about 90 percent complete, versus typical manufactured homes which arrive 98 percent complete.) As far as guarantees are concerned, a typical guarantee for setup is 90 days, while the home itself might be protected for a year. Even serious problems might not reveal themselves until after that time. A lot of dealerships have been known to leave their customers hanging after the setup crews leave even when the problems show up sooner. A search of consumer complaint archives found that some dealers and manufacturers refused to fix problems for *years* until they were publicized on local television stations. It's a safe bet that a lot of people just gave up complaining and lived not so happily forever after. So you will have to be proactive and vigilant.

As you may have noted by now, the subject of this book is largely about integrity — or the lack thereof in this industry. When we finally selected a dealership to buy our home from, we were made a lot of promises about how they had the *best* homes, would make *every* customer happy, and would fix *any* problems that arose. They even playfully chided us as a best friend might for being so inquisitive about the manufacturing process and construction of our new home. (That isn't how they talked to us later.) We were also informed repeatedly in no uncertain terms our local dealer had some of the best delivery and setup people in the business. The profuse tributes to each other among the various work crews began to make us smile knowingly after a while. (In actuality, the company who first set up our home wasn't even licensed to do business in the state, and the owner's young child was crawling under our home before it was properly supported. The child was even allowed to walk unsupervised all over the roof, standing on the edges 15 feet off the ground in places.) You need to remember: everything is for a reason, and the pitch never ends until they leave your property. We were left with no less than three separate bent areas in our frame by the "best" in the business, which produced bulges in our floors and walls. Vents were knocked off our home during delivery, and despite the fact we repeatedly told the dealership's general manager and the setup people about this problem, they refused to properly cover up the holes for over a month. By then, rain had poured in through our new ceiling and formed a small pond on our kitchen floor. Within a couple of weeks, the ceiling began to split apart in the wet areas. Don't forget the top of the food chain — the factory. We paid for R-28 insulation in our roof, which would have been 9.43" of rock wool insulation. The factory had paperwork to "prove" we received that, too. What we actually received was *3" to 4" of cellulose insulation* on average, with some areas which had *no* insulation. The actual R-value was probably approximately a factor of 10 or less. The factory claimed it was a "fluke" (just as they did when the tongue fell off our new home during delivery, dropping it on the highway—causing more problems). The general manager of the local dealership claimed all the mistakes were "bad karma." The setup folks said they were just glad to see us in the rear view mirror.

You can draw your own conclusions, but I would like to say this: so many things went wrong in our home (purchased from the Manufactured Housing Institute's "Manufacturer of the Year" for the previous four years in a row) that there is no possibility they were all chance occurrences. Furthermore, in doing research for this book I have heard from and read accounts of many other manufactured home owners from nearly every brand home and virtually every region of the country who have their own horror stories. This problem is truly industrywide. Even though we tried to be as careful as possible the first time around, we had to force the company to deliver us another home. Even then, the problems continued — the dealer and the manufacturer made many of the same mistakes on the substitute home that they did on the first one (and some new ones).

Manufactured homes aren't necessarily what they used to be. This is a picture of the interior of Champion's 2002 Genesis® model, the "Bainbridge." These homes are sold direct to builders and developers and are targeted directly at the relatively affluent and growing baby boomer market. The company has ten factories dedicated to this model. Although this line represented 10 percent of their sales volume last year, it represented 15 percent of Champion's total manufacturing revenues. (Courtesy Champion Enterprises, Inc.)

Information is your best weapon because ignorance is only bliss when you don't have to live in it. Here is your information!

This book is also about saving money on your initial purchase and in operating expenses for many years down the road. Buying a home is a lot like entering a financial minefield, and this can be especially true for manufactured homes because of the nature of the industry. Many unscrupulous dealers turn what is supposed to be an economical housing alternative into a financial disaster for the unsuspecting. Throughout the book, financial and economical alternatives will be stressed, and guidance will be offered on how to get the absolute best deal for your money.

It's worth adding that buying a home — whether or not it's built in a factory — will likely be among the weightiest stressors a person is likely to face in life. (Although here is another area where manufactured housing offers an advantage: on the acute to chronic scale, the manufactured housing alternative is closer to acute stress because manufactured homes can be delivered and set up in much less time than a traditional house can be built, thus abbreviating the potential agony.) Little wonder it's stressful;

few other decisions you make are going to have as much impact on your quality of life and happiness for the next few years— or next few decades. If it is a first home or if you don't have any experienced friends or relatives to help you with the ins and outs, the considerations you are apt to face can seem even more mind boggling. This book also strives to help prospective buyers navigate this maze as easily as possible, serving as a checklist of sorts as you go through the process so you won't make a major mistake or omission which can mean the difference between a happy home and a very expensive learning experience. We lived through it, and we want to help others avoid the pitfalls. After reading this text, you will be armed with strategies to use before, during, and after the purchase of your new home. These strategies will eliminate many potential problems before they occur and will help to give you the tools and leverage you need to satisfactorily take care of any other problems which arise. The dealer has a different agenda than you do and has his or her own time-tested arsenal of sales strategies. A dealer's unspoken agenda is not to have a "satisfied customer," it is to maximize profits at your expense. I intend not only to give you the tools to make it a fair fight, but to give *you* the competitive edge.

CHAPTER 1

Doing Your Homework

You may be looking for a new home because you're currently constrained in too small a house or spending too much money on an apartment with no equity to show for it. It could be that you need a living room to decorate your way, but your spouse really needs a den to be comfortable in. Maybe financial considerations or an economic downturn made it impossible to stay where you have been. Perhaps all of your appliances are simply worn out, so the ability to replace them all at once with a new mortgage makes it more financially pragmatic to finally purchase that new home you've been wanting. Your first consideration when planning to buy a home is determining your needs. These include space, floor plan, storage capacity, and extra features— things that are almost as individual and unique as you are.

It may help you to make a couple of lists. First, write down the things you absolutely have to have. Maybe you require three bedrooms, two baths, new kitchen appliances, a pantry, a fireplace, and a den large enough to accommodate that wraparound sofa unit you don't want to part with. Your list is probably going to be longer. You may find out at this point a manufactured house won't work for you. If a steeply pitched roof with attic access is critical, or if you really need a spiral staircase leading to your writer's garret, then a manufactured home probably isn't for you because such homes are more limited than site-built homes when it comes to many construction features. When you're done listing what you must have — and if a manufactured house is still an option —compose a second list consisting of what you would really *like* to have — a wish list of sorts. It's here that one of the really great advantages of a manufactured home can come in — a lot of options can be had for minimal investment. Oddly enough, this is also an advantage salespeople usually neglect to mention. You can add modern glass skylights for around $200 each or get a Jacuzzi-type tub for less than you could probably buy one at your local home improvement store (not including saving the installation costs). You have to be smart, however, so you should be flexible with your wish list and change it according to the willingness of the dealership to give you deals. The salesperson or manager does have a lot of margin to work with (20 percent to 25 percent profit is common), so read the next few chapters to learn how to get your best deal. On our wish list, for example, we wanted ceiling fans in almost every major room. We found out we could have each room "wired and braced" (also known as "fan prep") for ceiling fans from the factory at $25 each, which seems like a pretty good bargain. To include the fans, however, the salesperson wanted a whopping $200 each for fans which were not the best quality. So we went to our local home improvement store and picked up top-of-the-line fans with beautiful light kits and digital remote controls for less than $85 each.

Dealership markups to factory options add considerably to your cost—for instance, we found out individual dealers often nearly double their actual cost of kitchen appliance packages to pad their profits. In one case, one particular brand's manufacturing plants were running a summer "firecracker" special on appliance packages in which they were selling the deluxe kitchen packages to dealerships for $1,198. The dealer (not knowing we learned about the actual cost direct from the factory) then offered us this same set for $1,998 — a markup of roughly 67 percent. Being willing to go elsewhere for some products and services can sometimes save you hundreds or thousands of dollars. In another case, the factory was charging $535 for upgrading the standard insulation package, but a dealer told us the "factory" charged $1,200 more for that option (the identical home being built at the exact same plant)! In this latter case it's unlikely that hiring someone else to insulate your home would be feasible, but that $665 of extra profit for the dealer should give you more incentive to bargain hard. Keep in mind, too, that you are financing whatever you add to the house (unless you have a lot of money), so it will cost you much more in the long run than the initial amount. A rough rule of thumb is that for every dollar you finance, you will pay two more dollars in interest. The general idea is that it pays to be flexible. An important part of doing your homework is figuring out the least expensive way to create the home you want.

Wish lists may also have to be modified depending on which manufacturer you choose — some can incorporate features others can't, so ask what is available from the factory for each brand and model you are considering. Sample requirements and wish lists can be found in appendices A and B. You can use them as they are or modify them to suit your particular requirements. Finally, as you go through this book you should probably take out a legal pad and be taking additional notes on what applies to you. When you get into negotiations or when you are ordering your home, it will be a lot easier to remember something you have written down.

If you can meet your needs with a manufactured home, and if you think it might be a good alternative, then you should make sure it will meet with the local codes. In short, does your existing lot or subdivision allow a manufactured home, or can you relocate to a place that does? If you finance a land/home package through a dealer, this will largely take care of itself because the dealer will select a site which will accept their homes—although you still need to be diligent about the setup meeting code. More about this later. If you have an existing lot or have a piece of property in mind, then it will be up to you to find out about any code or subdivision requirements. Depending on the knowledge (and that usually is directly related to the dealer's proximity) a dealer has, you may need to convey these requirements to your potential dealer. You may be limited to double-wide models; you may have to have brick skirting; brick over a certain height may need lateral reinforcement on the back (it certainly should be reinforced at heights over 36″, whether required or not); certain types of piers may be required; the landings might have to be a certain size. There are a lot of considerations, and many will impact your ultimate home expense considerably. This can pose a financial hardship in some cases, but it will also usually ensure that you end up with a safer, more valuable home. For instance, brick skirting can easily add $2,500 to $4,500 to the cost of your home (it depends on the home size, average height off the ground, and area where you live), but the home will be much more attractive and will maintain its value longer. Here again, you need to be proactive throughout this process—for example, brick skirting really requires a perimeter footer (see the section on foundations), but virtually every one of the scores of dealers we spoke with insisted there was *no need* for a perimeter footer. You are your own protector, and one of the main reasons for doing your homework (and presumably buying this book) is to prevent problems before they really become problems. Knowledge truly is power.

Another extremely important preliminary consideration is energy efficiency and the programs your local power provider offers. The former is important in any case no matter what climate you live in — you will most likely be heating and/or cooling your new home for most months of the year, and this ongoing expense will largely depend on how efficient your insulation package is. Manufactured homes used to be notorious for their *inefficiency*, but times have changed a great deal. In our area of the country (South Carolina), which is known as "zone 2" on the HUD energy map, we have relatively mild winters and frequently hot summers. Here what's referred to as the Duke Power "standard" is generally considered to be an adequate option: R-30 in the ceiling, R-11 in the walls, and R-19 in the floor. (The state of South Carolina also uses this guideline for what it refers to as "energy efficient housing.") The R means "resistance to heat flow," and the higher the number, the lower your heating and cooling bills will be. Others (often dealers) will recommend lower or higher numbers. (For example, the North American Insulation Manufacturer's Association recommends R-30, R-15, R-19 in zone 2.) To determine the R values you need, look at what "zone" you will live in, what other requirements your area may have (government or power company), and what options manufacturers in your area offer. (The same manufacturer will typically vary options depending on where the home is sold and what your budget is.) For our area, the government's Home Energy Advisor (available at www.energystar.gov) indicates the typical yearly home-energy cost is $1,620, but the same home brought up to *energy efficient standards* (defined by the government as 30 percent more efficient than average) has an annual energy cost of $1,068. That's quite a savings, and in many areas it adds up to even more. For instance, in Pennsylvania, the typical cost is $1,892, but an energy efficient home only costs $1,019 to operate per year.

We had hoped to get R-30 in the ceiling, R-15 in the walls, and R-19 in the floor of our new home. We found the highest ceiling option, however, was R-28. This was OK because the standard floor insulation was R-21 and because of the way agencies measure insulation trade-offs. Higher insulation in one area makes up for a lower value elsewhere. In the wall, however, the standard insulation was only R-11. There were only two options for us in the brand and model home we chose — to upgrade to R-13 for another $110 or to upgrade our walls from 3.5" to 6" wide so R-19 insulation could be installed. This latter option added a whopping $900+ to the cost of the home. We went to the engineers at our electric cooperative so they could do some math for us (hopefully yours will be helpful, too) and found it would probably take over a decade for this option to pay for itself (or longer, considering it would be financed with interest). Specifically, they found that a home with our square footage and number of windows would cost approximately $70 more per year to heat and cool with R-11 as opposed to R-19 walls. We then decided on the inexpensive R-13 option, for more modest savings over the long run. Some manufacturers do offer (in some areas) an R-15 option for the walls, which is arguably the best solution for many parts of the country. We requested it but were told it wasn't available from the particular plant that built our house. It is (or should be) inexpensive because R-15 batts are readily available which fit inside standard 3.5" walls—and it is the wood which is the primary cost for R-19 walls (stud grade 2" × 4" boards cost a lot less than 2" × 6" boards). Remember, everything is a trade-off, so you should make the decision which makes the most sense for you.

Do your research based on the area where you live. In the north and even in the upper midwest, you will probably want to get as much insulation as possible in your new home. In each area of the country you will find different recommended standards and incentives. One such standard in the Pacific Northwest was the Super Good Cents program. It was somewhat like the Duke Power standard in the Carolinas, but at one time it qualified homeowners for a $3,500 rebate for buying an energy efficient manufactured home. Super Good Cents certification required R-33 in the ceiling, R-19 in the walls, R-22 in the floor, and a number of other features like Low-E (low emissivity) glass and insulating gaskets around wall outlets. Even though this particular program is now defunct, it still provides a good goal for homeowners who want to save money in the long run, especially in cooler climates.

Here are some suggested minimum R-values for the United States (see map on page 18).

Zone	Ceiling	Wall	Floor
1	19	11	11
2	30	13	19
3	30	15	19
4	38	19	21
5	38	21	21

The Clayton Homes "standard" insulation package for our area (zone 2 on both the HUD map and the map on the next page) is R-11, R-11, R-21. That paltry roof insulation is going to cost you a *lot* of money down the road. It could also cost you more than you know. Many power companies offer discounts for homes which are "energy efficient" if you can document your insulation values. This can save you more money every day. Before you buy, find out what options your utility company offers. Ours gives the lowest electricity rate they offer for homes which meet or exceed the Duke Power standard (although our provider is not affiliated with Duke), so that was on our "must have" list. If we had accepted the standard insulation package, we would not only be using many more kilowatts of electricity per year, we would be buying them at a higher rate. Your power company can also give you good advice about what insulation you might need in your area. As mentioned before, ours even did a free energy comparison of different insulation ratings for us. Your home dealer should give you a "Consumer Insulation Information" sheet which verifies the

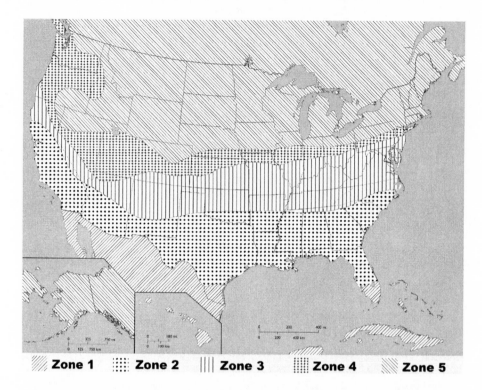

Zone 1   **Zone 2**   **Zone 3**   **Zone 4**   **Zone 5**

This map provides more accurate results than the three-zone map HUD uses.

insulation values in the three key areas (roof, walls, and floor) which you may need to bring to your utility company. (The best rate may also be tied to other factors as well — you may have to have perimeter heat ducts, a certain seasonal energy efficiency ratio [SEER] or efficiency rating on your air conditioner, etc. These latter type requirements are to your advantage, and I would highly recommend adding them to your wish list.) Your electric company may give you additional incentives, so find out what you need before you buy your home. Sometimes power utilities pay the consumer hundreds of dollars cash back for buying certain energy efficient water heaters or furnaces. Knowing what the requirements are in advance of buying your home can save you plenty. For instance, some customers are eligible for a $250 refund from the electric utility for something as simple as upgrading from a 40 gallon to a 50 gallon water heater — an upgrade which might only cost a few dollars at the dealership.

The savings can also be even more immediate. Some states (like South Carolina) encourage the purchase of energy efficient manufactured homes by offering tax incentives for homes which meet the standard (R-30, R-11,

R-19). Sales tax is limited to $300 (not counting tax on furniture and other items included which are not built-in) even if you purchase the home in another state and bring it in. This can be quite a savings. State sales taxes would have driven up the expenditures for our new home by an additional $5,550; however, because we ordered extra insulation, we paid $300 and saved $5,250. That more than paid for our added insulation. As in all other decisions, however, you have to protect yourself. The general manager of the lot where we purchased our home was in North Carolina and tried to charge us $600 in taxes, or $300 per section. Almost every quote we received in North Carolina used this same tactic. The law specifically states, however, the tax is per home — not per section. It took us several calls to the South Carolina state capitol to get the proof we needed to reduce our cost by $300. We had to bring a copy of the law to the dealership and give the manager a phone number to the state capitol to get him to charge the proper tax. Since dealers near the state line make these cross-state sales frequently, I suspect they already knew the law. We can't help but wonder who pockets that extra $300 such dealers seem to make on most all of their interstate sales.

Insulation does not end here, either. The government estimates the average household spends over 40 percent of its energy budget on heating and cooling costs (www.energystar.gov) and as much as 15 percent of your total energy bill could be eliminated by using Energy Star approved windows. In fact, our nation could save $134 billion in the next 15 years alone if all residential windows were replaced with Energy Star models. So you need to consider your windows, skylights, and doors as well. Energy efficient or Low-E windows are generally considered to be a good option if at all possible in whatever type of home you purchase. They can cost several hundred dollars extra (or over $1,000 on a large home), but most experts consider them worth the money. They not only help with insulation, these vinyl windows look better and are generally much easier to clean.

The typical industry option is a Low-E glass like the one AFG Industries makes. Low-E has a thin, invisible metallic coating which helps to block heat flow. In the summer, it deflects heat back outside, and in winter it redirects it back into the house. One of the nicest features of Low-E glass is that the coating raises the window's surface temperature on cold winter nights, so you don't feel as cold when standing or sitting near it. Low-E glass also helps block ultraviolet light so your furnishings and artwork don't fade so quickly. We paid for this option, and our U factor (heat retention) is supposed to be .38, which is great for the southern and mid–Atlantic states. The same window without this special coating has a

U factor of .48. Unlike R values, with U factors the lower the number, the more efficient the product.

It's likewise important to recognize that energy efficiency involves more than insulation; it's also about having energy- (and therefore, cost-) efficient appliances and utilizing intelligent conservation strategies. It's easy to compare the energy efficiency of major appliances with the yellow "Energy Guide" labels, and there are more energy efficient alternatives than ever before. Although many of these ideas are beyond the scope of this book, there are many other good books dedicated to just this subject that the prospective homeowner can turn to for more information. They include *Save Energy, Save Money* by Alvin Ubell and George Merlis; *Consumer Guide to Home Energy Savings* by Alex Wilson, Jennifer Thorne, and John Morill; and the *Energy Efficiency Manual* by Donald R. Wulfinghoff.

Enough about insulation and energy efficiency for now, but we will come back to this important topic in the chapters on salespeople and in delivery and setup. You don't want to miss that discussion — it could just be that you pay extra for that precious R-28 ceiling insulation, the dealer hands you paperwork "proving" you have it, and you end up with paltry R-11 anyway! We'll also cover some valuable energy saving tips in the chapter entitled "Making Your House a Home."

Doing your homework might also include going to a factory. When we found a floor plan we liked, we ended up going to the plant where it was produced in Bean Station, Tennessee, and spent a couple of hours there talking with a plant supervisor and touring the production facility. This can give you a much better understanding of what exactly goes into your home, what differentiates a manufactured home from a site-built house, and exactly what options are available. Even within the same company, available options will vary according to the particular manufacturing plant's capabilities. Dealerships, too, are often notoriously ignorant of available options for particular models. For instance, some plants literally don't have doors tall enough to put a steep roof pitch on 32' wide homes, but your local salesperson is almost certain to be unaware of this. If you are unsure in general about whether you want a manufactured home, a field trip of this sort could also be extremely helpful. We came away with the general impression that they could indeed build a satisfactory product. At Clayton Homes, Inc., one of the procedures they employ is to assemble the halves of multisection homes temporarily during construction, so they know everything should fit tolerably closely during the final setup. Not every company does this. If you have any doubts about the materials being used in manufactured homes, a plant tour will give you the opportunity to inspect them for yourself. Over the last couple of decades, tremendous strides have been made in both the quality and the range of available options.

We were somewhat disappointed by the quality of the plant we toured in some regards (just as you might be a little shocked to see what goes on sometimes during the construction of a site-built house). Frequently we found workers putting together rooms in the dark. They didn't even bother to drag in work lights as they were putting the finishing touches on various rooms. As we were looking at one kitchen, my wife noticed that the trim was upside down. The pattern of the wallpaper had flowers going up, but on the trim the flowers were going down. There were also siding pieces which were out of square, and some were not flush by 2" or 3" in comparison to others. When I asked why, a plant foreman and one of our tour guides said, "That's a good question!" Finished drywall (walls without trim strips) was not even an option in the homes we were most interested in, which was a surprise to us because we had been told by several salespeople it was available.

Doing your homework can also be made a lot easier if you have Internet access. Every major manufacturer has information on the Internet, and you can also frequently look up complaints about local dealers as well. On manufacturer Web sites, you can learn more about their construction features and capabilities as well as plant locations and contact information. You can then use these phone numbers and e-mail addresses to corroborate or supplement information from individual dealerships. Information from the factory is typically more reliable than what you will hear from salespeople that work on commission. Many company Web sites also show floor plans and offer virtual online walk-throughs of various featured homes. For complaints on area dealers, consumer "action" lines for local television or newspaper Web sites can be a treasure trove. If a dealership has too many complaints, avoid it. If you don't have a computer with Internet access, try your local library. Following is a partial list of Web sites for manufactured and modular homes.

American Homestar Corporation	http://www.americanhomestar.com/
Burlington Homes of Maine	http://www.burlingtonhomes.com/
Cavalier Homes, Inc.	http://www.cavalierhomebuilders.com/
Cavco Industries	http://www.cavco.com/
Champion Enterprises	http://www.championhomes.net/
Clayton Homes, Inc.	http://www.clayton.net/
Colony Factory Crafted Homes	http://www.colony-homes.com/models.htm
Commodore Homes of Pennsylvania	http://www.commodore-pa.com/
Fairmont Homes	http://www.fairmonthomes.com/
Fleetwood Enterprises, Inc.	http://www.fleetwoodhomes.com/

Four Seasons Housing, Inc.	http://www.fourseasonshousing.com/
Franklin Homes, Inc.	http://www.franklinhomesusa.com/
Giles Industries, Inc.	http://www.gilesindustries.com/
Hi-Tech Housing, Inc.	http://www.hi-techhousing.com/
Horton Homes, Inc.	http://www.hortonhomes.com/
Indies House	http://www.indieshouse.net/
Jacobsen Manufacturing	http://www.jachomes.com/
Karsten Homes	http://www.thekarstenco.com/index.asp
Liberty Homes	http://www.libertyhomesinc.com/
Manufactured Housing Enterprises, Inc.	http://www.mheinc.com/
New Era Building Systems	http://www.new-era-homes.com/
Oakwood Homes Corporation	http://www.oakwoodhomes.com/
Palm Harbor Homes	http://www.palmharbor.com/
Patriot Homes, Inc.	http://www.patriothomes.com/
Pine Grove Manufacturing	http://www.pinegrovehomes.com/
Pioneer Housing Systems	http://pioneerhousing.com/
R-Anell Housing Group	http://www.r-anell.com/
Schult Homes	http://www.schulthomes.com/
Skyline Corporation	http://www.skylinehomes.com/
Southern Energy Homes, Inc.	http://www.soenergyhomes.com/IE_ frameset.htm
Sunshine Homes	http://www.sunshinehomes-inc.com/
Wick Building Systems, Inc	http://www.wickmarshfield.com/

You may even save some extra money going to Web sites. We received a "coupon" for a $1,000 discount on our home as an incentive just for visiting the corporate Web site. There was a catch — the extremely fine print stipulated we could only use it if we financed our home through Vanderbilt Mortgage — which is owned by Clayton. We did finance through Clayton Homes because of a special six-month no-interest finance offer, which let us use the coupon, and then we refinanced at a better rate with a conventional mortgage after our home was set up and before we had started paying interest. (We couldn't get a conventional mortgage until after the home was set up, because the dealer wouldn't take a "letter of acceptance." Please see the mortgage section for more about the ins and outs on mortgages.) All things considered, our loan situation worked out wonderfully, but it was because of the extra research we did. Saving an extra $1,000 for simply clicking on a Web site was just icing on the cake. The Internet is just another tool in your arsenal. (By the way, if you get a coupon like this, keep it hidden until you get your best deal. If they won't honor it unless you disclose it to the dealer before financial negotiations, it isn't worth the paper it's printed on!)

The Manufactured Home Buyer's Handbook Web site has an exceptional list of up to date *consumer resources* also: www.manufactured

homebuyers.com. On the site you can find many links to Web pages which describe how to save money and energy, feature indoor air quality information, or detail the types of problems other manufactured home owners have had. Consumers Union reports and other consumer advocacy groups Web site addresses are provided, along with manufactured home owner's organizations from around the country which can help you learn more about the type of obstacles you may face as a manufactured home owner. Many of these Web sites are more region specific than this book as a whole can be, and some address the special concerns that manufactured home owners located in communities or parks or may face. You can also find complaint information, an online mortgage calculator, and much more!

CHAPTER 2

Custom Ordering Your New Home

Custom ordering your new home can pay dividends for you, and it goes hand in hand with doing your homework as just discussed. For example, custom ordering makes your "wish list" a lot more flexible, and visiting factories and Web sites will help you know a lot more about possible options. Custom ordering from an ideological standpoint also stands at the opposite end of the spectrum with *impulsiveness.* Impulse is the very response dealers want to trigger in their customers. As you start to visit sales centers, there is going to be a temptation to order something right off the lot. Indeed, you may find a home you're perfectly content with, and if it's an older model which the dealership wants to move off the lot, you might be offered a substantial financial incentive. There may well be points at which you would be willing to sign the papers (*any* papers— even if they have vague references to your first-born child and eternal soul) just to shut up an overbearing salesperson! Still, for most people, the best way to find a home they'll sincerely be happy with in the long term is to carefully reflect on their needs and custom order it. Who wouldn't be more satisfied in a home they helped design?

Salespeople play on your natural impulses to get the process over with as well. It is stressful buying any home, whether it's site-built or manufactured, and it is only natural to want to get everything done and over with as soon as you can. Custom ordering your home, however, can be done without adding too much time to the process, especially if you will have to make some type of improvements like clearing, grading, or foundation work to your property before the home arrives. Expect delivery to take about six to ten weeks after the order is placed, although if the factory is backlogged it could take longer.

As you visit dealerships, collect sales literature, and talk with salespeople. You should learn more and more about just what options are possible — but always keep in mind the source of the information. That is one of your mantras in this mission. Salespeople are usually the *least* reliable sources of information, and question everything you don't see with your own eyes!

We've already mentioned numerous possibilities about additional features, such as having your rooms "wired and braced" for fan/light kits (for virtually anyone, having this option makes a lot of sense), Jacuzzi tubs, ordering Low-E windows, and extra insulation — but that is only the tip of the iceberg. For roughly $100, you can have all four corners of most homes prewired for floodlights, with inside switches already installed. It costs a small fraction of what it would cost to add on later. You can choose from a number of other window types as well for various rooms, such as having windows topped with "fan" style panes or large bay windows or putting skylights virtually anywhere you choose. From floor covering to wall covering, you can choose what suits you. You may want to add a raised dining room floor or a sunken living room. There will probably be a choice in appliance packages (either basic or deluxe). Garbage disposals can usually be ordered with your home for a lot less than you would have to spend to install one later.

With most manufacturers you can even change fundamentals like the placement of doors. Suppose you need a home office, but all the spare rooms open into the kitchen/den area at the back of the house on the original floor plan. It's possible to have the door from one of the spare rooms moved to another wall which accesses the foyer, so guests could come in from the home's front door and walk directly into your new office (avoiding walking through a kitchen or den where you may or may not have been able to clean up lately). Get some sample floor plans and use your imagination, then find out just what the manufacturer can do for you. A word of caution, though. It can be a little hard to find out just what options are available. Persistence can pay off, however. We finally procured a list from Champion headquarters which showed all available home options — it wasn't meant for public consumption, but they blacked out all cost and confidential information to give it to us, and it was a tremendous help. Brochures which list features are seldom going to cover options like relocating doors — or hardly any of the options we discuss in this chapter. Charges for relocating doors often run about $200, but like everything else custom features and engineering fees are subject to wide variation (or big mark-ups) and negotiation. Also make sure you order the six-panel interior doors (although the better six panel doors are frequently standard now), and find out if it costs more to order full-length doors (standard doors are about 2½" off the floor).

Regarding "standard" versus "full-length" doors: some people really hate the shorter doors, and some people hardly notice them. You will need to make your own determination. One point, however, which people seldom consider in this regard is their heating and air conditioning system. Modern homes are pretty air-tight. Your heating/cooling system relies on return air to function properly. (This is the reason why you will often see a vent in the wall above the master bedroom in a manufactured home — allowing air to return back to the main part of the house.) Your guest/extra bedrooms will probably heat and cool somewhat more efficiently with that gap under the doors, and the air will be fresher because of increased circulation. If you want to do a simple test of this theory, put your hand at the base of one of the shorter doors while the heat or air is on — you will feel a steady rush of air exiting the room.

You can also add or move exterior doors or order a larger back or utility door. While you're walking around the various dealers' lots, as the next chapter discusses, use a tape measure (*always* bring a tape measure) to measure the width of the various entryways. You might be surprised to find a lot of 32" wide doors, especially in the back or on the side. You can order them all at the standard 36" width if you want. You do not want to try to move in (or out) any major appliances or large furniture through a 32" door. Even if you do succeed, you'll probably damage the furniture and possibly even the door or door frame. The standard "cottage" or "9-lite" door that is often used for the back or side of the home is notoriously fragile. The white plastic trim around the nine panes of glass (hence the name 9-lite) also quickly turns yellow in sunlight.

Hardwood flooring is one of many possible alternatives for some homes, but as with the discussion about ceiling fans earlier, always compare options. This is where getting itemized pricing can be really helpful. (Dealerships are often reluctant to give itemized pricing, but you can get it by either insisting on it or by being indirect. This will be discussed further in Chapter 5.) *Itemized pricing is the only way you can know exactly how much you are paying for what, and that in itself is another of the inherent advantages of custom ordering your home.* If you buy a home off a dealer's lot, you have no way of knowing what the individual features are costing. In our hardwood flooring example, we considered getting our dining room and foyer with real wood floors. The dealer wanted $1,900 for this option, however. We decided to go with faux wood vinyl floor covering instead, and quickly after moving in found Pergo on sale to finish our dining room with — it cost us $500 including the pad. The bottom line is that sometimes you save money by buying it from the factory, and sometimes you don't. As you can see, if you want to maximize the quality of home your money buys, your homework never ends.

Flooring also brings to mind carpet, and there are various schools of thought here. The basic carpet in most manufactured homes is pretty bad. Some professionals recommend not buying the carpet at all — that is, ordering the home without carpet in exchange for some small credit the dealer would give you (again, you can negotiate, but don't expect much here — the factory spends very little on their carpet). In this way, you could purchase all your carpeting at a local store and install it before you move in. I don't recommend that; it would take considerably more time and expense than many folks who may have just purchased a house have. Instead, spend a little more and get the best carpet and pad offered by the manufacturer. It may last a few years in moderately traveled rooms and longer in spare or guest rooms. Don't forget the pad — a good, thick pad makes an economical carpet feel better and last longer and makes an average carpet good. As the carpet wears out, you can then replace it room by room with what you really want. Chances are you will have more money, and you will almost certainly have more time later on. Moving is hard enough without laying carpet too.

One area that many people don't consider when looking for a new manufactured home is the roof. It is not obvious at first to most consumers that the roof can have a significant impact on how functional your new home will be and how satisfied you will be as a homeowner. We have previously discussed ceiling insulation options, and we're going to talk about dormers later, but I'd like to discuss two other structural considerations here: roof pitch and roof load. Standard roof pitch is usually the minimal 3:12. This means that roof rises 3" for every horizontal foot you transverse, resulting in a fairly low roof. This is the preferred roof for the factories because it costs less to produce and makes the home easier to transport (lighter weight and lower height). This can cause some major headaches for the consumer, though. One of the worst enemies your home will face is water, and it can quickly cause tremendous damage to your investment. Manufacturers also warn consumers at length about moisture damage in their setup manuals — which is why it saddens me they don't mandate steeper roof pitches even if it does cost more. The bottom line is the dollar, so if HUD doesn't act, the manufacturers won't. The shallow slope means water runs more slowly off the roof; this slow movement further interacts with the slight angle in that the latter allows the leisurely moving water to actually run back up the bottom sides of the shingles. If it contacts the decking of your roof, you will have to deal with fast deterioration and eventually leaks. It also means that adding expensive gutters to keep water from running over your doorways and to direct water away from your foundation can be an exercise in futility. Water will run around the edge of the shingles back to the house and pour out between the soffit and your new gutters. We were promised that a 3:12 roof pitch was more than adequate. Later, when we were having problems with water under our new home, the manufacturer advised us to install gutters as soon as possible to direct runoff from the roof away from the foundation. In the accompanying photographs, you can see just how ineffective these gutters are — about 75 percent of rainwater flows out between the roof and the gutter before falling against the ground at the foundation. Some water actually follows the soffit all the way to the side of the home, causing small rivers to flow against the sides of the house and discoloring the vinyl siding with roofing material.

Top, left: This 3:12 pitch roof actually becomes so flat near the edges that standing pools of water form on it. *Top, right:* Rain, rain, go away…. The camera's flash illuminates a torrent of water pouring out between the home's soffit and these properly installed gutters. Much of this water will now accumulate under this new home. *Left:* One purpose of gutters is to keep water from falling over entryways — but anyone walking in or out here will get an unwelcome bath!

Flatter roofs are also usually built using 2" by 3" trusses. Steeper pitches often employ larger truss pieces, and better, sturdier trusses typically support heavier roof "loads." If you're a large person, just walking on those smaller trusses can be a little too exciting, and at some points people will be walking and working on the roof. Common ratings are 20 PSF (pounds per square foot) for the south, 40 PSF for the north (to support snow), and 30 PSF for anything in between. Based on my experience, I would recommend you order a steeper pitch (4:12 or 5:12) if you can afford it (and if it's available in the home you choose) for both the appearance and the performance a higher pitch will provide. If you can't get a steeper pitch, make absolutely sure the manufacturer doesn't cut corners by not using roofing paper. Find out what size trusses your home will use, and consider ordering one size stronger roof load than you need. Specify that you want your trusses spaced 16" on center unless that's standard, especially if you are going with the small prefab trusses. (Many factories place them 24" on center, but every plant should be able to accommodate a request for 16" on center trusses.)

Another feature most people don't give a lot of thought to is the phone jack. The standard location for the phone jack is the kitchen. One phone jack is usually standard; some manufacturers don't put in any or won't add additional jacks. If you use a cordless phone, you may want to choose a different location for it or at least try to add additional jacks. The reason is that one of the major causes for interference with cordless phones are appliances, whether it's because the base unit is surrounded by large metal appliances or because of interference from being on the same electrical circuit with them. A cordless phone may work just fine surrounded by your refrigerator, range, and microwave — but don't count on it. If the manufacturer will only add one jack, and if the cost for the phone company to add more is too prohibitive, consider an expandable cordless phone system. Extra handsets can be added to these which will work off of the one base unit without the need for more phone outlets. Additional units cost around $50, which might be less than the local phone company will charge for adding phone jacks — and you would still need to purchase extra telephones if you have the manufacturer or phone company add more phone jacks.

Well, you have the idea. Just find out what things you can have done, how much they cost, and make your selections. Do yourself — and your bank account — a favor and make your selections with your spouse (or whomever you are consulting with, if anyone). Don't do it at the lot with the salesperson or manager. Do it over your kitchen table with a drink and a relaxed frame of mind. Take your time. Visualize the house, and consider where you want to be in the future. You will probably make smarter choices that way — both financially and in terms of the kind of house you'll be living in.

Even when you custom order your home you will still want to see the floor plan/model in advance if at all possible. Walking into an actual model will not only give you a better feel for the design than a drawing will, it will help you catch nonsensical features. As an example, allow me to explain one feature we missed. Our master bathroom light switch controls nine bulbs—two vanity light bars and one overhead ceiling light. Having this 400-watt monster on separate switches would not only be easier on the eyes for me and easier on our power bill, but the location of the switch is insane unless you live alone. It's located inside the bedroom area leading into the bathroom, so if you or your spouse has to visit the bathroom during the night, it unleashes a torrent of light which floods the bedroom on entry and exit of the bathroom. Even with the door shut you have enough light coming through beneath the door to work on your 1040 long form in bed. Had we had any clue, we would have insisted on the switch being placed *in* the bathroom, and also we would have had the two vanity light bars and the single bulb fixture wired separately so we could just turn on the solitary bulb at night or when we don't need so much light. Now, we are going to have to have these fixtures rewired and have the switch plate moved. This is going to involve running new wires through the ceiling cavity and walls—no easy job. It would have been an easy problem to correct at the factory. Catch everything you can before it's too late.

At a minimum, find a dealer with a home which is most similar in design and level of quality to the one you're interested in. A call to the factory is one of the easiest ways to locate dealerships carrying specific models. With luck, you should be able to find the exact model you're considering, although you may have to travel.

Whether you custom order your home or order it off the lot, there are many features you definitely want to avoid. Some are obvious when you see them in a home; others may not be easily noticeable until it's too late (like our light switch). One line of homes called the "Appalachian" series had some interior doors that were so narrow I had to turn sideways to get through them. Other features to avoid include plastic sinks which are easily and permanently damaged, wood backsplashes, kitchen cabinet doors which are some type of particle board covered by paper (the exterior quickly wears through, and then they look horrible), hollow-core doors, and rooms without overhead lights. Heat ducts in traffic areas are a real problem for numerous reasons and can be avoided by ordering perimeter heat. Many other bad features are seldom found today, like plastic toilets, plastic tubs and showers (make sure these are fiberglass), plastic skylights (they tend to fade or discolor with time), polybutylene plumbing, small 30-gallon water heaters, etc., but check just in case. Also, make absolutely sure there are water cut-offs at all fixtures. Finally, I try to avoid a home with no windows on the ends. Maybe it's just personal, but I think they make the home look too much like a "box" whether the home is manufactured or site-built.

Closets deserve an extra mention here. For most people, storage space is one of the main requirements in a home. Manufactured homes seldom offer any attic space or basement access, so you will want to make absolutely sure you have plenty of closets and cabinets. There is nothing quite like taking on a 30-year mortgage only to find your new home has a major deficiency *after* you start moving in groceries, clothes, and other possessions. Many new manufactured homes don't have pantries, and fewer still have hall or entryway closets. Consider looking for floor plans that incorporate them, or see if you can add them to a floor plan you like. Verify that your master bedroom closets and pantry will have light fixtures in them as well — some manufacturers omit these as a way to cut costs. There is also another closet disaster in wait in many of the floor plans — closets in extra bedrooms which are so shallow that when you fill them with clothes, you can only access the ones in front of the closet door. You can learn to spot these closets on the diagrams if you are careful, and you should certainly be able to tell when you walk in a display model with them. These closets only allow you to access what is directly in front of the door because the hung clothes come all the way to the front edge of the closet, blocking both reach and sight of the ends. On the diagrams/floor plans, they look like the accompanying diagram of an unacceptably small closet. The quick giveaway is the nearly equal distance from the line representing the closet rod to the wall on either side. This sort of closet is really only acceptable for a hall closet or a child's room (and children tend to grow). Extra bedrooms may be ordered with alternative-style closets (or even larger ones) if they don't already include them, as seen in the next two closet diagrams.

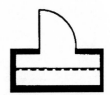

In this unacceptably small closet, notice how close the front wall is to the clothes rack.

One final and important caveat — even if you walk into a display home that is supposed to be just like the one you are custom ordering except for certain features you are asking to add — remember to still get everything in writing! Make sure every option or upgrade in the display model that you want is going to be built into your new home. Some dealers will add upgrades to their lot

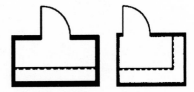

Left: A much more functional closet has greater room in front of the rod. *Right:* Another serviceable closet style uses an L-shaped hanging space.

models which are not standard, and specifications are also subject to change. Don't make any assumptions or rely on providence. *If you have it in writing that you ordered your home a certain way, then you have legal recourse.* Otherwise, it's very unlikely you can have problems corrected without a lot more money coming out of your pocket.

## CHAPTER 3

Illustration of Customization

We're about to enter the nitty gritty in the next chapter — actually working with dealerships. First, however, let's expand on the idea of customization in a more practical way. This should help prepare you for the floor plans you're going to be getting at dealerships, both from a fundamental understanding perspective if you haven't looked at them before and from the standpoint of using a basic floor plan of a model to visualize how you can transform it into the home you really want. You can't tell everything from a floor plan (you still want to walk in an actual model if possible), but you can tell a lot, and the floor plan is also a very useful tool for illustrating to the dealership or manufacturing plant what changes you want to make and in what locations. It can cut down drastically on errors and miscommunication. The general idea is to find a model that has as many design elements and "standard" features as possible that match your conceptualization of the perfect home and then modify it and upgrade it as possible. Following is a sample floor plan which includes some good features for a manufactured home; most noticeably, it has large, open rooms and even includes space for a pantry and entryway closet. Although you may walk into such a model on a dealership lot and be very impressed with the residential style 3" crown molding and the spacious kitchen, you hopefully will also look for features that don't work for you — like the absence of a back door, the carpeted bathroom, and the long drab line of the roof. The second sample shows some revisions and a redrawn floor plan.

As you can probably tell, we've made quite a few changes to this revised plan. You may want to look it over for a few minutes to see if you can spot them all, but if you're impatient I'll go ahead and list some for you:

1. One of the first things we did was "flip" this entire model end to end. You can tell this option is just like flipping a picture on your com-

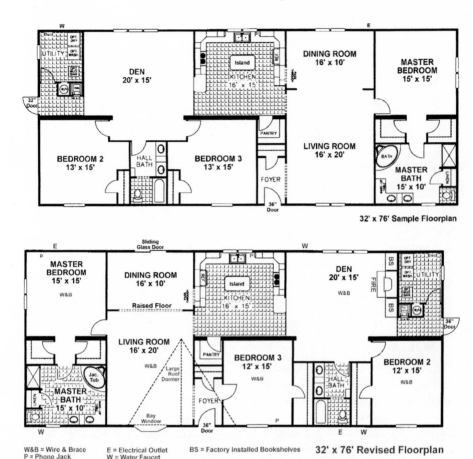

32' x 76' Sample Floorplan

32' x 76' Revised Floorplan

W&B = Wire & Brace   E = Electrical Outlet   BS = Factory Installed Bookshelves
P = Phone Jack   W = Water Faucet

puter screen horizontally — it has no effect on the vertical orientation of the home. The front door is still out front, the bedroom is in the back, etc. This option can often mean the difference between a model being perfect for you and totally unacceptable. For instance, if you have an established driveway and garage on the right side of your property, the side entrance on the left would have made your life miserable.

2. The next problem with our theoretical home was the lack of a back door. A lot of home designs are like this. Two exterior doors are common — one on the front and the other either on the back or one of the sides. Of course, if you want to have a secluded deck out back in the future, you will want a way to get onto it from the house. The two logical choices are putting a door in either the den or the dining room. We chose a patio-style door off the dining room, and of course it's made from thermal pane glass which matches the windows in the rest of the house.

3. We also moved an interior door to illustrate a point made earlier in the text. In bedroom 3, the door originally led in from the den area. In our earlier example, we talked about having a home office, and wanting access for clients to come straight in the office from the foyer without walking through the "living" areas of the home. This simple and inexpensive change can make a dramatic difference in the functionality of your home.

4. One final "door" change — we increased the standard opening for the side door from 32" to 36" so we could more easily get appliances and furniture in and out near our driveway. Don't expect the floor plans you see at dealerships to be this detailed, however; you'll have to find out smaller details like this on your own, so don't forget that tape measure!

5. Something else you will have to draw in yourself on the plans will be the location of exterior electrical outlets, water faucets, and phone jacks— they are very important to your home's practicality. You can see this model originally had one electrical outlet and one water faucet on the back side. We added one more electrical outlet in the front, and two water outlets there. If you are planning to have front walkway lights and flowerbeds in the front yard, you'll probably want something similar. Otherwise, with a large home like this, you could find yourself fighting a couple of hundred feet of water hose or electrical cord pretty quickly. We added two more phone jacks inside for convenience (in the office and master bedroom); just in case the standard kitchen jack has problems with interference.

6. In all the major rooms, we had the manufacturer "wire and brace" the ceilings. This means we will have ceiling light fixtures with a wall switch preinstalled in these locations. (Don't assume all rooms will have ceiling fixtures unless you buy a home off the lot with them or you order your home that way — you may be limited to lamps or major rewiring if you do.) Each of these locations will also be "braced" or physically reinforced with wood so you can safely hang ceiling fans or other heavy fixtures from the ceiling. Do not attempt to hang a fan from an electrical junction box in the ceiling which is not reinforced! Something else this diagram doesn't show is that we had the four exterior corners prewired for floodlights. (In the actual home we bought, we had seven rooms "wired and braced" and all four corners pre-wired at a total cost of less than $250.)

7. Linoleum flooring is usually standard in the kitchen and utility rooms and sometimes in the bathrooms and foyers. On the floor plans, it is usually indicated by some kind of pattern similar to what our example uses. You'll note here we added more vinyl to the bathrooms— both of which primarily used it around the area of the toilet. While stepping out

of the shower or master bath onto carpet every day may feel good, it's not a very good idea (consistently wet carpet will quickly lead to deterioration and mildew/fungus growth). You should probably go a step farther with this plan and put linoleum in the foyer as well (this is standard in many homes now). Most manufacturing plants use name brand linoleum, and if you take proper care of it you should get many years of use from it. Standard carpet in high traffic areas like entryways will quickly be destroyed unless you use vinyl carpet runners or take some other preventative measures.

8. While we're in the bathroom area, we threw in a Jacuzzi tub for two. If you do this, you'll want to make sure you have a big water heater or else buy an add-on heater which is available from home improvement stores for around $100 to $150. The add-on heater is good for prolonged baths, so you don't have to keep adding hot water. This isn't usually a factory option.

9. The original plan in this example shows two impractically small closets in bedrooms 2 and 3. We replaced these with two deeper closets which run the length of one of the walls. This may be overkill for your situation, but it's certainly one way to get some concealed storage space. In a home this spacious, you can afford the floor space for them.

10. We've made a lot of practical changes to our sample floor plan so far, but don't forget the aesthetic. You want the home to be attractive; you want to maximize your enjoyment while you're living in it. In this plan, one thing we did was add a large bay window off the living room. This addition combines with the extensive surface area of the patio door directly opposite it to effectively highlight the large, open area between them (cathedral ceilings further enhance the airy image). Once you decide on a particular model home, the factory can tell you exactly what your window options are, but bay windows and "fan" windows (small semi-circular windows placed above the lower main window) are common options.

11. In the revised plan, the dining room floor has also been raised up to break up the living room and dining room somewhat. This effect can be enhanced by placing hardwood flooring or faux wood linoleum in the dining room area as well; it will be a lot easier to clean up spills, and we won't have to worry about our carpet near our new patio door.

12. We put in a 36" fireplace in our den in this example as well. They do feel good in the wintertime (especially if the power goes out), but this is probably chosen at least as much for ambiance as for practical reasons. You can purchase various styles, corner or wall, wood or gas, half hearth or full hearth. Make sure you see an example of one before you order it, but some of these are very nice.

Left: This is an example of a full-hearth fireplace. *Right:* A dormer breaks up the long line of the roof.

13. On either side of our fireplace, we've added factory-installed bookshelves. This is a common option to surround fireplaces in the center of the wall. (You can often add extra cabinetry in various areas of the house if it isn't standard.) This was an option we chose in our actual home, and the bookshelves were fine. The were enclosed on the bottom and had adjustable shelves on top. They were wide enough to set a 27" television on. See examples of the product if at all possible before adding it. Built-in furniture leaves holes and damage if you remove it because you don't like its appearance or find out it's too cheaply made. For items like medicine cabinets, if you have basic installation skills you'll get a better product if you go to a local home improvement store to pick out one yourself.

14. Finally, we put a large dormer option on this home as well. Initially, it will serve a couple of functions. It will help keep a lot of dripping water from falling at the front door. (Make sure, however, you don't have the edge of the dormer exactly over the door, or it will be like you're standing under an open spigot when it rains!) More importantly, a dormer will break up the flat line of the roof and make your house look much more like a traditional home. In the future, or immediately after setup, you could use this dormer as a natural location to extend the roof of your home out over a front porch.

CHAPTER 4

Dealing with Salespeople

The word *dealing* might seem to have overly harsh connotations. We're talking about people, right? Shouldn't we say "working with" or maybe even "collaborating with"? Actually, the verb *dealing* was chosen with a great deal of thought. This might be the most difficult part of the process of buying a manufactured home or the easiest — it depends largely on your own personality and attitude. If you are like most people, you want to be a friendly and trusting person, and unfortunately that posture will not serve you well at all. You must assert yourself and take charge of the process— you must adopt an aggressive and dominant posture even if that is not your normal nature. The salespeople have been immersed in a culture where you are seen as a meal ticket and little else, and they are apt to do or say whatever they think will win you over. They are going to try and manipulate you into making the highest payment you can afford. If you allow them to take over the process, it will destroy your bargaining position, and you could be ushered into making decisions you will regret for many years. If you haven't had a lot of experience shopping for a manufactured home, this must seem like overly strong or inordinately generalized sentiment. I've been to literally dozens of sales centers in four states and dealt with scores of salespeople in depth. The major difference is the polish or the technique the salesperson uses— the underlying disdain for the customer and for the truth remains pretty constant. Going above the salesperson to the manager — if the former crosses the boundaries of civility or honesty by so much that you feel the need — seldom earns much more than an insincere apology and a new angle on the sales pitch. The managers are salespeople that are relatively good at the game, and they are, therefore, harder to see through. (Indeed, through experience I concluded that this attitude and culture extends right into upper management of these corporations.) I'm sure there are probably a few exceptions, but I doubt any such souls could survive long in that milieu. A second problem seems to be fairly widespread ignorance regarding the products they are trying to sell; ignorance always seems to be a close relative of indiscriminate disdain. This lack of accurate knowledge, however, only seems to make the lies more common. If they don't really know the answer, they'll make it up! Every error, however, will be in favor of the dealer and the dealer's product quality.

I'll give you some examples of the sales pitches and distortions, but allow me to preface them this way. You have only three choices: to allow them to manipulate you and talk you into a bad purchase, to walk away to pursue other housing options (and there is no entirely safe home purchase — whether it is manufactured housing, traditional site-built construction, or any other option), or to steel yourself and go into the foray armed with information and strategies. The latter is what I recommend, and it will allow you to best them at their own game. Visit multiple dealers as well, always taking notes and gleaning information and always noting discrepancies. A prior visit to a manufacturing plant can be a tremendous asset at this point, but you can also ask for the plant's 800 number or find them over the Internet as a backup. That way, when you have several items which you feel are in doubt, you can verify this at the source (factory or corporate offices) by phone or e-mail and feel relatively confident. Plant employees are much less likely to stretch the truth than employees in the sales chain, and they are more likely to have access to accurate specifications.

To help explain what may seem like this overly pessimistic attitude at the outset, allow me to explain what our manufacturer's regional manager told us *after* we had encountered numerous quality problems in our new home and after we had complained repeatedly about false promises. This manager stated with a wide grin in a rare moment of candor — "What do you expect us to tell you [when you're shopping for a home on one of our lots], we are trying to sell you something." The grinning was especially irksome because we were standing in our new kitchen next to a pool of water several feet in diameter on the floor, while more water dripped down out of the ceiling through a light fixture. This regional manager not only showed disdain for our plight, he seemed to revel in it. He had our money; he had won, and we had lost. His smirk seemed to indicate "so what if they now know the horrible truth about how we do business? *We got 'em.*"

This was by no means an isolated incident for us, and I've heard similar tales of terror from customers of most major and numerous minor brands. After having this leak and multiple other problems in our home, we were forced into waiting for a replacement home to be built at the factory and brought out to us. In the replacement home alone, we had five water leaks in addition to several more leaks in the septic lines under the house because the septic's end caps weren't tightened (allowing a rather unpleasant smell to surround our new home). These leaks included a major roof leak (which let many gallons of water into our bathroom floor and the exterior wall during one hard rainstorm), a leak around the shower stall, a loose fitting on the refrigerator water line, a defective faucet (which sprayed water into the wall cavities) in the guest bath, and a leak in a water line under the home caused when a staple or nail had penetrated the line at the factory. This latter leak didn't show up for over a week; I spotted it while inspecting for problems underneath the home. Many more gallons of water had accumulated in our "belly board" (in the plastic which holds the insulation under the floor), soaking our insulation and soaking the floor joists. The only clue was the sound of a slow drip under the house.

I couldn't determine the source of a pool of water on our new kitchen floor at first, but removing this light fixture quickly revealed the problem. Our manufacturer's regional manager dismissed this water leak with a laugh. He also assured us water above our ceiling wouldn't harm our home in any way! He did take decisive action, though; he instructed the setup crews not to allow us in our home until all work was done. This is one case where what you don't know can definitely hurt you! (If you suspect water may be above your ceiling, *do not* check any light fixtures until all power has been turned off.)

I couldn't visually spot it until my knee sank into several inches of water which had amassed under the vapor barrier over the ground. I could go on with a host of other problems, but for now the point is this: the salespeople are trying to sell you something. That is their sole mission, no matter how sweet they sound. *Your mission is to protect yourself.* If you can't be hard-nosed, bring someone you trust who will stand up for you. It's easier to get tough with dealers and factories after you've been burned by them, but I'm telling you this so your learning curve can be shorter and so your reason won't be stretched quite so thin by the deception you're apt to face. If you start to weaken, remember our horror story and shore up your resolve!

Always remember: if you can't verify it for yourself or get it in writing, anything is suspect. Bring your requirements/wish list, a pad which you can easily write on, a stud finder (good ones can be bought for as little as $10), a tape measure, and a good, bright flashlight. The lists are a great way to focus you and to quickly eliminate models which can't be ordered with the features you have identified as necessities. The pad helps you keep track of your questions—both those to ask the salesperson and those which develop during your visit that you need to follow up on later. Just the act of taking notes and writing down names sometimes makes the salesperson a little more helpful and honest. A digital camera is also an outstanding tool to use to help you remember what various features and models look like. If you shop around very much, it can quickly become confusing. A camera with two-megapixel resolution (or higher) should be fine. The stud finder and tape measure are for verification. You might be amazed how much fun you can have with these and the average salesperson.... Besides, the tape measure will also help you figure out if existing furniture will fit in certain rooms. Most display homes don't have electricity, so your flashlight can frequently illuminate dark areas, sometimes revealing defects or problems you would otherwise miss. Check out everything; look in every room, every closet, and under every sink. Bring your notes from other dealers, too, from both same brand and other brand manufacturers. Keep these out of sight, though, in front of the salespeople. More on this later.

It will help you focus if you start out by telling the salesperson the size and general description of the home you want. You should be friendly but businesslike and not overly verbose. If you are good at visualizing from a floor plan, there should be brochures available which show the various models they have on the lot or can order. The floor plans will look much like the home drawings in this book and are often grouped according to size and a particular series of homes. These brochures can also be very helpful in that they sometimes list the "standard" features of the homes and sometimes list upgrade options. Such lists can help avoid tremendous numbers of fact-finding calls. You should take control insofar as directing the selection of homes to look at. Salespeople generally have certain models which they have been instructed to "push"; extra bonuses or "spiffs" are paid to them for selling particular homes. Home size is one good way to constrain your visit. There might not be any point in seeing homes which are smaller than 1,500 square feet or larger than 2,000 square feet, for instance. The only exception to such a rule that I can imagine is to look at another size model to see a specific feature which you are interested in. For instance, there might be a 2,400 square foot home on the lot which has a stone fireplace which extends to the ceiling, and this might be a feature you would like to see an example of before you invest in one.

It is likely the salesperson will ask you early on if you've been visiting other lots. It is to your advantage not to elaborate too much in this regard. Many salespeople become less than helpful once they learn you've really looked around, and you do need to really look around — getting a good deal takes time and patience. They generally do not want to compete for your business unless they've already invested considerable time and effort themselves— if they know you've looked at 20 dealerships or are going to, they would rather move on to the next fish because the odds are better at reeling that one in. Furthermore, salespeople and dealerships don't want to end up in a price war (although before you sign the dotted line, that is exactly where you want them) because that means their hefty commissions/markups will be smaller. They play the percentages, so you should too, and keep your cards close to your vest. You also don't know just who knows whom in this business. Salespeople move from lot to lot frequently, and even lots which appear to be competitors often aren't. Clayton Homes, Inc., frequently uses this tactic by placing "Clayton" dealerships adjacent to or across from "Luv Homes" dealerships. The same company runs and supplies both lots. Champion is a prime example of a manufacturer that has a lot of different "competing" brands which are in reality all now owned by Champion. (Champion now owns and operates Redman, Moduline, Summit Crest, Silvercrest, Atlantic, Titan, Fortune, Commander, Dutch, Gateway, Advantage Homes, Homes of Legend, Homes of Merit, and Chandeleur.) Just tell the salesperson something innocuous like "We've looked around a little, but haven't seen what we want yet."

Do ask questions— plenty of them about construction and features. Have important questions written down in advance, and jot the answers down as you go. The salesperson will know you're serious and be less likely to lead you along. If you want all 2" × 4" studs, ask if that feature is standard or available. Ask if all construction is 16" on center (that means the wall's support studs are 16" apart). If they say that's standard, write down their answer and verify it later. (They will often tell you this when only exterior load-bearing walls are 16" on center, as required by HUD — interior walls are most likely 24" on center by default.) In addition, ask about any other features you might need or be interested in, although as discussed previously some lots don't seem to have much of a grasp of just what the factory can do. Also mentioned earlier, one option is to "flip" a floor plan end-to-end if you like the house but the doors or room position do not conform to your property. Ask the salesperson how much this costs if you might require it. Some might tell you there's no charge; others may add a charge of $1,500 or more. Chances are that there will be an "engineering" fee from the factory to flip the plan (even if they've flipped the plan before and therefore already done all the engineering work), and then the dealer may add on to the fee. If the salesperson says there is "no charge," however, you should *write down the answer with the person's name, the time, and the date.* Then after you get your best price for everything else, say, "And, oh yes, don't forget to have the floor plan flipped as we discussed with our salesperson." If you are told it will cost extra, bring out those notes which are now almost as valuable as cash.

You will have to work with the salespeople to find out about the options you are considering in your home and whether or not they are available in the different models, but as indicated earlier this process can become very frustrating so stay focused. Oriented strand board (OSB) "wrap" in the exterior walls is one good example of something you'll want to get. "Bill" (to protect the not-quite so innocent) at Luv Homes in one city said that would cost us "about $800" extra. Then, when Bill found out we had looked around, OSB became a "standard" feature. He also told us it was "real smart" of us to ask about "such things"— he would not buy a home without such features, and most of the homes they sell don't come with them. We already knew from our homework, however, that OSB wrap was standard on every one of those models, and strongly suspected Bill just wanted a little extra pocket money. I later asked Bill over the phone how thick the wrap was, and he finally settled on ⅝" thick. When asked if he was sure, he said "Yeah—I'm reading it right off the sheet in front of me." A quick call to the factory, however, acquainted me with the truth: it is only ⁷⁄₁₆" thick. (In still further conversations I told Bill what the factory said about the OSB wrap being ⁷⁄₁₆" instead of ⅝", and he said they must have changed that specification. The factory said it was always ⁷⁄₁₆", however. Did Bill just read me a misprint over the phone, or were we just told ⅝" to make the product look better than it was? Given our experiences, the latter is a pretty safe bet.

One setup worker told us a horror story about a family member for whom he had helped to purchase a manufactured home. Since he worked in the industry and with this certain dealership extensively, he thought he could really help her out. He advised her to order it with the "OSB wrap" and the Oakwood Homes dealer sold her the multisection home. During setup, however, the gentleman found they wrapped only the two ends of the home in OSB—the only parts exposed and visible during setup. Without his intimate knowledge of manufactured home construction, this omission probably would never have been caught. When the family complained, the dealership "looked up" the order form and claimed they had ordered it that way! Why would anyone want OSB wrap, but only on the two ends? Two-thirds of the exterior walls had only thin siding stapled over the insulation. So the dealer made extra money for an "upgrade" while essentially leaving the structural deficiency the customer had specifically said she wanted corrected. The worst part is that the dealer did it in such a way as to deceive the customer — for all intents and purposes, the ordinary buyer would not know for years, or possibly ever, that they didn't really get what they had paid for. Once again, be vigilant and have everything spelled out in writing so this doesn't happen to you!

Our most enlightening visit to a dealership might have been in Lexington, South Carolina. It took "Sue" (again, not her real name) weeks to call us back in response to our e-mail inquiries regarding a particular model their lot was supposed to have because no one there was really "technology oriented" enough to figure out how to read the e-mail according to Sue. The next day, as we were leaving the lot, she told us she didn't know much about the homes because she was new (as an explanation for why she told us so many things that turned out to be untrue). She said she was instead like me — her "real" background was in computer technology just like my own background. I guess she forgot the earlier conversation, and how she didn't know how to open e-mail.

Soon after I went up the steps to this particular dealership in Lexington using my cane and advancing upward with my right leg only (I contend with Reiter's Syndrome, a rare arthritic condition), she was telling us about Clayton being the "Manufacturer of the Year" and how great the Clayton company president was. Then she said to our astonishment how Clayton Homes is a fantastic company in part because "*we even hire the handicapped and junk like that.*" "Junk" was her exact word; I felt a warm spot in my heart for her and Clayton right there — even before she told me the part about the bet with her manager that we couldn't be the couple from York because we drove up in a Mustang and that little "hick village" just couldn't have any Mustangs. Oh yes, the Lamborghini of the redneck world. "Sue" had the same inner attitude toward customers as most of the salespeople we worked with; she just lacked the polish. She never stopped smiling, though.

Later, as we were viewing a Greenbriar model (GB32764A) we were very interested in, she explained to me that walls which were exactly 3.5" thick in total were constructed with 2" by 4" lumber. Their technology is amazing if they can squeeze 3.5" (the actual width of a 2" by 4" board) of wood and two thicknesses of sheet rock in the same 3.5" of space! Sue also explained to me how studs in the laundry room wall which measured 24" apart were really 16" apart. We had told her that there were several features we really needed; for instance, we wanted water and electrical outlets on both the front and back of the home. She assured us that in "high end" homes like this that is standard. I asked her again, "Are you sure?" She once more said, "Yes." As we walked out of the model, I insisted on walking around the exterior of the home. Sue seemed to protest. I asked her to show me the water outlet in the front — she couldn't because there wasn't one. The moral is that salespeople will lie to their customers. Period. No nicer term does this justice. "Sue" was one of the worst, but we saw it to varying degrees on almost every lot we went to. If somewhere there are manufactured home salespeople who don't lie — I apologize to them and also wish them luck because they won't have the job for long in this cut-throat field.

If you aren't familiar with construction, you may wonder if there is any substantive difference between 16" versus 24" on center construction. HUD sets the standards for manufactured housing, not local ordinances, and according to HUD 24" is a satisfactory minimum standard for inte-rior walls (exterior walls are required to be 16" on center). From the man-ufacturer's perspective, 24" construction means lighter, easier-to-transport homes and significantly less material and labor costs. For you, it means somewhat less structural integrity in your home (obviously, the wall load-bearing capacity is reduced approximately 25 percent), and it also means that you will also have fewer studs with nonstandard spacing when you try to add shelving, wall units, or anything of that nature later. This latter point alone makes it worthwhile to have 16" construction for me, and the for-mer one makes it mandatory to my sensibilities.

On the other hand, some construction features were not worth the extra cost based on our research of HUD requirements. For instance, we were informed that while HUD allows the use of 2" × 3" studs on interior walls, they had to be at least grade 2 lumber or better. If you specified all 2" × 4" construction as a minimum, then the manufacturer can legally use "utility" grade lumber. (They can — and will — use this in the exterior walls anyway.) I've been told the only difference is "cosmetic." I've also inspected these boards after the home they are in has been transported several hun-dred miles. It's not true. Many utility-grade boards are either split when installed or of poor enough quality to crack apart during transit. We stuck with the 2" × 3" grade 2 interior walls and saved money. Because of HUD regulations concerning the grades of lumber manufacturers can use, I don't feel we gave up much if anything in terms of structural integrity there. If you are in doubt about the HUD requirements, contact the Manufactured Housing Board or the equivalent in your state (see appendix C for list-ings).

After you test the waters on your area dealership lots, pull out your tape measures and stud finders in these homes — you will still be misled, but the salespeople just don't act as sure as before. They will say things like, "I'm *pretty sure* that wall has 2" × 4" studs." (In one case, a stud was exposed and was obviously a 2" × 3"; I even put a tape measure across it in front of them — and the salesperson still swore it was a 2" × 4"! If you're new to lumber, be aware that you need to always add ½" when you measure. For instance, a 2" × 4" is really 1½" × 3½".) Just know what you are looking for, know who you are dealing with, and take the notes (and pictures if you have that digital camera) so you can sit down later to select the home you are really interested in. Most homes on lots will have exposed edges of carpet in a number of areas—bend down and check just how plush or thin they feel. Ask about the weight, the pad, and warranty. Do not buy a home with extremely cheap carpet which will need to be replaced in a year (unless you're in the carpet business). How detailed you want to get is up to you and your available time, but you may want to ask questions and do research on areas from lumber to windows— but verification will really be up to you. The more homework you do in advance, the less chance there will be for misery later. Insist the salesperson call the factory if anything is in doubt, or in the contract stage make the manager put what you need or what is being promised in writing.

While we were shopping, we were often given false assurances. For instance, many Clayton salespeople promised every "Greenbriar" model was high-end and thus came from the factory with the Duke Power energy standard. Actually, standard in that model was R-11, R-11, R-21—far shy of the Duke standard. We were also promised the window package upgrade we eventually bought was Energy Star certified. All the salespeople we asked proudly pointed to the prominent Low-E stickers on the windows. (In 2004, Clayton Homes' Web site proudly announced they were the 2003 "Energy Star Partner of the Year" and claimed Clayton was the only home manufacturer to offer Energy Star certified homes from every one of its manufacturing plants.) Only after we moved in did I discover Low-E is not equivalent to Energy Star and that, in fact, every Energy Star window is specifically labeled as such (look for the National Fenestration Rating Council, or NFRC, label). Our windows are not so marked, and while they do meet the winter Energy Star requirements in our geographic region, they do not meet the summer requirements. The labels they do carry are actually somewhat misleading, implying outstanding performance in both seasons. Ironically, a window's insulation efficiency can be a considerably more important factor in a hot climate — according to the Environmental Protection Agency (EPA), window loss accounts for up to 25 percent of a home's heating load but up to *50 percent of a home's cooling load*. Knowledge is power, so try to be as informed as you can. If your salesperson asserts the windows you are considering are Energy Star certified, ask to see the NFRC label. In fact, and please forgive the repetition: get *every-*

thing that is important to you in writing — before you sign the contract. The truth of the matter is that these were probably still the best window options we had available to us from the factory, but we should not have been mislead about their ratings or capabilities!

Left: Salespersons would point to these stickers while promising Energy Star features. Despite the phrase "year round energy savings," this expensive window option does not meet summer Energy Star requirements. *Right:* The sun and snowflake symbols also tend to indicate year round performance.

Entire homes can also be rated as qualifying for the Energy Star standard, and many people are surprised that manufactured homes can fall into this category as well. The general Environmental Protection Agency guideline for this standard is that the home uses 30 percent less energy than homes built to the older "Model Energy Code" standards while maintaining or improving indoor air quality. These are great homes which are cheaper to own and which will maintain a higher resale value — but *ask for proof in the form of the blue EPA Energy Star label.* If they cannot show it to you, then the salesperson is not telling the truth. The EPA uses five related features to evaluate these homes:

1. improved insulation
2. high-performance windows
3. tight construction
4. tight ducts
5. energy-efficient heating and cooling equipment

Also, don't be embarrassed about verifying what salespeople tell you. We were told over and over again by salespersons that certain models could come from the factory with finished drywall throughout — only to find out later that one could have up to three rooms finished, and another one came from a factory which never did any finished drywall. If the feature is important to you, double check. Have the dealership check with the factory, or check yourself unless you are buying a home right off the lot which you've already seen. Salespeople often don't know, they are frequently new, and, as I hope you've seen by now, they are quick to stretch the truth even when they do know the facts. Many of them need to make a sale to keep their jobs, and that's a pretty good motivator. So ask questions and verify information regularly. I operated a retail computer business for a number of years, and, if anything, I learned to respect the customers who asked a lot of questions. They were the ones who had done their homework and spent their money wisely. Honest people generally aren't bothered by questions, so if your salesperson or dealership doesn't like questions, ask yourself *why*.

There are other types of dishonesty you can expect to encounter at dealerships. One is misleading printed information. As we noted earlier, "Sue" and many other salespeople frequently bragged about being the "Manufactured Housing Institute's Manufacturer of the Year" three years running. The Manufactured Housing Institute sounds like a very dignified academic bastion of integrity, doesn't it? Flashy vinyl stickers attached to every model home's front door and scattered through the offices touted it. Clayton Homes, Inc., employees would always respond to my inquiries about what this "reward" was based on by making vague general statements about "quality" and "customer satisfaction." I contacted the Manufactured Housing Institute several times by phone and in writing to find out just what the "Manufacturer of the Year" award was based on. No one at the Institute could or would tell me why Clayton

Salespeople indicated that this award was based on overall quality or customer satisfaction. Calls to the Manufactured Housing Institute, who supposedly issue this award, could not verify this. In fact, employees at the Manufactured Housing Institute repeatedly said they did not know what the significance of "Manufacturer of the Year" was.

Homes won that distinction or provide me with any details about the award in general. Since *most of the members of the "Institute" are businesses — specifically manufactured home parts suppliers/vendors,* I suspect it is based on who buys the most product and has nothing to do with quality.

There are a couple of ploys or techniques used by salespersons that you need to avoid at all costs. One of the first things they are likely to ask about is a trade in. If you do have a home to trade-in, this is *not* the time to mention it. Just tell them that a trade-in isn't an issue or that you are considering a home for a new property, or if they somehow get it out of you that you do have an existing home you'll need to move (and if you've read this book you have no excuse to fail that badly) then tell them Uncle Jimmy has already agreed to buy it from you. Why, you might rightly ask at this point, why must I begin to deceive when I find it so egregious when they treat me that way? The answer is simple, they are specifically learning information to negate your trade-in value; that is, *they are using it to shortchange you.* Upon learning you have a trade-in and finding out its model, and therefore its approximate value, they will inflate any prices they quote you by approximately that amount. For instance, if you have a 1,000-square-foot home ten years old and in excellent condition, it might be worth $7,500 or possibly more on the open market. Maybe you're looking at a 2,000-square-foot new home for which the dealership would have quoted you a base price of $60,000. Now that they know about your trade-in, that base price jumps up to $67,500. Of course, you'll get your $7,500 trade-in value, or maybe you'll only get $5,000 or so. *Your friendly little chat with the salesperson just cost you $7,500 to $10,000 plus interest for the next 20 to 30 years.* The dealership just got a used home to sell for nothing more than it costs them to move it. Always get your best price before you bring up your trade-in, and then fight to get a fair price for it. It's your money, so get your game face on and take it to them!

Focusing you on monthly payments is one of the most deadly traps salespeople are likely to set. In their training sessions at the dealerships this is drilled into them. It completely takes your perspective of comparing home prices and values away from you and turns your search for a home into a game of "how much can you afford." They ask you about your income, calculate how much they believe you can afford to pay, and then find the most expensive home package they can fit into it. Not only is this one of the reasons for a high rate of foreclosures on manufactured homes, it is an insult to every educated consumer, and you should recognize it as such. *You* should determine how much you can afford in home payments, and if you need help with this, a traditional bank or mortgage broker is a much safer bet than a salesperson or dealership manager. Always allow an extra margin of safety; never let a salesperson subtract your normal bills and expenses from your income and use the difference as "what you can afford." Furthermore, your goal is to save money by buying a quality manufactured home; it is not to spend as much as you can.

We've been talking specifics here, but there is an important general warning which you must observe just in case you are in that majority of the populace who really likes to be friendly and trusting of others: do not fall for emotional ploys. Do not. We heard two common themes with slight variations over and over: (1) this is just like the home I bought for my mother, or (2) this is just like the home I sold for cost to my preacher/reverend/priest. (Even one of a manufacturer's regional managers used a version of this one.) Other typical pitches include a slightly overly intimate admission that "This is the same home I chose for myself" (with the implication that the salesman could have had any of them). Some just tug at the heartstrings without reference to particular homes. One I liked was how this young saleswoman flew hundreds of miles every month to Florida to visit her sick grandmother — that was why she missed appointments with us. Funny, since she flew there every month, and presumably had the tickets and had arranged time off, she would have known in advance she wouldn't be at the dealership to meet us. Unfortunately, these ploys often work no matter how terrible they are because they do play with our emotions. If a lie manages to make the customer begin to like the salesperson, that commission is halfway in their pocket. Remember, this isn't about love or common bonds and interests. It's business. Underneath the facade, you had better understand the *real* dynamics of the relationship, or you'll certainly get taken. The truth of the matter is that *good salespeople make more sales by studying the weaknesses of the customers than by knowing their product.* Don't show weaknesses. Show only what you want them to see.

This emotional appeal is more than an effective sales technique, it's ingrained in the corporate philosophy. Companies use slogans like "Building the American Dream," and name models which they want to aggressively push on customers "Dream Homes." The last thing you want to do is succumb to this sentimental sales pitch, this calculated corporate ploy — or your dreamy state will likely soon turn into the American nightmare. *Keep your emotions in check* until you find the home you really want and until the ink is dry.

There are a hundred subtle things to look out for, but once you understand the game you can recognize them for what they are. Models will sometimes have expensive air-fresheners installed and beautiful furniture to inflate the appeal of the home beyond what it would otherwise be. These are the manufactured home equivalents of painting fast food restaurants in orange tones to make you hungry. Entryways are often posted with signs saying something to the effect of "Our homes are locked for our customers' protection"—they're really locked so customers can't browse without a salesperson's "guidance," instead you'll need to go to the sales office first and then be shepherded around the lot. Hokey promotions are common, such as "free" televisions and "free" vacations if you purchase a home. The televisions are usually cheap sets, and the vacations usually aren't entirely free. In one example, a free cruise offer, the "Mini Vacations" company more than doubles port charges you're responsible for and tries to make extra money on "upgrades" which aren't really upgrades. They may charge you hundreds extra to avoid sleeping in bunk beds, for instance, even when the actual cruise ship on that route uses twin lower beds as its most basic accommodation—therefore *you are tricked into paying extra for nothing.* You'll also most likely be sailing off season, or again you'll pay hundreds extra. The end result is that the "free" vacation may cost more than one you book through your local travel agent.

Sometimes the offers are so extravagant they are hard to resist. One lady from McAllen, Texas, filed a complaint with the Attorney General's office after she had visited a dealership because of an ad for a "free car" with the purchase of a manufactured home. She called before she went to the dealer to make sure the offer was legitimate, and they assured her it was. After she purchased her home, though, she was informed no car would be forthcoming; supposedly the salesperson who promised free cars had been terminated, and the dealer wasn't going to honor that offer. If it sounds too good to be true, it probably is, and anything you get from a dealership is going to be paid for with interest.

Even away from the dealership, the come-ons are terribly misleading. In the "homes for sale" section of the paper, countless ads which look like great opportunities from individuals are usually really just made up by creative lot managers with extra time on their hands. If the advertisement talks about a great deal due to a divorce, just "taking over payments," living in a great "pool" community, touts something like "Please help me save my credit," or simply offers too good a price to be true, you'll probably see more fake ads with different gimmicks using the *same phone number.* That's your tip-off that it's a rip-off!

Probably the most popular scam that dealerships use is called "bait and switch." There are a myriad of variations, and this general technique has sold manufactured homes by the millions. One variant has the dealer advertising extremely low prices on a repossessed or older model home. The customer comes in and makes an offer, but the loan doesn't get approved. Fortunately for him, however, the general manager ran his credit application for a new model, and he was approved for that one! (Please note the sarcasm.) Of course, his payments would be a lot higher, but, after all, this would be a brand new home. Another popular variant is to advertise non-existent homes and non-existent salespeople. The name of the non-existent salesperson the potential customer uses when they call or drop by alerts the real salesperson to what type of fish they have nibbling at the worm (that is, what ad they fell for). Of course, the model home they want to see has just been "sold," but they do have a great deal on another new home which is just loaded with features!

If you don't see a home model you're interested in while shopping on a sales lot, or if they can't order something you're interested in, don't be persuaded into just "coming into the office" for a talk or so they can get your information. You are there to get information for yourself, *not* to give it out. If they do have models that interest you or can be ordered to your liking, just get an approximate price (and be sure you know roughly what that includes—landings, brick skirting, heat pump/AC, etc.) and leave unless *you're* ready to start earnest negotiations. Do not let them pressure you into filling out any kind of papers right then and there. Finally, be willing to walk off the lot or out of the office at any time. There are other dealers; in fact, there are probably more just across the street or within a mile down the road. The strategy of walking out can also be extremely helpful right through the contract stage. If not overdone, it's a very effective way of getting the salesperson's attention or winning important concessions.

After you've found at least two or three models you really like, then make sure you visit at least two or three different dealerships that carry them. Again, don't be specific about where you've been and how much you know, or you will only hurt yourself in negotiations. Some companies will even forbid competition among dealers, knowing it cuts into revenues. You might find major differences in price or in setup charges. Going to dealerships 50 or 75 miles away is sometimes helpful and will seldom greatly affect your final cost negatively (most dealerships within that range claim not to charge extra for delivery). Some dealerships or salespeople also need sales more badly, and this often affects mark-ups. Just beware of using a dealership which looks like it is about to fold because it looks run-down or has very few models on it. A bargain may be no bargain if you have no after-sale support or worse if they go bankrupt before your new home is delivered or completely set up. Ask for references if you are suspicious.

To illustrate the need for comparison shopping, consider a new Consumers Union report released January 27, 2005, which found customers who shopped at three or fewer dealerships paid substantially more (about 10 percent more on average) than those who compared more than three prices. This Texas study cited one example in Dallas County where a new "Alamo" model by Clayton Homes (a 76' by 16' single-wide home) was sold to a consumer for $42,000, yet in neighboring Franklin County the exact same model was selling for $33,800, a savings of roughly 20 percent. The more you shop, the more you save....

After you have the models, specifications, and general pricing in hand, you're ready to start serious negotiations. Then you can take the best price or try to get one or more dealers to lower their quote based on another one. If you get far enough along in negotiations greed kicks in, and pitting one dealer against another one regarding price is much more apt to work for you. At this stage, you can make the often unsavory nature of the business work for you.

Following are some common traps to avoid while dealing with salespersons:

    1. letting the salesperson take control of your visit

    2. not bringing your tools (pad and pen, tape measure, stud finder, flashlight, and digital camera)

    3. telling the salesperson you have a trade-in up front

    4. telling the salesperson what other lots you've seen, what prices you've been given, or letting the person see any of your written notes—play it close to the vest!

    5. getting walked into the office to "talk" before you even know if they have what you want

    6. falling for misleading "awards" or general assertions of how this brand or series home has the highest "quality" in the business or the lot the best service — none of it is legitimate information

    7. not getting written documentation of features and floor plans or not taking notes

    8. getting in a premature discussion of how large a monthly payment you can afford

    9. emotionally bonding with the enemy (that is, the salesperson)

    10. being pressured into *anything*

CHAPTER 5

The Devil Is in the Details: Responsibilities and Contracts

If you've gotten this far in the process, you've done a lot of research, visited numerous dealerships, and found at least a couple of homes you like. Now you're ready to start talking seriously about money. Roughly a third of the hard work is done. By now you've also seen that a book on this subject by its nature repeats common themes — you are continually doing your homework, customizing and changing your home plans, and constantly bargaining with dealership representatives. At this point, it should be second nature to you, and you're getting better at it. That's outstanding, because presently you're about to start dealing with the biggest, fastest shark in the sea — the sales manager. Sales managers know all the tricks of the salesperson plus a few more. In addition, now they (the salesperson and the boss) most probably will work in tandem against you.

First, you want to do your best to determine exactly what your money is paying for. As you've gathered by now, dealerships tend to want to lump things together and keep things hazy. You want to get itemized pricing to the extent possible. That means you want to begin with a price for the base home you're interested in — just the home and its standard features. You're now at the stage where you can begin to apply pressure on their asking price, or bargain. Remember that they have a substantial margin to work with, and don't be timid. If they are asking for $50,000 and you'd be happy with $45,000, you might start by asking them to take $40,000. At this point, keep setup and delivery charges out of the picture entirely, or you'll never be able to make accurate "apples to apples" price comparisons with other dealers. Don't let them "bump" you up by more than $100 or $200 at a time.

Once you have your starting price, begin to ask about your cost for the various extras you are "considering" individually. Keep in mind that something you are only considering usually costs less than something you *have* to have. Need is a terrible bargaining position, so even if in your heart of hearts you undeniably must have the fireplace, the salesperson does not necessarily have to know that. In fact, only let the salesperson or manager see that inner sanctum at your peril. Now you can begin to get individual prices for the items you require in your new home as well as for those on your wish list. This is fairly easy — just bring copies of the wish list you made earlier. If there are notes on it from other dealerships, do not let the salesperson or manager look at it — *ever*. If you want, you can give them a list of options without any notes just so they can jot down some prices for you. If something seems high, it's OK to say something to the effect of, "At Bill's American Home dealership, they only charge $150 for installing factory ceiling fans." (Give a specific dealer name only if you have to.) This tactic is most effective if you use it sparingly and on items where it truly looks like there is too much markup. Never, at any point of the negotiations, tell the dealership they have the best prices — that will virtually ensure that something else gets marked up to make up the difference. Like everything else, get these price quotes in writing.

At this stage of the process, you will begin dealing not just with the cost of the home but with the legal responsibilities of both parties — who is required to do what. Part of this involves preparing the land for the home, moving the home to the site, securing it properly, and finishing the trim work. Now that you know how much home you can purchase for a given amount of money, find out about setup charges. These can vary tremendously — I've seen setup charges for identical home installations vary by over $10,000. It is extremely important to look at these costs individually. Many dealerships advertise fantastic prices on homes to get you on the lot and make a sale and then make a large percentage of their profit on outrageous setup fees. Use the same process that you used before. Compare prices, and remember that everything is negotiable. Bargain hard for the best deal. Don't let anyone tell you something to the effect of, "Yes, our setup charges are higher, but that's because we use the best people in the business." That is one of the standard industry lines.

This book is dedicated to the principle that the guarantee of your new home's setup rests with you — you will make sure the home is right before you accept it, because relying on the dealership management or the professionalism of the work crew will often let you down regardless of what anyone says. The manager typically hires the cheapest crew, and turnover among setup workers is sometimes as high as it is among salespeople. If you talk to the former for very long, you'll soon find out that discontent runs high, and discontent is not a breeding ground for quality. I mention this point here so that you aren't willing to pay more for some reverie of higher quality which exists only in a pitch; we'll cover the specifics of how you supervise your setup later.

This stage also represents an opportunity to save some money if you or someone you know well has the skills or ability to do some of the setup work or if you shop around and find a professional who will do some of the work for a lot less than the dealer charges. If your best friend happens to be a mobile home mover, or if you are a brick mason, you could save substantially by doing major elements of the job yourselves. Just brick skirting alone can cost several thousand dollars on larger homes, and that doesn't even include the concrete footing. This can be a double-edged sword, however. You will have to make sure that nothing you do will negatively impact your legal rights under your home warranty, and if time is a factor, contracting out or doing some of the work yourself may slow the overall process. For instance, what if your friend is delivering your home and the hitch literally falls off one of the sections of the house, dropping the home on the road? This actually happened to us, only it was the dealer's driver. Would the manufacturer or dealer contend it happened because your friend was driving recklessly? You could lose far more money than you saved. Even if the friend were insured, this could drag out the whole process for many months. This latter point brings up another: if the dealer makes all the arrangements, he or she is responsible for the timing and coordination of the various independent contractors/work crews, and they tend to work quickly to get on to the next job. They usually use workers who are accustomed to operating together.

In other areas, there is less reason for concern about locating your own contracted work crews. For instance, our dealer-arranged "trim" crew wanted $6,000 to do three rooms in finished drywall (as opposed to having the seams covered by trim strips typical in manufactured houses). After a few phone calls, we found a drywall company that would do the same job for only $1,800. Drywall work performed after the rest of your setup is finished should in no way interfere with the dealer's workers or affect your warranty. Again, it's a matter of doing a little investigative work. Just make sure that you don't save money in some way that can hurt you in the long run. If you're doing a land-home deal, you may want to shop around regarding prices for installing wells or septic tanks in rural areas. These are big ticket items: They can be done fairly independently of other setup issues and represent a good potential source of savings. If in doubt regarding anything, pay the dealer to assume the responsibility. Also, if you feel the dealer's price is high for some aspect of the setup, there is nothing to keep you from getting quotes from other contractors even if you don't necessarily intend to use them. (If this is the case, be respectful of those contractors' time by not taking too much advantage of it.) If they quote substantially lower prices for identical work, *you can then use those quotes as leverage to get the dealer to lower his prices.* Let the dealer know you are cost conscious and will not be taken advantage of.

At this point, you also need to consider another wish list of sorts as well. Fortunately, this one is comparatively simple. It involves your home's setup: what elements do you require or simply desire for the sake of economy, convenience, or aesthetics. A competent and honest dealer should be able to handle most of this for you, but there is no guarantee your dealer is competent and even less likelihood he or she is honest. First, the property must be ready for the home. The dealer will usually come out (or send someone out) to check the land, but usually they only want to see if the home can be physically moved there. If you look in your contract, you'll likely find you're responsible for other critical elements like site grading and water drainage — which can affect your warranty — so explicitly ask if these will be issues. If you are purchasing a land-home package (buying the property through the dealership as well), the dealership will probably assume more responsibility for land suitability, but be sure. Get responsibilities in writing. You may want to ask about who the individual contractors will be so you can obtain references. Regrettably, this seldom helps. The only references you will likely receive will be from customers who are satisfied — even if 90 percent of their former customers criticized their work in actuality.

Major considerations during the contract stage include your heating and air conditioning options. From the factory, most manufactured homes come with a generic "one size fits all" electric heater and are "air conditioning ready." Typically now, these factory heaters are used for an emergency or back-up heat source. They are not efficient and will likely be expensive to use. The dealer normally contracts a local heating and air-conditioning company to hook up a more suitable unit (based, of course, on who offers the dealer the lowest cost) and adds it as part of the "setup" cost. In our region of the country, the Southeast, that usually consists of a heat pump. (Heat pumps provide both heating and cooling.) The dealer we eventually selected told us they installed 3½ ton units in all of their large homes, and that's what they tried to install for us— even though our home was almost 400 square feet larger than any home they had sold before. (The smaller the unit, the lower the dealer cost. Do you recognize a trend here?) Other dealers had recommended a 4 ton unit, and we insisted on that instead. The best way to determine what you really need is to consult an expert in heating and cooling before you sign the paperwork. If the unit is too small, it will run continuously and not properly heat or cool; if it is oversized it will short-cycle, or shut off before it reaches peak efficiency. Short-cycling means equipment will wear out more quickly and will be more costly to operate. Air conditioners, for instance, reach peak efficiency in about ten minutes according to the Environmental Protection Agency. If your run times are considerably shorter, your unit is probably much too large.

Energy efficiency is also a cardinal consideration in this regard. Space conditioning typically accounts for at least 40 percent of a home's budget. Heat pumps are rated for heating efficiency (HSPF, or heating season performance factor) and cooling efficiency (SEER, or seasonal energy efficiency ratio). Several dealers bragged to us about how they used only high-efficiency units rated 10 SEER. (Air-conditioning can become a major issue here in the summer!) Curiously, a little research revealed that currently federal law actually prohibits the sale of any heat pump with a SEER rating below 10, or a HSPF rating below 6.85. Energy Star heat pumps have SEER ratings of 12 or higher, and HSPF ratings of 7 and up. Don't be taken in — units with SEER ratings of 12 are widely available for little extra cost, and they will save you money for many years to come. Also, find out about the unit's warranty. Ours was covered by a buyer protection plan for five years; alternatively the manufacturer (Goodman) offered a comprehensive five-year warranty for only $20 at the time of installation. Heating and air-conditioning repairs are expensive enough to justify inquiring about warranties in advance.

There are also a host of smaller considerations, some of which have been touched on. What kind of steps or landings will the dealer provide? Will they use a perimeter footer under brick skirting? Will the mason give you a choice of brick colors, or do you have to settle for whatever is in stock? If you don't find out about all the details, you will have to be satisfied with whatever the dealer provides. In our case, for instance, the fine print noted we would have only one access door to underneath our home. Not wanting to have to crawl up to 80 or 90 feet in case of needed service, I said we would need two doors— one at each end of the home. The dealer checked and said that was fine, but the contractor (a brick mason in this case) wanted $250 to pay for the extra door. I called a local masonry supplier, found the *identical door for under $30*, and the contractor then agreed to let me supply the door and install it for no extra cost. Not only did we have better access to underneath our home, we saved $220 and demonstrated to the dealer and the contractor we weren't totally gullible.

Once you get pricing all ironed out, then it's time to talk about trade-ins if you have one. This may well cause quite a fuss— because dealers like to mark up their prices accordingly for trades. They may even say that they don't accept trade-ins. Not very many dealers could stay in business without doing that, however. Being a savvy consumer, you've already probably spotted a number of trade-ins on the lot, and you've probably called around to check on the blue book value of your home (hint!) so you know what it's *really* worth before the dickering starts. Our dealer told us he wouldn't accept a trade-in, so we said that was a deal breaker and walked out. It was already after a great deal of soul searching and haggling, and it was very hard to walk out the door. We really liked the home, and we had gotten a pretty good price. You have to remember the flip side of the equation, though. The salesperson really needed a sale. The manager knew very well that the dealership still stood to make a great deal of money. They had also invested a lot of time "working us over." Before we drove off the lot, the salesperson literally ran out the door and asked us to come back. After we called his bluff, the manager changed his mind, and we got almost as much money as we had asked for. Of course, we asked for more than we expected, and we were taking our time walking to our car. We were fairly sure they would come after us. It was a calculated risk, but recognizing that at this point their incentive was even greater than ours, we played it, and it paid off. If not, we had two or three other dealers we were interested in. As it was, the dealership sent out a crew to move the old home off our property the day before the new one arrived. We didn't have to search for a buyer or make any arrangements for home movers. There were no timing issues to coordinate.

Once you have all the details ironed out to your satisfaction — and only then — should you get to the contract or "sales agreement." This is a critical point, and one you should not rush into. You will likely be dealing direct with the sales manager or the equivalent of such. Sales managers will have a well-rehearsed pitch, going over what points they want to, and glossing over what they don't. The contracts are long and complicated, even before financing is considered (which we'll soon cover). Managers will push through and try to get everything done in one meeting usually. Often, customers will be required to watch a mandatory short film — which covers some of the company's perceived legal responsibilities in the safest way possible. This is about like watching a film in elementary school, and most customers won't remember to ask relevant questions about it later. If you are required to watch a film, jot down any things that are suspicious, and inquire about those points later to determine exactly what the legal import is. Some of it will likely deal with issues of your warranty and things which can void it. In covering the contract later after the film, don't be surprised if the sales manager also records critical parts— again a step to legally protect the dealership, getting a taped record that you understand and accept the contract. There is a slight problem here, though. It is doubtful that even an attorney could understand everything that is presented at this meeting fully and completely without studying the material. You will be whisked over it and asked to sign and state for the record that you do.

Red flags should be going off everywhere in your head, and the best thing you can do is not make a mistake. I'd like to cover one example of a possible point of contract contention here in depth, but first a simple piece of advice: *refuse to sign any contract until after you have had a chance to take it home and study it.* No matter what protest the dealer may make, insist on this. Go back to your kitchen table or office, have a family pow-wow, and read every word. When in doubt, call someone who knows more about such matters. If you're friends with a lawyer, give that person a call regarding suspicious passages. At the least, note any concerns and make sure the dealer can adequately explain them or insist on the contract being changed. A contract is an agreement between two or more parties— you are not totally at the company's mercy unless you agree to it. You have a right to insist on amending the document until it is satisfactory to all parties or to walk away if you can't. If the dealer doesn't want to let you take a copy of what he or she wants you to sign with you, ask him or her — and ask yourself — why not.

That said, let's get on to our example. This was a point of dissonance in the case of the home we eventually purchased and the contract we signed. My wife and I had the full contract faxed to us in advance of the signing. We both noticed one particular passage which concerned us. We, in turn, faxed it to someone else to review it — and that person had the same concern. The passage regarded arbitration:

> **ARBITRATION:** All disputes, claims or controversies arising from or relating to this contract, or the subject hereof, or the parties, including the enforceability or applicability of this arbitration agreement or provision and any acts, omissions, representations and discussions leading up to this agreement, hereto, including this agreement to arbitrate, shall be resolved by mandatory binding arbitration by one arbitrator selected by Seller with Buyer's consent. This agreement is made pursuant to a transaction in interstate commerce and shall be governed by the Federal Arbitration Act at 9 U.S.C. Section 1. Judgment upon the award rendered may be entered in any court having jurisdiction. The parties agree and understand that they choose arbitration instead of litigation to resolve disputes. The parties understand that they have a right to litigate disputes in court, but that they prefer to resolve their disputes through arbitration, except as provided herein. **THE PARTIES VOLUNTARILY**

AND KNOWINGLY WAIVE ANY RIGHT THEY HAVE TO A
JURY TRIAL. The parties agree and understand that all disputes
arising under case law, statutory law and all other laws including,
but not limited to, all contract, tort and property disputes will be
subject to binding arbitration in accord with this contract. The parties agree that the arbitrator shall have all powers provided by law,
the contract and the agreement of the parties. These powers shall
include all legal and equitable remedies including, but not limited
to, money damages, declaratory relief and injunctive relief.
Notwithstanding anything hereunto the contrary, Seller retains an
option to use judicial (filing a lawsuit) or non-judicial relief to
enforce a security agreement relating to the Manufactured Home
secured in a transaction underlying this arbitration agreement, to
enforce the monetary obligation secured by the Manufactured Home
or to foreclose on the Manufactured Home. The institution and
maintenance of a lawsuit to foreclose upon any collateral, to obtain
a monetary judgment or to enforce the security agreement shall not
constitute a waiver of the right of any party to compel arbitration
regarding any other dispute or remedy subject to arbitration in this
contract, including the filing of a counterclaim in a suit brought by
Seller pursuant to this provision.

In short, *the customer is waiving substantial legal rights in signing the
contract*, giving up "judicial relief" for binding arbitration. The company
is giving itself a safety blanket, avoiding any chance of costly litigation/law-
suits no matter what actions they might take or omit to take in the sale
and setup of the home. Furthermore, the buyer is agreeing to settle any
disputes by an arbitrator of the *seller's choice*. At the same time, note that
the seller (in this case Clayton Homes, Inc.) carefully reserves the right to
sue the customer. It's pretty obvious which of the two parties involved
crafted this document. We complained to the dealership's general manager when he glossed over this point in going over the contract with us;
we made it known we didn't like the provision. Apparently, someone else
had complained before because he had a ready-made spiel: "This is America. Everybody has the right to sue!" He went on to explain that this provision was mainly to keep the customer's cost down in the event there was
a problem, so they wouldn't need to hire attorneys. He added that if we
weren't happy with the results of arbitration, we were free to take the manufacturer or the dealership where we purchased the home to court and sue
them. He insisted this was the case even when we asked him to explain
what "binding" arbitration meant. In other words, the general manager
looked us straight in the eye and unequivocally lied to us regarding this
legal document. When it came time to record our understanding and
agreement, we kept trying to get his "clarification" of the arbitration

language on tape (that is, to record his saying that we did in fact have the right to take them to court if they were dishonest or negligent), but he didn't want to record *that* part.

Are points like this a big deal? Does the company really intentionally mislead you — that is, are they genuinely aware of the legal realities? Maybe you feel that possibly the employees don't understand the meaning of the language themselves. When we later had problems with our home, however, and threatened to seek out legal remedies when company representatives had abused our trust repeatedly, the Clayton regional manager literally laughed at me and told me point blank: "You signed a legal contract. You *can't* sue us." They know exactly what they are doing. I'm telling you now so you can see through the subterfuge and avoid the pitfalls. If there is a stipulation you can't live with, make amendments to the contract or find another manufacturer or dealer who will work with you. Our first home was defective from the factory and further damaged beyond repair during delivery from the dealership. It was flawed so badly that the dealer and manufacturer had little choice but to replace it. That involved a new contract — or a "Settlement and Release" in which Clayton Homes asked us to wave even more of our rights. We refused to sign the company's version; instead, we insisted on a revised version which the regional manager finally agreed to in which we did retain some rights. Here is one small section which might illustrate why we refused to sign the new contract — in effect, the manufacturer had so thoroughly protected itself they could have probably just dumped any replacement home on the site without even setting it up:

> Buyer(s), on behalf of themselves and their heirs and assigns, jointly and severally, do hereby forever release, discharge, indemnify and agree to hold harmless Clayton Homes, Inc., the above referenced Manufacturer, Seller and Contract Holder, and their respective directors, officers, employees, agents, subsidiaries, affiliates, successors, assigns, suppliers and insurance carriers, from any and all claims, liability, damages and expenses whatsoever, whether now existing or hereafter arising, including, without limitation, any and all claims relating to the manufacture, sale, delivery, setup or servicing of the Original Home or Substitute Home.

This manufacturer and owner of the dealership covered themselves pretty completely, didn't they? Always be aware of what you're signing; take as much time as you need to review the documents with family or professionals, and only obligate yourself to reasonable contracts. As in every other stage, *the company you are dealing with is looking to maximize their position at your expense.* This contract excerpt should amply demonstrate that; you have to be alert and protect your own interests vigorously. Many people without experience in legal matters or the corporate world don't realize they can request changes in legal documents—if they want the home, car, or job, they feel they have to blindly follow along with the powers that be and sign whatever is presented to them. Sometimes that is the case but certainly not always. When you are talking about an investment of $25,000 to $100,000 or more, you are paying for the right to have leverage yourself. Don't be embarrassed; use it. The dealer or manufacturer certainly won't hesitate to exercise its rights. This principle is certainly not only limited to the manufactured housing industry either, but given its nature and past history you should certainly exercise maximum vigilance when dealing with these companies.

The real truth is that forced arbitration in and of itself gives the manufacturer a very substantial advantage in any conflicts which may arise. Even Daniel Weinstein, a former superior court judge and senior judicial officer for Judicial Arbitration & Mediation Services, Inc., admitted the probability of "unconscious as well as conscious bias" toward the companies that hire the arbitrators repeatedly. In effect, the manufacturers are paying the salary of the persons responsible for determining who is right and who is wrong. According to court filings, the credit card company First USA arbitrated roughly 19,000 disputes, and in the process paid over $5 million in fees to the arbitrators they used. Bottom line: out of 19,000 cases they only lost 87 times, which is less than 1 in 200. How do you like those odds? (*"Paper Tiger, Missing Dragon,"* Consumers Union Southwest Regional Office, November 2002.)

There is another significant aspect to arbitration agreements that you should also be aware of: they may not be binding in all states and under all circumstances. Some states have specific stipulations such as requiring that arbitration clauses in contracts be in boldface type for them to be legal (note in the excerpt above Clayton Homes was careful to do that). Other factors can also come into play; for instance, if you have an FHA loan the arbitration clause may not be binding. To know for certain, you'll probably need to contact a qualified attorney. Try to find one with experience in this area of the law.

Contract or sales agreement details must also be worked out and scrutinized in other ways. It should list the *home and setup options,* and should have a place for the *seller's and buyer's responsibilities.* In addition to concerns already discussed, the contract should mention who is responsible for paying off any required property taxes and obtaining any permits. *It's a good idea to insist on having "set up to county code" or a similar line listed;* that way it leaves less room for misunderstandings. I told our dealer up front our county required landings which were one foot larger in one direction than the county in which we purchased the home. As a result, he gouged us for fully half the cost of our landings. It's just another example of how what you say can cost you hundreds of dollars. Silence really can be golden.

There might also be other *features you need which aren't required by code — get these spelled out in writing under the setup options or seller's responsibilities.* For instance, our homework taught us we needed lateral reinforcement on any perimeter brick work over 36" high. Our county code doesn't require it. In such a case, if the contract doesn't specifically call for it, the installer can really gouge you for this reinforcement later. (The same goes for other items previously discussed, like perimeter footers.) Taxes are another matter to check — dealers often try to charge (and succeed) for each section of multisection homes even when it's illegal. As previously mentioned, the state of South Carolina caps the tax on energy efficient manufactured homes at $300, but the dealer tried to get away with charging us $300 tax *per section*, or $600. We brought in the full text of the South Carolina law (available on the state government's Web site) and only paid the correct amount, saving another $300.

I just mentioned the problem of saying too much, and it's been highlighted before in the section on working with salespeople. Allow me to give you one last example here because sometimes as you get to the end of this long process you tend to relax. Salesman extraordinaire and bestselling author Harvey Mackay wrote a book called *Swim with the Sharks Without Being Eaten Alive* in which he described a sales routine designated as "Calling Mr. Otis." This scam is extremely common in the manufactured housing trade, at car dealerships, and other sales centers where sacrificial lambs are routinely slaughtered. Let's assume you've worked really hard, have gotten a good price on a home design you really love, and you're feeling justifiably proud. Everything is spelled out in writing, including the price, and although the papers aren't signed yet, they're drawn up and you're ready to go. Who could blame you when you mention with a satisfied smile that you were bargaining for the same exact model in the next city, but they wanted $5,000 more for the house and another $4,500 extra to set it up. The salesperson and sales manager share a laugh with you over that because they know you worked them over pretty good. You might not even bring it up first if you've let this dealer know you've been looking around. They might inquire what price you had been quoted elsewhere, just for "future reference." At this juncture, there's no point holding back anything, you've already landed the fish, right?

At this point, the sales manager will make a comment to the effect of,

"Well, that's all we have to do except to clear it with the general manager!" He or she seems to be just as excited as you are, and the person then sticks his or her head out in the hall or gets on an intercom and calls for Mr. Otis. Your five-pound bass just jumped right out of the boat. The name "Mr. Otis"—or whatever name this dealership uses—isn't real, it's code. Someone comes to the office (it might very well be the general manager, or it could be another salesperson) and probably politely greets you before extracting the salesperson or sales manager out of the room. "Mr. Otis" is long gone now, but the salesperson leaves you sitting there with your anticipation growing. When the manager or salesperson comes back from the "meeting," he or she sadly announces, "Mr. Otis won't go for the deal. I really wanted to help you out, so I quoted you a price that's way below our cost." The actual version used matters less than the fact that all your work has gone out the window. The quote is marked up to the same price the other dealer offered you, and it's take it or leave it. You showed them your cards, and you're playing poker. You never, ever, show your cards until everything is signed and delivered. If you are asked another dealer's price, say nothing (and pray you haven't given the name of the dealership because it can be called), or better still, say something like, "Really, their price was $3,000 *less* than yours, but we just felt good about working with the folks here. Y'all are *so nice.*" Now who's the salesperson? You can even do your own reverse version of Mr. Otis, and right before signing the deal receive a cell phone call from your father, who used to be a carpenter but now is in ailing health. (You can always excuse yourself to go to the bathroom and place a call to "Dad" from there, telling him or her to call you back in two minutes.) In fact, it turns out that dear old Dad is the reason you're buying a bigger place, so he doesn't have to move into a nursing home. Anyway, Dad is very upset you're buying this house because it doesn't have 6" walls with R-19 insulation. He says if they don't throw that in for the same price, you should walk out, and he is your father after all. If you're a gambler, and the dealer has your phone number, you might really walk out. (Make sure you have a hang-dog expression as you leave.) If there is financial room for the dealer to move, chances are you'll get a phone call. You probably won't get the call that day — the dealer will want you to convince Dad the home is OK as is. You'll probably get the call within a few days, though, before you could likely strike another deal elsewhere. If you are willing to fight fire with fire like this, be sure to take Dad (or Mom, Grandmother, Father Flannery, friend, etc.) out for a delicious celebratory meal if your gambit works.

Be willing to walk out at any time, even if you aren't a master gambler. That is the biggest weapon in your arsenal. Actually, if you don't threaten to walk out at least a time or two, then you probably haven't bargained hard enough! It's your money; fight for it. If a salesperson or dealer senses that you won't walk out, then *you're* facing the big guns, and what happens probably won't be pretty. It's not uncommon for dealers to mark up homes by 20 or 25 percent. This doesn't include what Kevin Burnside, the author of *Buying a Manufactured Home* and a former Fleetwood salesman, calls "kickbacks," or VIP money which is built into every invoice. These kickbacks are paid directly to the dealers by the manufacturers once a year and can amount to over 10 percent of the cost of every home invoice they have purchased during the year. It doesn't end there, either; dealers make more money through rebate programs, by padding the setup charges, and on the "back end." Back-end profit results from insurance and financing deals—whether because you purchase these directly from the dealership's own company or as referral fees and kickbacks from other companies for sending business their way.

Given what you now know about dealership profit margins, you should try not to pay more than 10 percent less than the starting price. This isn't set in stone, and some dealers and models may not have as much room to move, but it's a good rule of thumb. If the dealer starts out at $77,000, you might counter with $62,000, or about 20 percent less than the asking price. You'll never get that, but if you end up at $70,000 or below, you've helped your financial cause considerably, and the dealer is still making nice profit. As a reminder, always see if you can get the same thing for less elsewhere; you might be pleasantly surprised in the difference in markup, and the worst case scenario is that you gain more valuable information. Only offer more money in small increments of $100 or $200 at a time—you can be sure that's the way the dealer will offer monetary concessions. Maybe $7,000 doesn't seem like it's a whole lot to fight for. (If it doesn't seem like much, you're probably looking at other types of dwellings.) It would be worth it to most people, though, including most wealthy people—affluent people didn't get that way by being financially spontaneous. The sum of $77,000 financed at 7 percent (a rate most people should be able to easily get or get below at this time) would cost you $512.28 a month for 30 years. At the same rate, $70,000 would be $465.71 in monthly payments for the same duration. That's $46.57 less a month, or $16,765.20 over the life of the loan. (This might be enough to pay for your home insurance!) If your credit's not quite as good, though, or if you don't bargain for a good interest rate, that $7,000 difference becomes even greater. At 9 percent, for instance, the same sales price would cost you $56.32 more a month, and $20,275.20 more in interest. You can run these calculations yourself using a mortgage calculator, which is discussed in the chapter on financing. As you start getting final prices, these calculators can be a tremendous help in guiding your decisions without relying on salesperson's calculations, and they can also be a great motivator for making you dicker harder! In fact, I'm pretty sure we could shave another thousand or two off that price.... Put on your poker face, and be a lean, mean negotiating machine.

While on the subject of saving money, you should be aware of another potential tool in your arsenal: *timing*. Dealership lots are usually working with both monthly and yearly quota systems. The salespeople and retailer as a whole are under a considerable amount of pressure to meet these quotas. That can work to your advantage in that dealerships may be more eager to bargain to make a deal near the end of the month or in the latter part of December. The end of the year can be especially enticing to the general managers of dealerships because of the "kickbacks" they are paid then on their sales for the year.

There is another potential trap at this stage which can be easily side-stepped: *never agree to a large, nonrefundable deposit*. The dealer may ask for 5 or 10 percent down, but $100 to $200 should suffice unless you are custom ordering your home. Then you may need to pay as much as $1,000 or more. You should have in writing that the deposit is refundable if the financing does not go through or make certain you are preapproved at your choice of lenders before giving a deposit. Dealers often make money by trying to insist on substantial, nonrefundable deposits. If you give them a $5,000 deposit, are dependent on dealer financing, and it falls through, you could be in a very bad situation depending on the fine print in your contracts. You have to take charge and set the terms yourself. If the dealer insists on an outlandish arrangement, go elsewhere. Also make sure that any deposit is applied to the purchase price as opposed to becoming some "fee."

There will be other aspects in the contract, including attorney fees, title fees, and more. Look them over, and if you need to, make some calls to be sure they are fair. The biggest extra item should be insurance. Unless you are buying your home with cash, you are going to be required to have it. Like taxes, it can be escrowed into your payments (some lenders may insist on this, but not all), or it can be paid by you separately. This insurance protects the home, and since the bank will hold your title, it protects the bank. These expenses need to be closely examined. While companies have used financing and insurance for years as ways to pad in extra profit, they are taking it to new levels. Clayton Homes, Inc., may be the best at it. While other huge manufactured housing companies like Fleetwood were "gushing red ink" (according to the *Los Angeles Times* reporter Jesus

Sanchez in the article "Mobile Homes Await Rebound," June 8, 2003) during the recent "correction" mode, Clayton Homes remained profitable. Clayton offers home buyers home insurance in-house (that is, they own the insurance company — the HomeFirst Agency, Inc.), and they also own a finance company (Vanderbilt Mortgage and Finance). Clayton Homes doesn't tout the fact they own these companies to their customers, and without a doubt many people just purchase/choose Clayton's financial services without ever realizing that they are sinking more money into the very same business. What would clearly be a conflict of interest in any professional field is just good business for this industry.

It doesn't end there, though. The transaction is set up to "encourage" you to use their services. We'll see more details of this later in mortgages, but our dealership refused to take a letter of acceptance from a bank, which in effect forced us to use Vanderbilt Mortgage (Clayton Homes) to finance our home or spend thousands of extra dollars. Then, to get the best rate, we had to take out not only insurance with Clayton Homes, but a Home Buyer Protection Policy as well. That's right, if we didn't use the insurance products they suggested to us, we would be punished with a substantially higher mortgage rate which would have again cost us thousands of dollars. The Home Buyer Protection Policy (HBPP on our contract) cost an additional $580 up front, and of course we would be paying interest on it (more money which went into Clayton Homes' "back end"). This HBPP plan covered major appliances for five years. Can you see why this company has thrived? There's not any way that I can tell you exactly what you will face; it will depend on your location, the company and their current policies. Given Clayton's success, there is no doubt that many other manufacturers have taken notice and are implementing similar strategies.

In the chapter on mortgages, I will tell you how we dealt with our particular financing and insurance situation to come out on top, even with the deck stacked against us. For now, let me say this: make sure you can switch insurance companies at any time without any penalty. If you can choose a different insurance carrier up front without being penalized, shop around and compare several companies. Compare apples to apples — make sure you are looking at policies with the same dollar amounts, deductibles, etc. Be careful — at first the Clayton Homes' quote (HomeFirst/Voyager) looked pretty competitive. When we actually received the policy and read the fine print, however, we found out it was terrible! The bank (in this case Clayton Homes) was well protected, but the home buyer was not. For example, where most companies will normally group personal effects such as jewelry, silverware, electronics, CD collections, firearms, computers/ software, and so on into categories each of which has a cap such as $500 (and optionally let you pay more to increase this amount), our HomeFirst policy put a $250 cap on each individual category and a $500 total limit on all of them. If someone came in and stole every personal item in the home listed above, the policy would pay $500 minus the $250 deductible, or just $250. If someone came in and just stole a $2,000 wedding ring, your $500 college ring, and whatever other jewelry they could find, because of the caps and the deductible the insured would be entitled to *nothing*. Why is this policy so bad? Because it's worthless, and the home manufacturer therefore has increased profit. Shop around, and ask about the policy details. By now you probably see this admonition coming, but repetition engenders retention: the dealership looks out for itself, so you should too.

Finally, you should also carefully clarify warranties before you sign. Read them in full, and make sure they are something you can live with. Normally, setup carries a 90-day warranty, while the home itself is limited to defects which appear within one year. Increasingly now, some manufactured housing companies are offering longer warranties (several are currently offering five-year home warranties) as a selling point. The warranty date usually starts when the setup is complete — even if you don't move in for six months. Also make sure the local dealer will provide warranty service as opposed to the factory — the factory should be a last resort unless you happen to live near it. If a dealership were to go out of business, and that's fairly common, you might have to depend on the factory or another dealership. In many cases, the dealer and manufacturer may share warranty responsibilities — and squabbles between them can affect your home. Find out who does what. Even in the warranty, everything is negotiable. Cracks fairly commonly form in the ceiling sheet rock, and since the local dealer has a trim crew basically on call, you may get it to extend coverage of such problems. Get it in writing, though; a verbal promise doesn't mean much. Individual items like the subfloor, linoleum, shingles, etc., typically have their own extended warranties. Make sure you get paperwork regarding those additional warranties for reference and put them in a safe place. Find out who services any extra warranties as well.

## CHAPTER 6

Cases from the
Manufactured Housing Board

We've just spent the last two chapters wrangling with the difficulties of working with salespersons, sales managers, and general managers. To those who know me, they know I am by most measures open-minded and nonjudgmental. Frankly, I am somewhat bothered by my own stereotyping (with some limited caveats) of this relatively large group of human beings. If I am distressed by it, I suspect that you, the reader, may be as well. My experience with literally scores of salespersons and managers, however, presses me forward in my convictions. This book is primarily for the consumer, and to do the consumer justice, the story needs to be told without rose colored glasses. Forgive me then, if you can, for my indelicacy, and let these words stand as your weapon in this financial and emotional battlefield where you dare to tread. If such preconceived notions seem too harsh for you to bear willingly, then I have chosen to enlist another weapon of words with which to sway you to take heed: the South Carolina Freedom of Information Act. I have looked through the public documents regarding actions the South Carolina Manufactured Housing Board has taken (and not taken) to illustrate a few of the character flaws you may encounter. This chapter might just as appropriately be entitled "Dumb Crook News."

These are relatively recent cases, and I've tried to choose representative examples. There are many others which have been omitted —cases involving more misappropriated funds, "omission" of material facts during a manufactured home transaction, and salespeople using cocaine seem all too common. The names have been changed to protect the innocent (and the not so innocent), but the dates are real, and you can look these up yourself to verify them at the South Carolina Manufactured Housing Board. The added italics are mine, highlighting in most instances the specifics of the violations in the particular case. If you think South Carolina is different from the rest of the nation, think again. Consumer complaint files abound everywhere. According to findings of the Consumer Union (presented elsewhere in this book), Texas may be worse. Even the president of one of the leading manufacturers admitted to us it was a "shame" that the salespeople were the way they were, but that was the state of the "industry as a whole." It's true — there seems to be no correlation between location or brand and the quality of people you deal with. In part, this no doubt results from frequent turnover; an employee working for Oakwood this week might well be working for Champion next week.

BEFORE THE SOUTH CAROLINA MANUFACTURED HOUSING BOARD

In the Matter of:

ORDER

I. M. Lyon

    Applicant.

    This matter is before the Board pursuant to the application of I. M. Lyon (Applicant) for a license to engage in the business of selling as a manufactured home retail salesperson in this state. Upon staff review of the application, questions arose regarding Applicant's conduct and character and fitness for licensure. At the Board's meeting on May 13, 2003, Applicant appeared in support of the application. At that time it was established that *Applicant was previously denied licensure by Order, dated March 26, 2002, for misrepresentation or omission of material facts in a manufactured home transaction and employment of unfair, fraudulent, or deceptive acts or practices. It was further established that at the time of violation, Applicant was on probation pursuant to an Agreement with the Board, dated March 13, 2001, following a previous denial of licensure by Order, dated April 5, 2000, for misrepresenting or omitting material facts in manufactured home transactions and using fraudulent or deceptive practices.* Therefore, the record reveals a pattern of misconduct by Applicant while previously licensed, which clearly indicates, in the Board's estimation, a lack of the requisite character and fitness for licensure. After due consideration, the Board voted unanimously to deny the application and issue this Order.

The denial of Applicant's application is made pursuant to Section 40-1-130 of the 1976 Code of Laws of South Carolina, as amended, and is based upon Applicant's failure to satisfy the Board that he meets all requirements for the issuance of a license, including, among other things, possession of the character and fitness for licensure and requisite familiarity with the statutes and regulations of this Board, such as those specifically concerning the misrepresentation or omission of material facts in a manufactured home transaction and employment of unfair, fraudulent, or deceptive acts or practices, as evidenced by, among other things, the acts and omissions referenced above. Furthermore, the denial of Applicant's application is based upon Applicant's having committed acts that would be grounds for disciplinary action in this State, as evidenced by *Applicant's misrepresentation or omission of material facts in a manufactured home transaction and employment of unfair, fraudulent, or deceptive acts or practices, as evidenced by, among other things, the acts and omissions referenced above, in violation of Sections 40-29-150(4), (9) and (10), and 40-1-110(d), (f), and (g) of the 1976 Code of Laws of South Carolina,* as amended.

THEREFORE, IT IS ORDERED that Applicant's application for a license to engage in the business of selling as a manufactured home retail salesperson in this State be and hereby is **DENIED.**

AND IT IS SO ORDERED.

SOUTH CAROLINA MANUFACTURED HOUSING BOARD

6/9/03   BY: *John Doe*

Date   Vice Chairman of the Board

Page 1 of 1

BEFORE THE SOUTH CAROLINA MANUFACTURED HOUSING BOARD

In the Matter of:

ORDER

Bill Bruiser, III

Applicant.

This matter is before the Board pursuant to the application of Bill (Bully) Bruiser, III (Applicant) for a license to engage in the business of selling as a manufactured home retail salesperson in this state. Upon staff review of the application, questions arose regarding Applicant's conduct and character and fitness for licensure. At the Board's meeting on May 13, 2003, Applicant appeared with counsel, Ron Smith, V, Esquire, in support of the application. At that time, it was established that *Applicant has been the subject of numerous actions by this Board in the past for violation of the licensing laws, unpaid administrative penalties, and professional misconduct. The record discloses that Applicant's dealership license was suspended on or about December 1, 1989, and revoked on or about January 10, 1990, following a consumer complaint hearing. Applicant was subsequently cited for selling manufactured homes without a license on or about October 2, 1990, and July 1, 1992. The record further reveals that Applicant attacked a Board investigator on or about July 28, 1993, for which he was charged and pled guilty to assault and battery of a high and aggravated nature on June 20, 1994. It further appears that Applicant engaged without a license in a sale of manufactured homes in this State in a transaction with Jane Jones, on or about October 19, 1999. It further appears that Applicant has been involved in the delivery, setup, repair, underskirting, advertising and marketing of land/home sales pursuant to an Agreement, dated November 22, 1996. South Carolina requires that persons who engage in these activities be licensed, and Applicant is unlicensed. Therefore, Applicant has engaged in a pattern of conduct indicating a blatant disregard for lawful authority and applicable requirements of law, which supports the conclusion that Applicant lacks the character and fitness for licensure.* After due consideration, the Board voted to deny the application and issue this Order.

The denial of Applicant's application is made pursuant to Section 40-1-130, of the 1976 Code of Laws of South Carolina, as amended, based upon Applicant's failure to satisfy the Board that he meets all requirements for the issuance of a license, including, among other things, possession of the character and fitness for licensure and requisite familiarity with the statutes and regulations of this Board, such as those specifically concerning licensure and the regulation of manufactured home sales in this State, as evidenced by, among other things, Applicant's extensive record of blatant violations. Furthermore, the denial of Applicant's application is based upon Applicant's having committed acts that would be grounds for disciplinary action in this State, as evidenced by Applicant's engaging in the business of selling as a manufactured home retail salesperson in this State without a license and in violation of applicable provisions of law, as mentioned above, *in violation of Sections 40-29-30, 40-29-80(A)(8), (10), (12), (14), (15), and (B), and 40-1-110(d), (f), and (g) of the 1976 Code of Laws of South Carolina,* as amended.

THEREFORE, IT IS ORDERED THAT Applicant's application for a license to engage in the business of selling as a manufactured home retail salesperson in this State be and hereby is **DENIED.**

AND IT IS SO ORDERED.

SOUTH CAROLINA MANUFACTURED HOUSING BOARD

6/9/03	BY: *John Doe*
Date	Vice Chairman of the Board

Page 1 of 1

BEFORE THE SOUTH CAROLINA MANUFACTURED HOUSING BOARD

In the Matter of:

<u>ORDER</u>

Willie Wheeler

    Applicant.

This matter is before the Board pursuant to the application of (Slick) Willie Wheeler (Applicant) for a license to engage in the business of selling as a manufactured home retail salesperson in this state. Upon staff review of the application, questions arose regarding Applicant's conduct and character and fitness for licensure. At the Board's meeting on May 13, 2003, Applicant appeared without counsel in support of the application. At that time it was established that *Applicant has an outstanding citation dated September 20, 2002, for unlicensed practice. Neither the dealership nor the Applicant, as general manager, was properly licensed. Applicant admitted that violation and acknowledged his responsibility to satisfy the outstanding citation. It was further established that on or about January 31, 2001, Applicant engaged in a manufactured housing sales transaction with Mrs. Jane Doe and her husband, John.* Mrs. Doe was present along with Ms. Jill Jones and Mr. Isaac Johnson of the South Carolina Department of Consumer Affairs and Mr. Ivan Jordan of the Board staff, all of whom testified before the Board. From the evidence and testimony received, it appears that *the Doe transaction involved a failure to pay debts from the loan proceeds received and an unrecorded dealer held second mortgage known as a "throwaway mortgage," which essentially allowed the buyer to avoid making a down payment and paying the closing costs, as required by the purchase agreement and loan application filed with the lending institution. In this instance, Applicant admitted that he entered into a second mortgage agreement on behalf of the dealership, which allowed the Does to purchase the home without making the payments represented to the lender. The dealer's second mortgage was not filed of record, therefore, the lending institution had no notice of its existence. Applicant, for his part, denied involvement in any failure to disclose material facts or attempt to provide false or fraudulent information, asserting instead that there was no intent to defraud and that the failures to properly file and disburse funds were the result of oversight. Applicant's denial and explanation are unpersuasive.* After due consideration, the Board voted unanimously to deny the application and issue this Order.

The denial of Applicant's application is made pursuant to Section 40-1-130 of the 1976 Code of Laws of South Carolina, as amended, based upon Applicant's failure to satisfy the Board that he meets all requirements for the issuance of a license, among other things, possession of the character and fitness for licensure and requisite familiarity with the statutes and regulations of this Board, such as those specifically concerning the failure to satisfy the outstanding citation for unlicensed practice and misrepresentation or omission of material facts in a manufactured home transaction and employment of unfair, fraudulent, or deceptive acts or practices, as evidenced by, among other things, the acts and omissions referenced above. Furthermore, *the denial of Applicant's application is based upon the Applicant's having committed acts that would be grounds for disciplinary action in this State, as evidenced by Applicant's misrepresentation or omission of material facts in a manufactured home transaction and employment of unfair, fraudulent, or deceptive acts or practices, as evidenced by, among other things, the acts and omissions referenced above, in violation of Sections 40-29-80(4), (9) he and (10), and 41-1-110(d), (f), and (g) of the 1976 Code of Laws of South Carolina, as amended.*

THEREFORE, IT IS ORDERED that Applicant's application for a license to engage in the business of selling as a manufactured home retail salesperson in this State be and hereby is **DENIED**. Applicant shall not be eligible to apply again for licensure until such time, if ever, in the future as the outstanding citation has been satisfied and the Doe matter has been satisfactorily resolved with the Department of Consumer Affairs.

AND IT IS SO ORDERED.

SOUTH CAROLINA MANUFACTURED HOUSING BOARD

March 25th, 2003	BY: *Randolph Scott*
Date	Chairman of the Board

SOUTH CAROLINA DEPARTMENT OF LABOR,
LICENSING & REGULATION
BEFORE THE SOUTH CAROLINA HOUSING BOARD

In the Matter of:

Pants O. Fire
License Nos.: 32563   <u>FINAL ORDER</u>

Respondent.

This matter came before the South Carolina Manufactured Housing Board (the Board) for hearing on March 11, 2003, as a result of the Notice of Hearing and Complaint dated February 5, 2003 which was served upon the Respondent and filed with the Board. The hearing was conducted pursuant to S.C. Code Ann. §§40-1-90 and 40-29-10 (1976), as amended, and the provisions of the South Carolina Administrative Procedures Act (The APA), S.C. Code Ann. § 1-23-10 et seq (1976), as amended. The State was represented by Joe Smith, Esquire. The Respondent appeared and was not represented by counsel.

The Respondent was charged with violation of SC Code Ann. §§40-1-110, 40-29-80(4), 40-29-80(9), 40-29-80(10), 40-29-80(12), (Supp. 2001), and S. C. Code of Reg. 19-425.44 (1976), as amended.

FINDINGS OF FACT

Based upon the preponderance of the evidence on the whole record, the Board finds the facts of the case to be as follows:

1. The Respondent is licensed by the Board as a retail salesman, and as such, is authorized by the laws of the State of South Carolina to sell manufactured homes in the State. At all times relevant to the actions alleged in the complaint, the Respondent was employed as a retail salesman with Gold Mine Homes of West Columbia, South Carolina.

2. An investigator for the Board testified that *an investigation was conducted after receipt of a complaint from a lender who was asked to provide financing for a land/home transaction in which the Respondent was involved.* The complaining individual apparently alleged that *the Respondent provided the lender with a forged installment contract.* During the course of the investigation, a copy of the installment contract, dated August 8, 2001, was obtained from the files of the lender, and was placed into evidence without objection from the Respondent. The buyer and seller whose purported signatures appeared at the bottom of the installment contract testified during the hearing. *Both the buyer and seller denied that was their signatures on the contract.* However, both testified that they had signed the contract of sale for the land in question on or about August 8, 2002. The contract of sale of the buyer and seller admitted signing was on the letterhead of Friendly Realty, the listing agents for the property.

3. Further, the investigator testified that on or about October 2, 2002, he along with the Administrator for the Manufactured Housing Board met with the Respondent to discuss the forged installment contract. He testified during the meeting, *the Respondent admitted that he traced the signatures of the buyer*

and seller as they appeared on the contract of sale dated August 8, 2002, onto the installment contract dated August 8, 2001. During his testimony *the Respondent denied that he forged to signatures, but admitted that he traced the signatures onto the installment contract. The Respondent testified further that he created the installment contract with the August 8, 2001 date at the request of a lender representative, and that the representative always had knowledge that the installment contract was not personally signed by the individuals.* He also stated during his testimony that he is now fully aware of the seriousness of his actions, and would not repeat it in the future.

4. The State also presented testimony which shows that the Respondent's license expired owner about June 30, 2002 and was renewed August 29, 2002. *On or about August 10, 2002, following the license expiration date but prior to the renewal date, the Respondent signed as the authorized agent for Gold Mine Homes on the Form 500 that accompanied the installment contract.* The Respondent admitted that he signed the Form 500, and testified further that because the renewal application was processed through the business office, he was unaware that there was a lapse between the time the license expired and when it was renewed.

5. Further, the Board finds from the evidence presented that *the Respondent has violated the Board's Practice Act.*

CONCLUSIONS OF LAW

Based upon careful consideration of the facts in this matter, the Board finds it includes is a matter of law of that:

1. The Board has jurisdiction in this matter and, upon finding that a licensee has violated any of the provisions of S. C. Code Ann. §40-29-80 (Supp. 2002), has the authority to suspend for a determinate period, revoke or restrict a license issued to a licensee and may impose a civil penalty of not more than $2500 or any combination thereof. Further, upon finding that grounds for discipline exist, S. C. Code Ann. §40-1-120 (1976), as amended, provides that the Board has the authority to: issue a public reprimand; place a licensee on probation or restrict the entity's license for a definite or indefinite time and prescribe conditions to be met during probation, restriction or suspension including, but not limited to, satisfactory completion of additional education, of a supervisory period, or of continuing education programs; and impose the reasonable costs of the investigation and prosecution of a case.

2. The Respondent has violated S. C. Code Ann. §40-1-110(f), (1976), as amended, in that *the Respondent, as evidenced by the conduct described herein above, has committed a dishonorable, unethical and unprofessional act that is likely to deceive or harm the public.*

3. The Respondent has violated S. C. Code Ann. §40-29-80(4) (Supp. 2002) in that *the Respondent misrepresented a material fact in a manufactured home transaction when he traced to signatures of the buyer and seller from a sales contract onto an installment contract that was given to a prospective lender.*

4. The Respondent has violated S. C. Code Ann. §40-29-80(9) (Supp. 2002) in that *the Respondent employed fraudulent practices* in connection with a manufactured home transaction when he traced the signatures of the buyer and seller from a sales contract onto an installment contract that was given to a prospective lender.

5. The Respondent has violated S. C. Code Ann. §40-29-80(10) (Supp. 2002) in that the Respondent, as evidenced by the conduct described herein above, *used a deceptive act in an attempt to obtain financing for potential customer.*
6. The Respondent has violated S. C. Code Ann. §40-29-80(12) (Supp. 2002) in that the Respondent, as evidenced by the conduct described herein above, *acted as a representative of a license manufactured housing retail dealer when his license was inactive.*
7. The sanction imposed is consistent with the purpose of these proceedings and has been made after weighing the public interest in the need for continuing services of qualified manufactured home manufacturers against the countervailing concern that society be protected from professional ineptitude and misconduct.
8. The sanction imposed is designed not to punish the Respondent, but to protect the life, health, and welfare of the people at large.

NOW, THEREFORE, IT IS ORDERED, ADJUDGED AND DECREED that:

1. The Respondent shall pay a fine in the amount of $1,000. Said fine shall be paid within sixty (60) days of the date of this final order, and shall not be deemed paid until received by the Board.
2. The Respondent's license shall be placed in a probationary status for a period of one (1) year from the date of this final order, with the following terms and conditions to apply during the probationary term:
   a. The Respondent shall, within thirty (30) days of the date of the final order, furnish a corporate surety bond or other security in the form prescribed by the Board in the amount of $30,000.
   b. The Respondent shall, within ninety (90) days of the date of this final order, attend the salesman course offered through the South Carolina Manufactured Housing Academy, and submit to and receive the passing grade on the manufactured homes retail salesman's examination.
   c. Any additional violation(s) of the Board's Practice during the term of probation shall result in the immediate suspension of the Respondent's license until further order from the Board.
3. It's still the Respondent's responsibility to demonstrate compliance with the provisions of this final order, failure by the Respondent to comply with any of the provisions of the final order may result in the immediate temporary suspension of the Respondent's licensing pending hearing into the matter and until further order of the Board.
4. This final order shall take effect immediately upon service of the order upon the Respondent or Respondent's counsel.

AND IT IS SO ORDERED.

SC MANUFACTURED HOUSING BOARD

April 4th, 2003   BY: *John Doe*

Date   Chairman of the Board

BEFORE THE SOUTH CAROLINA MANUFACTURED HOUSING BOARD

In the Matter of:

<u>ORDER</u>

I. B. SELLER

　　Applicant.

　　This matter is before the Board pursuant to the application of I. B. Seller (Applicant) for a license to engage in the business of selling as a manufactured home retail salesperson in this state. Upon review of the application, questions arose regarding applicant's conduct and character and fitness for licensure. *Applicant has been denied licensure in the past based upon findings that she employed unfair, fraudulent, or deceptive acts or practices during a period of prior licensed practice.* See the Order of this Board dated April 10th, 2001. Applicant appeared before the Board at its regular meeting on June 11th, 2002, without counsel. She offered her own testimony concerning what she had learned from the disciplinary actions of the Board and her intentions of practicing as responsible manufactured home retail salesperson in this State. She also indicated to the Board for willingness to submit to probationary conditions in order to allow the Board to address the special risk that she presents to the public safety and welfare due to her history with this Board. After due consideration, the Board voted (with one vote in opposition) to grant the application with conditions and to issue this Order.

THEREFORE, IT IS ORDERED AND AGREED THAT

　　1. Applicant's application for a license to engage in the business of selling as a manufactured home salesperson is hereby granted subject to the following conditions:
　　　　a. The license will be placed on probation for a period of not less than one year. At the end of that period and upon showing of satisfactory practice as a manufactured home retail salesperson, Applicant may petition the Board to release her from the terms of this probation.
　　　　b. Applicant will furnish a surety bond or other security acceptable to the Board in the amount of $30,000 and will maintain this bond amount for a period of not less than one year.
　　　　c. Applicant's employer, a licensed manufactured home retail dealer in this state, will furnish a surety bond or other security acceptable to the Board in the amount of $60,000 and will maintain this bond amount for a period of not less than one year.
　　　　d. Applicant and her employer shall appear and report to the Board as requested by the Board.
　　　　e. Applicant shall promptly advise this Board in writing of any changes in management at her place of employment. Correspondence and copies of reports and notices mentioned here and shall be directed to:
　　　　　　LLR — Manufactured Housing Board
　　　　　　P.O. Box 11329
　　　　　　Columbia, South Carolina 29211—1329
　　2. It is further understood and agreed that if Applicant fails to abide by any of

the aforementioned terms and conditions, or if it should be indicated from a liable report submitted to the Board or to the Department of Labor, Licensing and Regulation, that Applicant has engaged in any activity in violation of the statutes and regulations which govern her practice, then Applicant's license may be immediately temporarily suspended until further Order of the Board following hearing into the matter. It is understood and agreed that by executing this Agreement, Applicant specifically consents to consideration by the Board of any appropriate sanction under §40-1-120 after the hearing required by this paragraph.

3. It is further understood and agreed that, pursuant to the South Carolina Freedom of Information Act, this Agreement is a public document.

4. It is further understood and agreed that this Agreement does not satisfy, prejudice, or stay any disciplinary action currently pending before the Board or which may be filed in the future.

5. Applicant shall cooperate with the Board, its attorneys, investigators, and other representatives in the investigation of Applicant's practice and compliance with the provisions of this Agreement. Applicant maybe required to furnish the Board with additional information as may be deemed necessary by the Board or its representatives. In addition to such request, the Board in its discretion may require Applicant to submit further documentation regarding Applicant's practice and it is Applicant's responsibility to fully comply with all such requests in a timely fashion. Failure to satisfactorily comply with such requests will be deemed a violation of this Agreement.

AND IT IS SO AGREED.

I AGREE:

I. B. Seller
Applicant

I AGREE:

Josh Dealer
Employer of Applicant

AND IT IS SO ORDERED.

SOUTH CAROLINA MANUFACTURED HOUSING BOARD

June 27th, 2002   BY: *John Smith*
Date   Chairman of the Board

Page 2 of 2

BEFORE THE SOUTH CAROLINA MANUFACTURED HOUSING BOARD

In the Matter of:

I. (Fireball) Steele,

                                        AGREEMENT

Applicant.

WHEREAS, this matter is before the Board pursuant to the application of I. (Fireball) Steele (Applicant) for a license to engage in the business of selling as a manufactured home salesperson in this state. Upon review of the application, questions arose regarding Applicant's conduct and character and fitness for licensure. At the Board's meeting on July 9, 2002, Applicant appeared without counsel in support of the application at which time it was established that *Applicant had multiple felony convictions for burglary and arson.* Applicant provided evidence that he is now released from the terms of probation for those convictions and that he has married and become a father since the time of the incidents involved in the criminal convictions. Applicant also presented letters of reference from employers and evidence of a job opportunity, if licensed. Applicant advised the Board of a willingness to restrict his practice and to submit to any other conditions as the Board may desire from time to time, to assure it of Applicant's continued fitness and qualifications; and

WHEREAS, the Board believes that it is in the public interest to issue a license to Applicant upon certain terms and conditions as provided below.

THEREFORE, IT IS UNDERSTOOD AND AGREED THAT:

1. Applicant shall be issued a license to engage in the business of selling as a manufactured home salesperson in this state, which shall be in a probationary status upon the following terms and conditions of probation, which shall continue in effect for a period of not less than one year and until further Order of the Board:

   a. Applicant shall comply with the terms of this Agreement and all state and federal laws, including those governing the sale of manufactured homes.

   b. Applicant shall appear and report to the Board as requested by the Board.

   c. Applicant shall Promptly advise the Board in writing of any changes in address, business, professional status, or compliance with this Agreement. Correspondence and copies of reports and notices mentioned here and shall be directed to:

   LLR — Manufactured Housing Board
   P.O. Box 11329
   Columbia, South Carolina 29211—1329

2. After a period of not less than one year of continuous compliance with the terms and conditions of this Agreement, Applicant shall be eligible to petition the Board for termination of this Agreement in the Board's discretion. At that time, Applicant shall appear and demonstrate to the Board's satisfaction that all of the terms and conditions of this Agreement have been fulfilled and that he should he granted full, unrestricted licensure status. At that time, the Board, in its discretion may grant or deny Applicant's petition in whole or part, or otherwise modify this Agreement as the Board may deem appropriate.

3. It is further understood and agreed that if Applicant fails to abide by any of the aforementioned terms and conditions, or if it should be indicated from reliable reports submitted to the Board that Applicant is otherwise unable to practice with reasonable skill and safety, then Applicant's license may be immediately temporarily suspended until further Order of the Board fol-

lowing hearing into the matter. It is understood and agreed that by executing this Agreement, Applicant specifically consents to waive the procedural requirements of S.C. Code Ann. §40-1-90. It is understood and agreed that by executing this Agreement, Applicant specifically consents to consideration by the Board of any appropriate sanction under §40-1-120 after the hearing required by this paragraph.

4. It is further understood and agreed that this Agreement does not satisfy, prejudice, or stay any disciplinary action currently pending before the Board or which may be filed in the future.

5. It is further understood and agreed that each provision of this Agreement shall be subject to review by the Board. Applicant shall cooperate with the Board, its attorneys, investigators, and other representatives in the investigation of Applicant's practice and compliance with the provisions of this Agreement. Applicant may be required to furnish the Board with additional information as may be deemed necessary by the Board or its representatives. In addition to such requests, the Board in its discretion may require Applicant to submit further documentation regarding Applicant's practice, and it is Applicant's responsibility to fully comply with all such requests in a timely fashion. Failure to satisfactorily comply with such requests will be deemed a violation of this Agreement.

AND IT IS SO AGREED.

SOUTH CAROLINA MANUFACTURED HOUSING BOARD

June 17th, 2002	BY: *Paul Drake*
Date	Chairman of the Board

I AGREE:

I. Fireball Steele	*July 24th, 02*
Applicant	Date
John Hancock	*July 24th, 02*
Witness	Date

Page 2 of 2

SOUTH CAROLINA DEPARTMENT OF LABOR, LICENSING & REGULATION
BEFORE THE SOUTH CAROLINA MANUFACTURED HOUSING BOARD

In the Matter of:

Marcus (Buzz) Tripp
License Nos.: 8174   **FINAL ORDER**

Respondent.

This matter came before the South Carolina Manufactured Housing Board (the Board) for hearing on March 11, 2003, as a result of the Notice of Hearing and Complaint dated February 6, 2003, which was served upon the Respondent and filed with the Board. The hearing was conducted pursuant to S.C. Code Ann. §§40-1-90 and 40-29-10 (1976), as amended, and the provisions of the South Carolina Administrative Procedures Act (the APA), S.C. Code Ann. 1-23-10. *et seq.* (1976), as amended. The State was represented by Clark Kent, Esquire. The Respondent appeared and was represented by John Smith, Esquire.

The Respondent was charged with violation of S.C. Code Ann. §40-29-80(3) and (18) (Supp. 2002); however the parties stipulated to the amendment of the complaint to reflect that the Respondent was charged with violation of S.C. Code Ann. §40-29-150(3) and (7) (1976), as amended.

FINDINGS OF FACT

Based upon the preponderance of the evidence on the whole record, the Board finds the facts of the case to be as follows:

1. The Respondent is licensed by the Board as a retail salesman, and as such, is authorized by the laws of the State of South Carolina to sell manufactured homes in the State.
2. The State alleges in the complaint that *the Respondent failed to disclose the fact that he had been convicted of a felony in his renewal applications for the years 1994, 1995, 1996, 1998, 1999 and 2000.* However, the State withdrew the allegations with respect to the years 1996 and 1998. The Respondent, who was represented by legal Counsel, did not contest the charges, and admitted that he failed to disclose in the renewal applications that *on or about August 3, 1993, he was convicted of a felony, specifically, distribution of cocaine. Although the Respondent was incarcerated from approximately August 1993 through June 1994, he was allowed to work under the work release program.*
3. By stipulation of the parties, a copy of the Respondent's arrest record that was obtained from the South Carolina Law Enforcement Division was placed into evidence. The record reflects that *the Respondent has an extensive history of arrests for crimes related to drugs which may indicate that the Respondent has a drug addiction problem.* However, none of the past charges are directly related to the Respondent's profession as a manufactured housing Salesman.
4. Based upon the evidence presented, the Board finds that the Respondent's failure to disclose his 1993 felony conviction is a violation of the Board's Practice Act.

Page 1 of 3

CONCLUSIONS OF LAW

Based upon careful consideration of the facts in this matter, the Board finds and concludes as a matter of law that:

1. The Board has jurisdiction in this matter and, upon finding that a licensee has violated any of the provisions of S.C. Code Ann. §40-29-80 (Supp. 2002), has the authority to suspend for a determinate period, revoke or restrict the license of a manufactured home manufacturer licensed in this State and may impose a civil penalty of not more than two thousand five hundred dollars or any combination thereof. Further, upon finding that grounds for disci-

pline exist, S.C. Code Ann. §40-1-120 (1976), as amended, provides that the Board has the authority to: issue a public reprimand; place a licensee on probation or restrict the entity's license for a definite or indefinite time and prescribe conditions to be met during probation, restriction or suspension including, but not limited to, satisfactory completion of additional education, of a supervisory period, or of continuing education programs; and impose the reasonable costs of the investigation and prosecution of a case.

2. *The Respondent has violated S.C. Code Ann. §40-29-150(3) (1976), as amended, in that the Respondent, as evidenced by the conduct described herein above, misrepresented a material fact in obtaining his license when he failed to disclose his felony conviction on his license renewal applications for the years 1994, 1995, 1999, and 2000.*

3. *The Respondent has violated S.C. Code Ann. §40-29-150(7) (1976), as amended, in that on or about August 3, 1993, the Respondent was convicted of a felony, specifically, distribution of cocaine.*

4. The sanction imposed is consistent with the purpose of these proceedings and has been made after weighing the public interest and the need for the continuing services of qualified manufactured home manufacturers against the countervailing concern that society be protected from professional ineptitude and misconduct.

5. The sanction imposed is designed not to punish the Respondent, but to protect the life, health, and welfare of the people at large.

NOW, THEREFORE, IT IS ORDERED, ADJUDGED AND DECREED THAT:

1. The Respondent's license shall be placed in a probationary status for a period of four (4) years from the date of this final order, with the following conditions to apply during the probationary term:
    a. The Respondent shall, within thirty (30) days of the date of the final order, furnish a corporate surety bond or other security in the form prescribed by the Board in the amount of Thirty Thousand ($30,000.00) Dollars.
    b. The Respondent shall attach a recent SLED arrest report to each renewal application submitted during the probationary period. To be deemed recent, the report must include verification that it was obtained from SLED no earlier than ten days prior to the date the renewal application is submitted to the Board.
    c. Should the SLED report reflect that the Respondent was convicted of a felony or crime of moral turpitude during the probationary period, his license shall be immediately suspended until such time as the matter can be heard by the Board.

2. It shall be the Respondent's responsibility to demonstrate compliance with the provisions of this final order, failure by the Respondent to comply with any of the provisions of the final order may result in the immediate temporary suspension of the Respondent's licensing pending hearing into the matter and until further order of the Board.

3. This final order shall take effect immediately upon service of the order upon the Respondent or Respondent's counsel.

AND IT IS SO ORDERED.

SC MANUFACTURED HOUSING BOARD

April 4th, 2003   BY: *Edward Teach, Jr.*

Date   Chairman of the Board

Page 3 of 3

SOUTH CAROLINA DEPARTMENT OF LABOR,
LICENSING & REGULATION
BEFORE THE SOUTH CAROLINA MANUFACTURED HOUSING BOARD

In the Matter of:

PIONEER HOUSING SYSTEMS, INC.
License Nos.: 12707   **FINAL ORDER**

        Respondent.

This matter came before the South Carolina Manufactured Housing Board (the Board) for hearing on March 11, 2003, as a result of the Notice of Hearing and Complaint dated February 7, 2003, which was served upon the Respondent and filed with the Board. The hearing was conducted pursuant to S.C. Code Ann. §§40-1-90 and 40-29-10 (1976), as amended, and the provisions of the South Carolina Administrative Procedures Act (the APA), S.C. Code Ann. §1-23-10, *et seq.* (1976), as amended. The State was represented by John Doe, Esquire. The Respondent was properly notified of the date, time and place of the hearing, however, the Respondent did not appear and was not represented by counsel.

The Respondent was charged with violation of S.C. Code Ann. §§40-29-80(5) and (14) (Supp. 2002).

FINDINGS OF FACT

Based upon the preponderance of the evidence on the whole record, the Board finds the facts of the case to be as follows:

1. The Respondent is licensed by the Board as a manufactured housing manufacturer and as such, is authorized by the laws of the State of South Carolina to engage in the design, construction, or production of manufactured homes in the State. Further, on or about January 31, 2003, pursuant to the authority granted by S.C. Code Ann. 1-23-370(c) (1986), as amended, the Respondent's license was temporarily suspended after the Board received information which indicated that the public health, safety or welfare was imperatively threatened by the Respondent's conduct.
2. The testimony received by the Board indicates that on January 3, 2003, Board staff received a complaint from Ted and Alice Smith alleging an electrical defect at their manufactured home. An investigation was conducted which

revealed that the Respondent manufactured the home ordered by and delivered to the Smiths on or about August 14, 2002. The investigation further revealed the existence of electrical detects in the Smith's manufactured home. Specifically, *numerous electrical outlets were not functional, the use of certain appliances caused the breaker to trip or the lights to dim, and the Jacuzzi could only be turned off by turning off the breaker.* On or about January 9, 2003, the Respondent was given both verbal and written notice of the problems with the Smith's home, and was further notified that *the Board's staff had determined that the electrical problems constituted a possible imminent safety hazard.* The Respondent was given five (5) days to remedy the problems, and was notified that failure to address the problems within the allotted time could result in the temporary suspension of its license in this State. *Following the Respondent's failure to respond to the written notification or to remedy the electrical defects in the Smith's home, the Respondent's license was temporarily suspended on or about January 31, 2003.*

3. On or about January 6, 2003, the Board's staff received *another complaint* concerning a home manufactured by the Respondent. The home that is the subject of the second complaint was ordered by and delivered to Bill Jones on or about October 17, 2002. *An investigation was conducted which revealed that the home contained an electrical defect in the wiring of the light fixture in the master bedroom.* The Respondent was notified of the existence of the defect and was given five (5) days to remedy the problem, and notified that failure to do so could result in the temporary suspension of its license. According to the testimony presented, *the Respondent did not respond to the notification from the Board, and failed to remedy the electrical defect in the Mr. Jones' [sic] home.*

4. The testimony further revealed that *there has been significant time lapse since the Respondent was notified of the electrical defects in the homes of Mr. and Mrs. Smith and Mr. Jones, and the Respondent has not remedied the defects in either home.*

CONCLUSIONS OF LAW

Based upon careful consideration of the facts in this matter, the Board finds and concludes as a matter or law that:

1. The Board has jurisdiction in this matter and, upon finding that a licensee has violated any of the provisions of S.C. Code Ann. §§40-29-80 or 40-29-260 (Supp. 2002), has the authority to suspend for a determinate period, revoke or restrict the license of a manufactured home manufacturer licensed in this State and may impose a civil penalty of not more than two thousand five hundred dollars or any combination thereof. Further, upon finding that grounds for discipline exist, S.C. Code Ann. §40-1-120 (1976), as amended, provides that the Board has the authority to: issue a public reprimand; place a licensee on probation or restrict the entity's license for a definite or indefinite time and prescribe conditions to be met during probation, restriction or suspension including, but not limited to, satisfactory completion of additional education, of a supervisory period, or of continuing education programs; and impose the reasonable costs of the investigation and prosecution of a case.

2. The Respondent has violated S.C. Code Ann. §40-29-80(5) (Supp. 2002) in that the Respondent, as evidenced by the conduct described herein above, failed to comply with the warranty requirements established by the Board as set forth in S.C. Code Ann. §40-29-260 (Supp. 2002).

3. The Respondent has violated S.C. Code Ann. §40-29-80(14) (Supp. 2002) in that the Respondent, as evidenced by the conduct described herein above, failed to follow directives of the Board.

4. The sanction imposed is consistent with the purpose of these proceedings and has been made after weighing the public interest and the need for the continuing services of qualified manufactured home manufacturers against the countervailing concern that society be protected from professional ineptitude and misconduct.

5. The sanction imposed is designed not to punish the Respondent, but to protect the life, health, and welfare of the people at large.

NOW, THEREFORE, IT IS ORDERED, ADJUDGED AND DECREED that the Respondent's license shall be, and hereby is, **revoked.**

IT IS FURTHER ORDERED that this final order shall take effect immediately upon service of the order upon the Respondent or Respondent's counsel.

   AND IT IS SO ORDERED.

                              SC MANUFACTURED HOUSING BOARD
April 4th, 2003   BY: *John Doe*
Date   Chairman of the Board

                          Page 2 of 2

   There seem to be some common themes running through this sample of material. One of the first that comes to mind is that there are many repeat offenders, and that taking away their license to sell homes doesn't necessarily prevent them from doing so. The Housing Board also seems relatively charitable in its considerations of offenders. In fact, the word "lax" might be more appropriate. Allowing someone with a history of felony burglaries and arson access to the keys of customers' houses might even seem to be inviting culpability on the part of the state agency if the felon's past tendencies resurface. (See the chapter "Making Your House a Home" for more information on keys and the locks to your home.) Letting a convicted crack cocaine dealer who lied about his past and is suspected of being a current addict work in a field where many thousands of dollars trade hands and which is already notorious for "misappropriation of funds" scandals might be a little too magnanimous as well. Kudos to the state, however, for giving someone caught forging loan documents, among other crimes, a second chance in the exact same job. This was the case of "Pants O. Fire," where Mr. Fire tried his best to implicate the lender who caught him and turned him in as a knowing conspirator. I'm sure that Mr. Fire, who admitted he "traced" the signatures, and yet still denies he forged them, will be better than ever at doing what he does after his one year of probation is up. Horace Walpole once said, "This world is a comedy to those that think, a tragedy to those that feel." If you become enmeshed in this milieu for long, let us hope that you focus on the cognitive aspects of it. (Unless you're on the money making end of the spectrum, and if that's the case, emotions or empathy aren't likely to be of much concern to you.)

There are other aspects here that my research and personal experience seemed to confirm. One owner, for instance, told me how within a week of moving into his new home, sparks and flame began to leap out of his breaker panel. (This was a different brand home than the one described here, and older — a 1985 Redman to be exact.) He was fortunate that the breaker panel happened to be in a bedroom where he slept, so he quickly noticed the sparks and was able to shut off the main power. Generally, though, the electrical systems now seem much improved over years past. I thought the case of the "Bruiser" was also very interesting. The Bruiser was very reminiscent of a sales manager in Charlotte, North Carolina, that my wife and I encountered. He quickly became extremely verbally abusive because we told him we wanted to explore alternative financing (that is, financing which was not through the dealership). He literally began to shout profanity and insults and attempted to become physically threatening. Fortunately, I'm not easily intimidated, but this manager's behavior in the presence of my wife was extremely offensive. All of this was the result of us quite calmly saying we must insist on looking at other finance options. Not wanting to be arrested, I walked my wife out the door while his rants continued behind us.

Another point which these cases illustrate is that fines of $500 or $1,000 are typical on those rare occasions dealerships are caught engaging in fraudulent and deceptive practices. *A fine of $500 means nothing to dealerships when at a minimum there are thousands of dollars made on each sale.* Furthermore, are any of the levied fines going to victims? From my understanding, none. It reminds me of a smalls claim court case I once observed. The defendant was found guilty of causing $100 in damages to the complainant, and the judge ruled the defendant did in fact owe $100. The court kept the money, and when the complainant expressed displeasure because he came to court to actually get reimbursed, the judge threatened to fine him as well if he didn't drop the matter. The court had theirs, so who cares about justice?

Along this same pessimistic vein, very few actions seem to be taken against manufacturers. Only the last case described here did, and it seems that only safety issues force the governing bodies to put their feet down. The corporations seem to have more protection than the consumer — again something Consumers Union seemed to note as well. The Consumers Union found, for example, that the Texas Manufactured Housing Division acted "*more as a service agency for the industry than a protector of home buyers.*" It's little wonder that the manufactured housing boards tend to favor the industry. A typical eight-member board might have two members which represent manufacturers, two which represent dealers, two which represent home installers, and just two members meant to represent the public at large. Guess who gets the short end of the proverbial stick with this arrangement?

This is a sad state of affairs which needs to change. Note these two recurring themes in the South Carolina cases above under "Conclusions of Law":

1. The sanction imposed is consistent with the purpose of these proceedings and has been made after weighing the public interest and the need for the continuing services of qualified manufactured home manufacturers against the countervailing concern that society be protected from professional ineptitude and misconduct.
2. The sanction imposed is designed not to punish the Respondent, but to protect the life, health, and welfare of the people at large.

The facts clearly seem to indicate that professional ineptitude and misconduct is winning out on a regular basis; in fact, dishonesty is almost being rewarded by the current system. Too much consideration is given to manufacturers, dealerships, and their employees, and not nearly enough to the consumers. Let's face it, the companies hold most of the cards and are much more likely to have attorneys on retainer than the average customer. It's time to tilt the scales back and give consumers the protection they deserve. I do make some recommendations in the conclusion of this book toward that direction, and I hope these recommendations receive some consideration from lawmakers and consumer groups. (For the legislators in the audience, please note that there are many millions of voters who live in manufactured housing.) Furthermore, why should we *not* punish a respondent who has broken the law and defrauded customers time and again? If we truly wanted to protect the welfare of the people, shouldn't we want to punish those who fleece the flock?

A draft of this book was sent to Mr. David Bennett, administrator of the South Carolina Department of Labor, Licensing & Regulation (and over the South Carolina Manufactured Housing Board) for his comments on it many months before it went to press. He never replied to my inquiries. (In fairness to Mr. Bennett, this chapter was not in the manuscript yet.)

Again, I'd like to emphasize that I'm not picking on South Carolina. In fact, let's look at another state briefly in the interest of fairness. West Virginia had a performance review of their Manufactured Housing Construction and Safety Board completed in May 2002. The report indicated West Virginia had 188 active manufactured home dealers and 88 active manufacturers. The West Virginia board conducted 241 disciplinary hearings from 1999 to 2001, most of them resulting in some type of fine, while three licenses were suspended and four were revoked. It took the board an average of 119 days to investigate complaints and take action on them in the year 2001. (West Virginia law—§21-9-11a—allows the board 90 days maximum for this task.) Part of the board's duty involves conducting dealer "lot audits" to make sure homes comply with HUD standards and regulations. In fact, the Division of Labor receives $9 per floor from HUD for every manufactured home shipped into West Virginia to help with such HUD code enforcement. Compliance officers are supposed to check for transit damage, check for improper dealer alterations (and outright dealer theft of components), etc. At the time of this report (May 2002), zero (0) dealer lot audits had been conducted at the licensed home dealers in West Virginia since 1999. Zero inspections on a performance measurement which is *required* by HUD over a period of three years. (I used to think Texas was the worst state for HUD compliance, but there retailers are audited at a relatively blistering pace: *once every 37 years* on average. Don't you know that really keeps the dealers on their toes!) The West Virginia board is also supposed to conduct regular installation audits to check for safety, construction, and foundation problems. In 1999 they conducted 48 such audits, in 2000 they conducted 35 installation audits, and in 2001 they conducted 2 audits (despite the fact that the West Virginia legislature provided $154,000 in 2001 to hire three additional compliance officers). There was a Manufactured Housing Recovery Fund set up for consumers' protection in West Virginia in 1991. It's been utilized 14 times to help consumers since 1995, paying out $78,098 in total, or $5,578.43 on average per complaint. The Manufactured Housing Recovery Fund currently has a balance of over $1,300,000, money which comes from one-time fees on licensees. So while the federal government (by way of HUD) is paying the West Virginia Manufactured Housing Construction and Safety Board for services they aren't providing, it seems the consumer protection fund is remarkably underutilized. They must be saving for a rainy day.

In fact, West Virginia should now be earning more income annually off this victim's Recovery Fund interest than they have paid out in the entire history of the program! This is the conclusion of the Performance Review conducted by the Office of Legislative Auditor:

> By not conducting dealer lot audits, the Manufactured Housing Section is not adhering to a performance measurement required by HUD, and the drop-off in installation audits implies that goals and objectives are not being met as they should. As a result, the chances of not detecting transit damage, dealer alterations, and improper installation are increased. This could have an adverse impact on the consumer by way of safety concerns as well as having to wait longer to have any problems corrected. Although this has never happened, HUD does have the authority to impose sanctions such as with-holding some or all of the portion of the funding that it provides to the Manufactured Housing Section. Therefore, it is essential that the Manufactured Housing Section start conducting dealer lot audits and increase the number of installation audits performed.

I guess that I am a natural skeptic in some ways, in part because of my now extensive experience in this field. The preceding passage immediately struck me in three ways, however: (1) the forthrightness of the assessment, (2) the pronounced suspicion that the "essential" nature of the last sentence is derived more from the possible lack of future funds rather than the safety issue, and (3) why hasn't HUD withheld any money for inspections which aren't being performed? Who's looking out for the consumer?

Let's go to one more state, for a more down-to-earth example of something that commonly happens to the average consumer. This is based on an actual reported case from Oklahoma in 2001, with the names omitted. A young couple starting out found a good deal on a manufactured home they really liked. They were going to be getting married and were having the home sent over the state line to some property they had purchased in neighboring Texas. The dealership was having a "Grand Opening Sale"—every home was discounted, and all kinds of incentives were being given away, too. With any home bought, the buyer received a choice of a brand spanking new lawnmower, carport, or storage building. These are items that any family starting out could really use. This was going to be a turn-key setup, and everything was supposed to be included in the price the salesperson gave them: utility hook-ups; septic tank; driveway; and the big three appliances, refrigerator/freezer, washer, and dryer. Sadly, though, before they were done, it turned out the salesperson had made a "mistake" in his calculations. After they were all ready to sign on the dotted line, they found out the only way they could get their septic was to *not* receive the three major appliances *and* the storage building they had picked out. At this point, the sympathetic manager came into the negotiations, but there was just nothing he could do. It turns out that the poor dealership was just about losing money on the deal as it was. (I know you're catching the subtle sarcasm.)

That wasn't the end to this Oklahoma disaster, either. Our protagonists soon found out that even without these items, the price was *still* too low. Those nice folks at the dealership had really been trying hard to help them out. (Of course, by now our heroes had no need of satire, and they realized they were in a terrible fix.) The only way the dealer could set up their new home for the promised price (even without the refrigerator/ freezer, washer, dryer, and storage building) was by bypassing state and county codes (and those irritating permits). The couple wisely alerted the Texas authorities to make the dealer comply with the law, but then they even got short-changed on their septic tank—costing them another $2,300. It seems somehow the company had two sets of contracts they used — the one which went to the finance company didn't even mention a septic tank, the driveway, the utility hook-ups, etc. (I guess Oklahoma has forgers, misappropriaters, and maybe crack heads, too.)

This innocent but naive couple started out with the best of intentions and high hopes. They were entitled to those aspirations—but unscrupulous charlatans selling "dream homes" wasted their time and money, leaving them only with "headaches and heartache." (Although our heroine noted that despite all the problems, the home was still beautiful, and they felt no blame toward the manufacturer.) Wherever you live and whatever brands you consider purchasing, remember your lessons from this and the preceding two chapters. You can count on your own good wisdom (if you're reading this, you're halfway home), your family, and your friends. Do not trust salespersons, dealerships, or even your own government to look after your interests. Caveat emptor.

Consumers Union Southwest Regional Office has been extensively reporting on manufactured housing problems for several years, and in their article "In Over Our Heads" (February 2002) they noted that almost half of customer complaints involve dealer fraud. The typical complaints they found were as follows:

- the dealership substituted a different home (another model, year, or size) for the one the customer thought they were buying;
- the dealership falsified information on the loan application (often lying about the down payment amount or accepting borrowed money as a down payment);

- the dealership ended up charging more for the home than the price they originally quoted;
- the terms of the sale were changed on the customer midway through the deal (when momentum makes it hard to back out) and additional expenses were added like extra fees or higher interest rates;
- the dealership refused to give the customer copies of contracts they had to sign.

CHAPTER 7

Who Owns the Bank?: Financing

The scary part is almost over, but don't stop taking your medication yet. This last financial hurdle deserves its own chapter. Even if you've done everything right so far and have gotten a good deal on a great home, if you get locked into a terrible mortgage that warm and fuzzy feeling can go away quickly, right along with your new house. This is actually one of the exceedingly bright situations now because of recent trends in the lending industry and because of the prevailing interest rates. As I write, rates are now as low as 5.6 percent for 30-year fixed mortgages, which is one of the lowest interest rate points in the last half of a century. Interest rates bottomed out at around 5 percent just over one year ago, and in all likelihood we won't see these rates again in the near future. Tremendous opportunity for saving money currently exists. The savings already inherent in manufactured homes (if you don't let a salesperson take control of the process, and you carefully comparison shop) combined with the currently depressed prices and great available rates means that virtually anyone with average income can own a good home. With an above-average income, the sky is the limit!

One word of caution, however: be careful how far you extend yourself financially. One of the reasons manufactured housing prices have been in a funk is that greedy dealerships have talked many people into spending more than they can really afford in order to make more profit. Such *predatory lending* can take many forms: high interest rates, exorbitant fees, financing for insurance products, misleading advertising, failure to disclose pertinent loan information, and simply lending money without regard to the consumer's ability to pay. This has led to a glut of repossessed homes. You don't want to achieve the American dream only to have it taken away. This is no small concern whatever type home you are considering.

MSNBC.com reports that the weak economy has caused a record number of foreclosures across the board in the fourth quarter of 2002. Champion Enterprises, Inc.'s 2003 shareholder statement estimates about 90,000 manufactured homes were repossessed in 2002 and that repossessions could peak at 115,000 in 2003. Oakwood Homes alone sold 4,960 homes in the first quarter of 2001 in North Carolina. Raleigh's *News & Observer* reported that in the exact same period Oakwood repossessed 3,900 homes! Don't be a statistic. You also need to remember you will require insurance and have to pay taxes. (Both can be escrowed, and together they typically add anywhere from $50 to $150 more a month to your payments.) In addition, you may have to pay Private Mortgage Insurance (PMI). There will also inevitably be a number of other incidental expenses as you're setting up any new home — new furniture, items broken during the move will have to be replaced, permits you didn't know you needed, etc. So you need to hold a little emergency money back when you're figuring out your down payment and your monthly payments. These are all reasons to negotiate as hard as possible on price and on the interest rate.

The Manufactured Home Buyer's Handbook is largely about things the dealers and manufacturers *don't* want you to know: what to look for, what to avoid, what to ask, and how to save money. This exceedingly important chapter follows in the same vein. If you're already loan savvy, you may want to skim portions of this chapter, but don't skip it entirely. There are elements and trends distinct to manufactured home loans the consumer needs to be aware of. If you aren't experienced with loans, this chapter is filled with the terminology and know-how you need to get the best deal. It's also filled with charts and graphs to visually illustrate for the novice or intermediate borrower just how much you can save — or spend — by making certain decisions. Even financial gurus might glean insight from the amortization line charts included.

The title of this chapter, "Who Owns the Bank?," comes in part from the fact that you are increasingly likely to be financing "direct" from the manufacturer. In the example illustrated previously, Clayton Homes dealerships like to finance their homes through Vanderbilt Mortgage and Finance — which is a subsidiary of Clayton. Vanderbilt Mortgage services many thousands of customers, and no doubt increases the company's overall profit margins considerably. The interest rates they charge are consistently above the prevailing mortgage rates, although they have become somewhat more competitive in the last few years. In 2001, Vanderbilt Mortgage and Finance was charging 9.9 percent when traditional banks were offering 7 percent loans, but in 2002 they began offering rates as low as

7.49 percent while other lenders had dropped down to around 6 percent. Of course, you had to "qualify" for the best rate Vanderbilt offered, or you might have to pay considerably more. Champion Enterprises, Inc., is one of the major companies that has followed suit in this trend by acquiring HomePride Finance Corp. This move was a result of both decreasing revenues and the fact that some of the lenders they had been using were leaving this market due to competition, bankruptcy/Chapter 11, and high foreclosure rates. HomePride generated $56 million in new consumer home loans in 2002 alone.

Other dealerships work with a plethora of lending companies, ostensibly to get you the best rate. Unfortunately, these rates also tend to be higher than the prevailing competitive rate. The sad fact is that if you have to finance through the dealer, it is apt to select the finance company or

This is a copy of a certificate sent to us by Clayton Homes, Inc., for visiting their website. The fine print stipulates the home must be purchased through Clayton's subsidiary, Vanderbilt Mortage and Finance. Even with the "discount," this can be a pretty lucrative proposition for Clayton Homes and Vanderbilt who may earn $100,000 or $150,000 in interest over the life of the loan.

mortgage broker which offers the biggest commission or kickback (as much as 2 percent of the total loan — and you're the one footing the bill). Dealerships like to offer what I would refer to as "gimmick" loans, too. They might sound really attractive to the unsuspecting or naive shopper, but they can be to your detriment in the long run. These include graduated interest-rate or step-rate loans where your payment amount increases until it stabilizes at a higher rate later on. These are often pushed on home buyers who lack the credit history or employment record of more-qualified buyers; and these are the very customers who are more apt to have difficulty meeting their monthly payments when they start rising. Graduated loans are particularly a recipe for disaster for elderly consumers who are on a fixed income. Sales managers are quick to point out to anyone who appears to be catching on that you can "always refinance later" before the rates go up. Sometimes you can, but you'll be paying closing costs again — and if credit really is a problem, you'll be stuck.

Other gimmicks include loans which are "interest free" for some amount of time like six months, then revert to the usual rate. It's another ploy aimed at short-sighted or cash-strapped shoppers, although it's better than the graduated loans if the interest rate is acceptable. For instance, if you have a 30-year mortgage at 7.49 percent and the first six months are interest free (that is, all of your premium applies to the principal for those six months), you do build up equity a little faster. The actual interest rate would still work out to over 7 percent, however.

The final insult is that most dealerships will declare to you it's cheaper to finance through the dealership because "there are no closing costs." We heard this line over and over, even at the dealership where we purchased our home with dealer financing. On the contract, we were charged $800 for an attorney's fee (an exorbitant amount by any standard) and $250 for a title search. These are closing costs, and when we questioned the general manager about them, we were told simply that they weren't considered closing costs. As we looked incredulously at this gentleman, who somehow maintained a relatively straight face throughout our negotiations, we realized we were dealing with some sort of lesser demonic presence who had no regard for honesty and the principles of democracy, but fortunately alternatives now exist.

You may be thinking it can't really be this bad. Certainly, salespeople will tell you it's not. If you're uncertain, consider this: I recently corresponded with another person who bought a home from the very same dealership in the very same month as I did. At a time when the manufacturer was offering 7.49 percent and banks were readily offering loans below 6 percent, this person apparently had less than perfect credit, and had been evicted from where she had been living through no fault of her own. In short, she was in a major housing predicament, and didn't have many places to turn. The dealership offered her hope, and promised everything would be fine. The hidden cost of hope runs high at dealerships, though — our protagonist was stuck with an interest rate of 13.75 percent! She was already in deep financial water, and now she was committed to paying almost $300,000 for a manufactured home! She was paying over $150,000 more in interest than careful shoppers — enough to buy two more identical homes and still have money left over to buy a new car.

High interest rates and predatory lending aren't the only things to fear from dealership financing. Outright fraud (or predatory lending taken to the extreme) also seems to be fairly common. In 2004, there were 25 lawsuits in Texas alone alleging that Clayton Homes, Vanderbilt Mortgage and several Clayton associates forged customer signatures on loan documents to fraudulently procure their land! The basic modus operandi seemed to be that Clayton dealerships would forge signatures to claim customers' land (which was used as loan collateral in land-in-lieu-of transactions) when they couldn't make their payments. The customers involved were not in a position to finance a home; that is, a reputable lender would not have made the loan. President and CEO Kevin Clayton seemed to admit the wrong-doing, but claimed, "This is isolated to one location in one market and we see nothing in this case that suggests otherwise." David Rumley, an attorney involved in the case, strongly disagrees: "*Our investigation has shown the forgeries of deeds and trust and documents related to land has occurred in almost every state where Clayton Homes sells trailers.*" (Clayton Homes operates in more than 33 states.) In one instance, the customer lived in a nursing home, and previously had both her arms amputated. In another, the consumer was hospitalized and was having surgery on the day she allegedly signed the documents (Bill Brewer, August 4, 2004, Knoxville *News-Sentinel*).

The bottom line is that the entity who owns the bank might be the most important factor in your home-buying process. Not long ago, buying a manufactured home meant you were purchasing a piece of property like a car or a boat. You held a title to your house, and if you owned the land it sat on, you held a separate title for the latter. As manufactured homes have improved in quality, the financial climate has changed. Now, increasingly, state governments and lenders consider these homes as real estate versus a "trailer," provided they meet certain criteria and are set up according to certain rules. In large part, Freddie Mac's entrance into the manufactured housing market has spurred this trend. The title to the land and the home itself are, in effect, merged into one entity. This has several important advantages for home buyers. First, they have more financing options because traditional banks which would not consider manufactured houses before now will. Second, it means that truly competitive rates are now available for qualified buyers who were once forced to pay much more interest, rates which typically range anywhere from 1 to 4 percent below dealer financing. Yet another benefit of the new scenario is that if you already own land to place your home on, it means that you can start out with considerable "equity" (equity is the part of the property that you have already paid for) because it is rolled into the home mortgage loan. The downside is that if you default on your payments, you will lose your land as well. Finally, this new atmosphere in financing manufactured homes has forced dealerships to offer more competitive rates themselves in order to keep a significant share of the business. In essence, they were forced to accept a smaller profit margin on mortgage loans rather than make no profit from them at all.

Equity is an important concept in this process. In fact, it's the central most important consideration from the consumer's point of view. You want to build up equity as quickly as possible and limit the amount of interest you pay. The larger the down payment you can safely muster, the more equity you will have, and the lower your payments will be. If you have a manufactured home to trade in, that increases your down payment and your equity accordingly. Also, as mentioned previously, if you already own land to place a home on, that can increase your equity as well, although this latter asset won't decrease the price of the home and therefore won't lower your payments. All of this may seem obvious to the more experienced, but first-time buyers need to learn the basics. Intricately related to equity is the concept of being "upside down" in a mortgage; that's when you owe more on your loan than your home is worth. Upside down is a terrible position to work from, and many new manufactured home owners find themselves in this position in their new home for many years—meaning if they have made a bad deal, they are often unable to get out from under it for decades. Remember our victim who owes $300,000 for a manufactured home? If she tries to sell it, what can she expect to sell it for? In essence, unless she wins the lottery or goes bankrupt, she is stuck with that home and those payments for life. Equity also has a direct bearing on another potential major expense: *private mortgage insurance* or PMI.

Private mortgage insurance protects the lender against loss in case the customer defaults on the loan. It is typically required whenever the consumer is making less than a 20 percent down payment on the total cost. While premiums for PMI vary, the first year is typically about 5 percent of the loan amount but they may be slightly less thereafter. This usually has to be *paid in advance of closing.* Thereafter, your monthly payments will be increased to build up an escrow account for future PMI payments. You should be able to drop it after the loan-to-equity ratio drops below 78 percent. (That's right, if you can't make the 20 percent up front then you can be forced to reach 22 percent later on — often meaning paying another 12 months or so of PMI.) This can take longer than most people think — for the first part of the loan, you'll mostly be paying interest. For instance, if your loan amount was $100,000 (for simplicity) over 30 years at 7 percent, you would have to make 163 payments to get the required $22,000 in equity with no down payment. Even if you put down $10,000 as a down payment, you would still have to make 116 payments to eliminate the PMI unless you paid extra toward the principal. Lenders can also make you keep PMI longer if you have problems making your payments or your home depreciates in value. Conversely, if you make improvements to the property or if it otherwise appreciates in value, you can have an appraisal done to verify it and request that the lender drop PMI if the loan-to-equity drops below 78 percent. Private mortgage insurance could cost you several thousand dollars extra each year — this example would result in about $5,000 more. To avoid these substantial extra costs, you should always try to reach the 20 percent threshold, if not up front then as soon as possible into the loan. Save up as much money as you can for a down payment (but make sure you retain a couple of thousand dollars or so in the bank for incidentals and unexpected expenses), and utilize trade-ins and land that you own if possible. In the previous scenario, if you own a lot which is appraised at $20,000, for instance, you could avoid PMI even with no down payment. Avoiding PMI also means you can apply some of the money you save to extra payments — shaving years off your loan and possibly saving tens of thousands more. One last point here: dealership financing often doesn't require PMI insurance. The reason is that their mortgage rates and other fees have such high profit margins built in that they don't have to charge for PMI.

You can look for alternatives to dealership financing easily in your local Yellow Pages under "mortgages" — and you will likely have a wide selection to choose from. Try both companies that specialize in mortgages and banks that offer them. Sometimes the ad will specify whether the company offers manufactured house loans; at this point not all lenders will. Rates change almost daily, so you have to call to get specifics. The best time to start seriously shopping for a loan is when you have the approximate cost of the homes you are considering. A lender can't help you much until then, except to give you the prevailing rates. Following interest rates in the financial news can help you know the best time to buy, but be aware that mortgage rates don't always fluctuate exactly with the general interest rate. Oftentimes, homeowners with great rates didn't just get lucky — they were able to time their purchase by studying financial forecasts. Call at least a half dozen different lenders, and get enough details to make apples-to-apples comparisons. They will need to know the approximate loan amount, how much down payment you will have, and whether or not you already own the land where the home will be situated. There may also be some stipulations or requirements to qualify for the loan to qualify as a real estate loan, such as brick underpinning or skirting.

Never compare just the annual percentage rate (APR) alone — some lenders quote superficially low rates by using *points* or adding *origination fees*. Points "buy down" the interest rate at the expense of more loan overhead costs, and origination fees are another form of additional closing costs. Listen carefully to the specifics. You might have one lender offering 5.875 percent with one point (which amounts to 1 percent of the total loan) but no origination fee, and another offering 5.875 percent with no points but with a 1 percent origination fee. The former will tout their loan as the best one because of no origination fee, the latter will use no points as a selling feature. In truth, these two loans should be of equal value if other fees (like attorney's fees) are also equal. Just as in working with dealerships, you still have to be wary of unscrupulous loan officers, but you aren't in quite as much jeopardy here. Don't forget to search the Internet or television ads for deals. Some advertise "no closing costs" or offer to beat anyone else's deal by .25 percent. Make a call and see if it's for real. A lot of companies like these are actually "brokers"— that is, they don't really "service" anyone's mortgage, they just negotiate and then sell it to another mortgage company. Request written "good faith estimates" from the lenders that sound best — don't trust one that won't give you this. While there may not be as much room as when bargaining for a home price, remember that there is some room for negotiating here as well. Even with low rates, lenders stand to gain or lose many thousands of dollars on your potential business. Armed with one estimate, you can often get better terms from another lender. This might be a lower rate or lower closing costs. So shop around. Copy or draw up a form like the following to help you stay organized and compare costs:

Comparison Chart — Mortgage Rates for ____ / ____ / ____ (Date)					
Lender	Loan Officer	Phone	Rate	Closing Costs	Points/Orig.

Rates are going to be affected by a number of additional factors as well. "Conforming" loans are available to customers with excellent or "A" credit and a good employment history, and these feature the lender's best rate. "Nonconforming" loans for customers with less-than-perfect credit require higher interest rates and quite possibly higher down payments as well. Married couples may benefit significantly by listing the person with the best credit history as the principal borrower (or possibly by having a cosigner with solid credit). Larger loans often are eligible for lower percentage rates—in fact, some of the companies which advertise good rates won't even consider loans of less than $125,000 or $150,000. Loans with shorter terms may also offer a slighter better rate. At the moment I write this, a 30-year fixed-rate mortgage averages an astoundingly low 4.98 percent (with an average of .62 discount and origination points), while 15-year fixed mortgages in the United States stand at 4.42 percent (with an average of .58 discount and origination points). Adjustable rate mortgages with variable rates are another option, and they can offer lower initial rates of interest. Given the current low rates, though, it would probably be foolish to pursue an adjustable rate mortgage at this time *unless* you planned to sell your new home quickly. It's unlikely rates will remain this low as this book goes to press, but historically speaking, it should still be a great time to buy.

Some lenders may charge $200 to $300 as an "application" or processing fee. Generally, this is simply a fee to assure lenders you are serious and aren't wasting their time. If your loan is denied, you are still responsible for the fee. Since you can often get the lender to credit this fee toward your loan upon acceptance this is primarily just a concern if you have poor credit history. Don't forget to ask about this, and let the lender know that you are considering other financial institutions to get the credit or to have the fee waived entirely.

Given our previous discussions regarding unscrupulous dealers and better rates elsewhere, you might wonder why everyone doesn't go to a conventional bank or mortgage company as opposed to financing the new home at the dealership. There are a multitude of reasons, unfortunately. One is that dealers can often find financing (at exorbitant rates) for those who won't qualify elsewhere. They also offer incentives for you to use their financial services, like the $1,000 coupon toward a down payment — which is only valid with "their" bank. The number one reason is probably high sales pressure and customer ignorance. Sales managers herd their unsuspecting customers in the directions they've been trained to by promising they are offering the best possible deal, and many customers aren't even aware they are frequently taking out a mortgage (and possibly insurance) with the same company they are buying the home from. The solution is for you to know the score and take charge of the process.

There is one additional ace up the dealer's sleeve, however, which is sometimes harder to overcome. This involves a refusal to consent to a letter of acceptance from a bank or other mortgage company. When you and a bank come to terms on a mortgage loan, the bank gives you a letter to take to the dealership. It basically states that you have been approved for the home loan of a given amount, and that the dealership will be paid in full upon delivery and successful inspection. This is the ideal situation for the customer, since it encourages the dealer to work as quickly as possible and to make sure the home passes inspection the first time. A refusal to accept such a letter by the dealer is often a calculated attempt by the company to force you to accept the dealer's loan on its terms. You can still obtain a bank or other mortgage company loan, but it will have to be what is often referred to as a "construction" loan, where some money is issued at different times. Suffice it to say that loans of this type mean that you will be paying thousands more in closing costs and interest. When you get to the contract/negotiation stage, one of your first questions to the dealer should be, "Do you accept letters of acceptance from reputable banks?" If they say no, and unless they offer you a genuinely good financing alternative, you should *insist* on it. If the general manager refuses, ask to speak with the regional manager or company president if need be. If you have to, go somewhere else. Competition is tough, and you can find dealers who will work with you on this. It is often preferable, however, not to have to change dealerships at this stage because you will have so much work invested in ordering your home and negotiating pricing. That's why you may want to go up the chain of command if necessary to win on this point.

By now you know not to trust salespeople or sales managers to calculate how much home you can afford. Dealers have been known to falsify credit reports and even create phony paychecks and W-2 forms to have their customers approved for loans. It is considerably safer to let a loan officer do this for you — such people are less inclined to risk letting you default on a loan, leading to foreclosure. The best solution, however, is for you to take stock of your own situation. You might want to head back to your kitchen table or office one more time for some calculations. Take your income and subtract all your debts—credit cards, car payments, utilities, groceries— everything that applies to your particular circumstances. The remainder is what you have to work with, or your *expendable income.* At this point, you should also know approximately what your new home is going to cost. You know you're going to require home insurance, and that you'll owe taxes. The more expensive the home, the higher these costs will be. Calls to insurance brokers (and once more, be prepared to shop around for insurance, too) and the tax collector's office can give you fairly precise estimates. You should also figure out what amount of down payment you can make given your assets and whether or not you have a trade-in. If you have less than 20 percent to put down, you may need to add the cost of private mortgage insurance. The last step is to calculate what your monthly payments would be for the cost of the home you want minus your down payment.

While lenders will be glad to do this for you, it is to your advantage to do it yourself. You may find that you need to omit some home features or landscape expense you really wanted and to run the numbers again because your expendable income would just barely cover your anticipated costs. Alternatively, you may feel your analysis shows you can afford a better-built home than you hoped, and therefore you want to add the cost of some items on your wish list and see what the payments come to. It would also be very handy to be able to compare the relative benefits of loans of different terms (such as 15-year, 20-year, and 30-year loans) or rates. Furthermore, one of the best ways to save money on a loan comes *after* you have negotiated your best rate. That involves adjusting the amount you pay monthly upward in some systematic fashion in order to build up equity more quickly (therefore paying less interest). Both because lenders are often exceedingly busy (especially so with the current low rates) and because it is not in their best interest to concentrate on saving you interest, you should have access to a *mortgage calculator* which will let you analyze loans and print amortization tables.

If you own or otherwise have access to a personal computer and the Internet, the solution is readily available. A monthly mortgage payment and amortization calculator is available online at http://www.bankrate. com/brm/calculators/mortgages.asp and other financial sites (also on *The Manufactured Home Buyer's Handbook* Web site: www.manufacturedhome buyers.com). Web sites like these also offer a wealth of mortgage related information — you can even arrange to have them notify you by e-mail if rates drop down to a point you've preselected. If you're like me, you'd rather have a program ready to access anytime on your own local computer. They are readily available as well. One popular shareware software (shareware is "try it before you buy it" software) download site is http://downloads-zdnet.com.com/. A quick search on "loan" resulted in a list 95 shareware programs related to the topic — many of them mortgage calculators. My favorite is Mortgage Wizard Plus 6.6a for Windows 95/98/Me/NT/2000/XP. It's a quick download at only 1.4MB, and it includes a 21-day free trial. Mortgage Wizard Plus is $27 if you decide to buy it, and an uninstaller is included if you conclude it's not for you. This intuitive program can calculate payments, remaining balances, amortization periods, interest rates, and affordable amounts. An amortization schedule is in a scrollable spreadsheet format with screen splitting, formatting capabilities, and selectable row locking/unlocking. Payment distribution can be displayed in tabular form in various reports and in pie, line, and bar charts. It is capable of figuring American, Canadian, and foreign mortgages as well. If you don't have Internet or computer access, you can still find amortization tables in books. *Monthly Interest Amortization Tables*, published by Contemporary Books, is full of just that: it covers loan amounts from hundreds of dollars to hundreds of thousands, and interest rates from 2 percent to 27.75 percent. Such printed tables won't allow you to make changes in payments and see the effects, however. (Two such printed tables appear in this chapter as examples.)

To give you some idea of what a mortgage calculator can do for you and a better feel for the different ways to handle a mortgage, we're going to use some results from Mortgage Wizard Plus to illustrate different loan scenarios. We looked at this subject briefly in the chapter on contracts ("The Devil Is in the Details"). Using a mortgage calculator, we can determine that every dollar we reduce the loan amount by typically saves somewhere between two and three dollars over the life of the loan at current typical rates. For example, when we reduced the cost of the home from $77,000 to $70,000 at 7 percent interest over 30 years, it reduced our payoff amount by $16,765.20. Leaving every other factor unchanged, at 9 percent we would save $20,275.20. Software programs like Mortgage Wizard Plus let you quickly calculate payments along with the cumulative cost of all payments and interest paid.

Now consider what else a mortgage calculator can do for you. We're going to take the same loan to see what manipulating our payments in a systematic fashion does. This is something that lenders aren't always happy to point out to you themselves because you are manipulating their profit

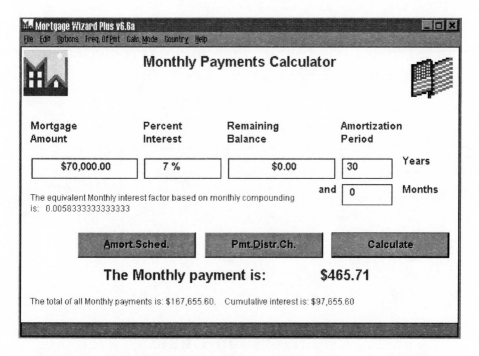

Shown is the initial screen for the software mortgage calculator Mortgage Wizard Plus Version 6.6a.

on the loan. Let's call the situation above scenario 1, where we took the $70,000 over 30 years at 7 percent. Then let's create scenario 2, where we apply extra money early in the loan toward the principal and see what happens. Two things are important to remember here: (1) You must be clear to specify to the lender any extra payment is to be applied directly to the principal and (2) The earlier in the payment cycle that you make extra payments the more it helps you. With simple interest loans, traditionally the vast majority of initial payments go to interest, and you build up equity very slowly. In scenario 2, we're going to pay just under an extra $100 a month for the first year, then $540 a month (less than $75 extra) for the next two years, and then $515 a month (about $50 extra) for the rest of the loan. Mortgage Wizard Plus will let you graphically chart the two different scenarios. I've done it here for your convenience in the two accompanying line graphs, scenario 1 and scenario 2.

Several factors become quickly evident. The solid line with circular points is the cumulative payments indicator. For the exact same $70,000 loan at the identical rate and term, you pay a total of $167,655.60 under scenario 1 and $135,485.50 for scenario 2 — a savings of $32,170.10. In the

Amortization Chart
30 Year Loan Subdivided into 5 Year Periods

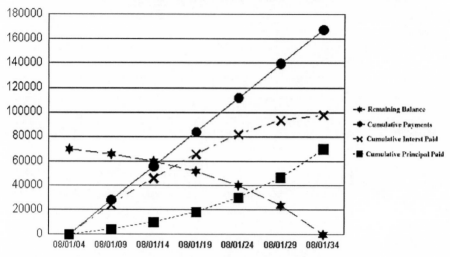

Amortization Chart
Scenario 2 -- Same Loan with Accelerated Payments

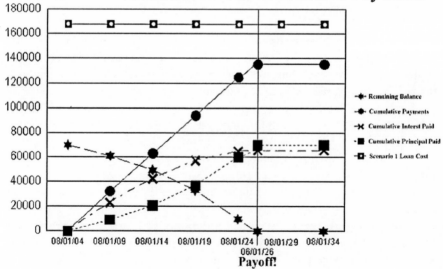

Top: Loan Scenario 1. *Bottom:* Loan Scenario 2.

first graph, you notice the dashed line (with *X*s for points) of cumulative interest payments rises sharply and stays well above the dashed line with squares, which reflects cumulative principal payments. By paying extra money which is applied directly to the principal, we have managed to keep this separation to a minimum, and by the end of the loan you have actually paid less interest than you have principal! A final important change is that the remaining balance of your loan, the line with the six-point stars, bottoms out very early — instead of stretching across all 360 months, you pay off the loan in just 261 months, or less than 22 years. Being able to pay extra money is a good reason not to buy more home than you can afford because having that margin to pay a little extra each month can make a tremendous difference in your financial future.

You've heard that *timing is everything,* and I've already explained how you may get a better price during some times of the year or by following rate trends closely to make your purchase. Timing is also crucial when you're paying extra money on your home. Part of the reason for the visual aids and amortization tables is to drive home *the importance of the first part of your loan.* That's when the lender is making their money, and you're doing little more than paying rent. In our scenario 1 example, in the first ten years you will have paid out almost $56,000, but you won't even have $10,000 in equity (or cumulative principal payments) to show for it. By carefully planning and budgeting your money, *scenario 2 more than doubles your equity in the same amount of time.*

The pie charts illustrating scenario 1 and scenario 2 are another way of comparing these two situations. Keep in mind these two loans began with identical amounts and terms. The area representing principal — the actual amount of money borrowed — remains equal. Both represent approximately $70,000, although in scenario 1 the actual figure comes to $69,920.19 because at the end of 360 payments, there is still a balance of $79.81 due. With any mortgage calculation, you may see slight differences depending on the whether the calculation uses months, exact days, or other minor differences. What has changed is the ratio of interest to principal. By paying the minimum payments, over 58 percent of your payments go to interest. By applying extra money toward the principal, we have changed the loan so that most of the money goes directly to principal. Let's take one final look at this through printed amortization tables, focusing special attention to the differences between the two tables in the last four columns to see how paying extra early can save you so much money:

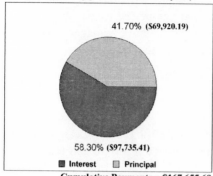

Scenario 1 -- $70,000 Loan
(A standard mortgage at 7% interest over 30 years.)

41.70% ($69,920.19)

58.30% ($97,735.41)

■ Interest   ▢ Principal

Cumulative Payments = $167,655.60
Data Derived from Mortgage Wizard Plus

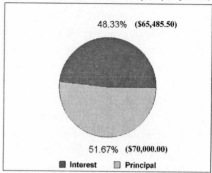

Scenario 2 -- $70,000 Loan
(Paying extra on principal each month - especially early in loan.)

48.33%   ($65,485.50)

51.67%   ($70,000.00)

■ Interest   ▢ Principal

Cumulative Payments = $135,485.50
Data Derived from Mortgage Wizard Plus

Amortization Schedule Scenario 1
($70,000 @ 7% over 30 years)

#	Date	Days	% Int.	Payment	Interest	Principal	Balance	Cum. Int.
1	08/01/2003	31	7.000	$465.71	$416.19	$49.52	$69,950.48	$416.19
2	09/01/2003	31	7.000	$465.71	$415.89	$49.82	$69,900.66	$832.08
3	10/01/2003	30	7.000	$465.71	$402.15	$63.56	$69,837.10	$1,234.23
4	11/01/2003	31	7.000	$465.71	$415.22	$50.49	$69,786.61	$1,649.45
5	12/01/2003	30	7.000	$465.71	$401.50	$64.21	$69,722.40	$2,050.95
6	01/01/2004	31	7.000	$465.71	$414.54	$51.17	$69,671.23	$2,465.49
7	02/01/2004	31	7.000	$465.71	$414.23	$51.48	$69,619.75	$2,879.72
8	03/01/2004	28	7.000	$465.71	$373.76	$91.95	$69,527.80	$3,253.48
9	04/01/2004	31	7.000	$465.71	$413.38	$52.33	$69,475.47	$3,666.86
10	05/01/2004	30	7.000	$465.71	$399.71	$66.00	$69,409.47	$4,066.57
11	06/01/2004	31	7.000	$465.71	$412.68	$53.03	$69,356.43	$4,479.24
12	07/01/2004	30	7.000	$465.71	$399.02	$66.69	$69,289.74	$4,878.26
13	08/01/2004	31	7.000	$465.71	$411.96	$53.75	$69,236.00	$5,290.23
14	09/01/2004	31	7.000	$465.71	$411.65	$54.06	$69,181.93	$5,701.87
15	10/01/2004	30	7.000	$465.71	$398.02	$67.69	$69,114.24	$6,099.89
16	11/01/2004	31	7.000	$465.71	$410.92	$54.79	$69,059.45	$6,510.81
17	12/01/2004	30	7.000	$465.71	$397.31	$68.40	$68,991.05	$6,908.12
18	01/01/2005	31	7.000	$465.71	$410.19	$55.52	$68,935.53	$7,318.31
19	02/01/2005	31	7.000	$465.71	$409.86	$55.85	$68,879.68	$7,728.17
20	03/01/2005	28	7.000	$465.71	$369.79	$95.92	$68,783.76	$8,097.96
21	04/01/2005	31	7.000	$465.71	$408.96	$56.75	$68,727.01	$8,506.92
22	05/01/2005	30	7.000	$465.71	$395.40	$70.31	$68,656.70	$8,902.32
23	06/01/2005	31	7.000	$465.71	$408.20	$57.51	$68,599.19	$9,310.52
24	07/01/2005	30	7.000	$465.71	$394.66	$71.05	$68,528.14	$9,705.18
25	08/01/2005	31	7.000	$465.71	$407.44	$58.27	$68,469.87	$10,112.62
26	09/01/2005	31	7.000	$465.71	$407.09	$58.62	$68,411.25	$10,519.71
27	10/01/2005	30	7.000	$465.71	$393.58	$72.13	$68,339.12	$10,913.29
28	11/01/2005	31	7.000	$465.71	$406.31	$59.40	$68,279.73	$11,319.61
29	12/01/2005	30	7.000	$465.71	$392.83	$72.88	$68,206.84	$11,712.43

#	Date	Days	% Int.	Payment	Interest	Principal	Balance	Cum. Int.
30	01/01/2006	31	7.000	$465.71	$405.53	$60.18	$68,146.66	$12,117.96
31	02/01/2006	31	7.000	$465.71	$405.17	$60.54	$68,086.12	$12,523.13
32	03/01/2006	28	7.000	$465.71	$365.53	$100.18	$67,985.94	$12,888.66
33	04/01/2006	31	7.000	$465.71	$404.21	$61.50	$67,924.44	$13,292.87
34	05/01/2006	30	7.000	$465.71	$390.78	$74.93	$67,849.51	$13,683.65
35	06/01/2006	31	7.000	$465.71	$403.40	$62.31	$67,787.20	$14,087.05
36	07/01/2006	30	7.000	$465.71	$389.99	$75.72	$67,711.49	$14,477.05
37	08/01/2006	31	7.000	$465.71	$402.58	$63.13	$67,648.36	$14,879.63
38	09/01/2006	31	7.000	$465.71	$402.21	$63.50	$67,584.85	$15,281.83
39	10/01/2006	30	7.000	$465.71	$388.83	$76.88	$67,507.97	$15,670.66
40	11/01/2006	31	7.000	$465.71	$401.37	$64.34	$67,443.63	$16,072.03
41	12/01/2006	30	7.000	$465.71	$388.02	$77.69	$67,365.94	$16,460.05
42	01/01/2007	31	7.000	$465.71	$400.53	$65.18	$67,300.76	$16,860.58
43	02/01/2007	31	7.000	$465.71	$400.14	$65.57	$67,235.19	$17,260.72
44	03/01/2007	28	7.000	$465.71	$360.96	$104.75	$67,130.44	$17,621.68
45	04/01/2007	31	7.000	$465.71	$399.13	$66.58	$67,063.85	$18,020.80
46	05/01/2007	30	7.000	$465.71	$385.83	$79.88	$66,983.97	$18,406.63
47	06/01/2007	31	7.000	$465.71	$398.26	$67.45	$66,916.52	$18,804.89
48	07/01/2007	30	7.000	$465.71	$384.98	$80.73	$66,835.79	$19,189.87
49	08/01/2007	31	7.000	$465.71	$397.37	$68.34	$66,767.46	$19,587.25
50	09/01/2007	31	7.000	$465.71	$396.97	$68.74	$66,698.72	$19,984.22
51	10/01/2007	30	7.000	$465.71	$383.73	$81.98	$66,616.74	$20,367.95
52	11/01/2007	31	7.000	$465.71	$396.07	$69.64	$66,547.10	$20,764.02
53	12/01/2007	30	7.000	$465.71	$382.86	$82.85	$66,464.25	$21,146.88
54	01/01/2008	31	7.000	$465.71	$395.17	$70.54	$66,393.70	$21,542.04
55	02/01/2008	31	7.000	$465.71	$394.75	$70.96	$66,322.74	$21,936.79
56	03/01/2008	28	7.000	$465.71	$356.06	$109.65	$66,213.09	$22,292.85
57	04/01/2008	31	7.000	$465.71	$393.67	$72.04	$66,141.05	$22,686.52
58	05/01/2008	30	7.000	$465.71	$380.52	$85.19	$66,055.87	$23,067.05
59	06/01/2008	31	7.000	$465.71	$392.74	$72.97	$65,982.89	$23,459.78
60	07/01/2008	30	7.000	$465.71	$379.61	$86.10	$65,896.80	$23,839.40
61	08/01/2008	31	7.000	$465.71	$391.79	$73.92	$65,822.88	$24,231.19
62	09/01/2008	31	7.000	$465.71	$391.35	$74.36	$65,748.52	$24,622.54
63	10/01/2008	30	7.000	$465.71	$378.26	$87.45	$65,661.08	$25,000.81
64	11/01/2008	31	7.000	$465.71	$390.39	$75.32	$65,585.76	$25,391.20
65	12/01/2008	30	7.000	$465.71	$377.33	$88.38	$65,497.37	$25,768.52
66	01/01/2009	31	7.000	$465.71	$389.42	$76.29	$65,421.08	$26,157.94
67	02/01/2009	31	7.000	$465.71	$388.96	$76.75	$65,344.33	$26,546.90
68	03/01/2009	28	7.000	$465.71	$350.81	$114.90	$65,229.43	$26,897.71
69	04/01/2009	31	7.000	$465.71	$387.82	$77.89	$65,151.55	$27,285.54
70	05/01/2009	30	7.000	$465.71	$374.83	$90.88	$65,060.67	$27,660.37
71	06/01/2009	31	7.000	$465.71	$386.82	$78.89	$64,981.78	$28,047.19
72	07/01/2009	30	7.000	$465.71	$373.85	$91.86	$64,889.92	$28,421.04
73	08/01/2009	31	7.000	$465.71	$385.81	$79.90	$64,810.02	$28,806.85
74	09/01/2009	31	7.000	$465.71	$385.33	$80.38	$64,729.64	$29,192.18
75	10/01/2009	30	7.000	$465.71	$372.40	$93.31	$64,636.33	$29,564.58
76	11/01/2009	31	7.000	$465.71	$384.30	$81.41	$64,554.92	$29,948.88
77	12/01/2009	30	7.000	$465.71	$371.40	$94.31	$64,460.60	$30,320.27
78	01/01/2010	31	7.000	$465.71	$383.25	$82.46	$64,378.15	$30,703.53
79	02/01/2010	31	7.000	$465.71	$382.76	$82.95	$64,295.20	$31,086.29

#	Date	Days	% Int.	Payment	Interest	Principal	Balance	Cum. Int.
80	03/01/2010	28	7.000	$465.71	$345.18	$120.53	$64,174.66	$31,431.46
81	04/01/2010	31	7.000	$465.71	$381.55	$84.16	$64,090.51	$31,813.02
82	05/01/2010	30	7.000	$465.71	$368.73	$96.98	$63,993.52	$32,181.74
83	06/01/2010	31	7.000	$465.71	$380.48	$85.23	$63,908.29	$32,562.22
84	07/01/2010	30	7.000	$465.71	$367.68	$98.03	$63,810.26	$32,929.90
85	08/01/2010	31	7.000	$465.71	$379.39	$86.32	$63,723.93	$33,309.28
86	09/01/2010	31	7.000	$465.71	$378.87	$86.84	$63,637.09	$33,688.15
87	10/01/2010	30	7.000	$465.71	$366.12	$99.59	$63,537.50	$34,054.27
88	11/01/2010	31	7.000	$465.71	$377.76	$87.95	$63,449.56	$34,432.04
89	12/01/2010	30	7.000	$465.71	$365.04	$100.67	$63,348.88	$34,797.07
90	01/01/2011	31	7.000	$465.71	$376.64	$89.07	$63,259.82	$35,173.72
91	02/01/2011	31	7.000	$465.71	$376.11	$89.60	$63,170.22	$35,549.83
92	03/01/2011	28	7.000	$465.71	$339.14	$126.57	$63,043.65	$35,888.97
93	04/01/2011	31	7.000	$465.71	$374.83	$90.88	$62,952.77	$36,263.80
94	05/01/2011	30	7.000	$465.71	$362.18	$103.53	$62,849.24	$36,625.98
95	06/01/2011	31	7.000	$465.71	$373.67	$92.04	$62,757.20	$36,999.65
96	07/01/2011	30	7.000	$465.71	$361.05	$104.66	$62,652.54	$37,360.70
97	08/01/2011	31	7.000	$465.71	$372.50	$93.21	$62,559.34	$37,733.21
98	09/01/2011	31	7.000	$465.71	$371.95	$93.76	$62,465.57	$38,105.15
99	10/01/2011	30	7.000	$465.71	$359.38	$106.33	$62,359.24	$38,464.53
100	11/01/2011	31	7.000	$465.71	$370.76	$94.95	$62,264.29	$38,835.29
101	12/01/2011	30	7.000	$465.71	$358.22	$107.49	$62,156.80	$39,193.51
102	01/01/2012	31	7.000	$465.71	$369.56	$96.15	$62,060.64	$39,563.06
103	02/01/2012	31	7.000	$465.71	$368.98	$96.73	$61,963.92	$39,932.05
104	03/01/2012	28	7.000	$465.71	$332.66	$133.05	$61,830.87	$40,264.71
105	04/01/2012	31	7.000	$465.71	$367.62	$98.09	$61,732.78	$40,632.33
106	05/01/2012	30	7.000	$465.71	$355.16	$110.55	$61,622.23	$40,987.49
107	06/01/2012	31	7.000	$465.71	$366.38	$99.33	$61,522.89	$41,353.86
108	07/01/2012	30	7.000	$465.71	$353.95	$111.76	$61,411.14	$41,707.82
109	08/01/2012	31	7.000	$465.71	$365.12	$100.59	$61,310.55	$42,072.94
110	09/01/2012	31	7.000	$465.71	$364.52	$101.19	$61,209.36	$42,437.46
111	10/01/2012	30	7.000	$465.71	$352.15	$113.56	$61,095.80	$42,789.61
112	11/01/2012	31	7.000	$465.71	$363.25	$102.46	$60,993.34	$43,152.86
113	12/01/2012	30	7.000	$465.71	$350.91	$114.80	$60,878.54	$43,503.77
114	01/01/2013	31	7.000	$465.71	$361.96	$103.75	$60,774.78	$43,865.72
115	02/01/2013	31	7.000	$465.71	$361.34	$104.37	$60,670.41	$44,227.06
116	03/01/2013	28	7.000	$465.71	$325.72	$139.99	$60,530.42	$44,552.78
117	04/01/2013	31	7.000	$465.71	$359.89	$105.82	$60,424.59	$44,912.66
118	05/01/2013	30	7.000	$465.71	$347.63	$118.08	$60,306.52	$45,260.30
119	06/01/2013	31	7.000	$465.71	$358.55	$107.16	$60,199.36	$45,618.85
120	07/01/2013	30	7.000	$465.71	$346.34	$119.37	$60,079.99	$45,965.19
121	08/01/2013	31	7.000	$465.71	$357.21	$108.50	$59,971.49	$46,322.40
122	09/01/2013	31	7.000	$465.71	$356.56	$109.15	$59,862.34	$46,678.96
123	10/01/2013	30	7.000	$465.71	$344.40	$121.31	$59,741.03	$47,023.36
124	11/01/2013	31	7.000	$465.71	$355.19	$110.52	$59,630.51	$47,378.55
125	12/01/2013	30	7.000	$465.71	$343.07	$122.64	$59,507.87	$47,721.62
126	01/01/2014	31	7.000	$465.71	$353.81	$111.90	$59,395.97	$48,075.43
127	02/01/2014	31	7.000	$465.71	$353.14	$112.57	$59,283.40	$48,428.57
128	03/01/2014	28	7.000	$465.71	$318.27	$147.44	$59,135.96	$48,746.84
129	04/01/2014	31	7.000	$465.71	$351.60	$114.11	$59,021.84	$49,098.43

#	Date	Days	% Int.	Payment	Interest	Principal	Balance	Cum. Int.
130	05/01/2014	30	7.000	$465.71	$339.56	$126.15	$58,895.70	$49,438.00
131	06/01/2014	31	7.000	$465.71	$350.17	$115.54	$58,780.15	$49,788.16
132	07/01/2014	30	7.000	$465.71	$338.17	$127.54	$58,652.62	$50,126.34
133	08/01/2014	31	7.000	$465.71	$348.72	$116.99	$58,535.63	$50,475.06
134	09/01/2014	31	7.000	$465.71	$348.03	$117.68	$58,417.94	$50,823.08
135	10/01/2014	30	7.000	$465.71	$336.09	$129.62	$58,288.32	$51,159.17
136	11/01/2014	31	7.000	$465.71	$346.56	$119.15	$58,169.17	$51,505.73
137	12/01/2014	30	7.000	$465.71	$334.66	$131.05	$58,038.12	$51,840.39
138	01/01/2015	31	7.000	$465.71	$345.07	$120.64	$57,917.48	$52,185.46
139	02/01/2015	31	7.000	$465.71	$344.35	$121.36	$57,796.12	$52,529.81
140	03/01/2015	28	7.000	$465.71	$310.29	$155.42	$57,640.69	$52,840.09
141	04/01/2015	31	7.000	$465.71	$342.70	$123.01	$57,517.69	$53,182.80
142	05/01/2015	30	7.000	$465.71	$330.91	$134.80	$57,382.89	$53,513.71
143	06/01/2015	31	7.000	$465.71	$341.17	$124.54	$57,258.35	$53,854.88
144	07/01/2015	30	7.000	$465.71	$329.42	$136.29	$57,122.06	$54,184.30
145	08/01/2015	31	7.000	$465.71	$339.62	$126.09	$56,995.97	$54,523.92
146	09/01/2015	31	7.000	$465.71	$338.87	$126.84	$56,869.13	$54,862.79
147	10/01/2015	30	7.000	$465.71	$327.18	$138.53	$56,730.60	$55,189.97
148	11/01/2015	31	7.000	$465.71	$337.29	$128.42	$56,602.18	$55,527.26
149	12/01/2015	30	7.000	$465.71	$325.64	$140.07	$56,462.12	$55,852.91
150	01/01/2016	31	7.000	$465.71	$335.70	$130.01	$56,332.11	$56,188.61
151	02/01/2016	31	7.000	$465.71	$334.92	$130.79	$56,201.32	$56,523.53
152	03/01/2016	28	7.000	$465.71	$301.72	$163.99	$56,037.33	$56,825.25
153	04/01/2016	31	7.000	$465.71	$333.17	$132.54	$55,904.80	$57,158.43
154	05/01/2016	30	7.000	$465.71	$321.63	$144.08	$55,760.72	$57,480.06
155	06/01/2016	31	7.000	$465.71	$331.53	$134.18	$55,626.53	$57,811.58
156	07/01/2016	30	7.000	$465.71	$320.03	$145.68	$55,480.85	$58,131.61
157	08/01/2016	31	7.000	$465.71	$329.86	$135.85	$55,345.01	$58,461.48
158	09/01/2016	31	7.000	$465.71	$329.06	$136.65	$55,208.35	$58,790.53
159	10/01/2016	30	7.000	$465.71	$317.62	$148.09	$55,060.27	$59,108.16
160	11/01/2016	31	7.000	$465.71	$327.36	$138.35	$54,921.92	$59,435.52
161	12/01/2016	30	7.000	$465.71	$315.98	$149.73	$54,772.19	$59,751.50
162	01/01/2017	31	7.000	$465.71	$325.65	$140.06	$54,632.13	$60,077.15
163	02/01/2017	31	7.000	$465.71	$324.82	$140.89	$54,491.24	$60,401.97
164	03/01/2017	28	7.000	$465.71	$292.54	$173.17	$54,318.07	$60,694.51
165	04/01/2017	31	7.000	$465.71	$322.95	$142.76	$54,175.31	$61,017.46
166	05/01/2017	30	7.000	$465.71	$311.68	$154.03	$54,021.28	$61,329.14
167	06/01/2017	31	7.000	$465.71	$321.19	$144.52	$53,876.76	$61,650.33
168	07/01/2017	30	7.000	$465.71	$309.96	$155.75	$53,721.01	$61,960.29
169	08/01/2017	31	7.000	$465.71	$319.40	$146.31	$53,574.70	$62,279.69
170	09/01/2017	31	7.000	$465.71	$318.53	$147.18	$53,427.52	$62,598.22
171	10/01/2017	30	7.000	$465.71	$307.38	$158.33	$53,269.19	$62,905.60
172	11/01/2017	31	7.000	$465.71	$316.71	$149.00	$53,120.19	$63,222.31
173	12/01/2017	30	7.000	$465.71	$305.61	$160.10	$52,960.09	$63,527.92
174	01/01/2018	31	7.000	$465.71	$314.88	$150.83	$52,809.26	$63,842.80
175	02/01/2018	31	7.000	$465.71	$313.98	$151.73	$52,657.53	$64,156.78
176	03/01/2018	28	7.000	$465.71	$282.70	$183.01	$52,474.52	$64,439.48
177	04/01/2018	31	7.000	$465.71	$311.99	$153.72	$52,320.80	$64,751.47
178	05/01/2018	30	7.000	$465.71	$301.01	$164.70	$52,156.10	$65,052.48
179	06/01/2018	31	7.000	$465.71	$310.10	$155.61	$52,000.48	$65,362.57

#	Date	Days	% Int.	Payment	Interest	Principal	Balance	Cum. Int.
180	07/01/2018	30	7.000	$465.71	$299.17	$166.54	$51,833.94	$65,661.74
181	08/01/2018	31	7.000	$465.71	$308.18	$157.53	$51,676.41	$65,969.92
182	09/01/2018	31	7.000	$465.71	$307.24	$158.47	$51,517.95	$66,277.17
183	10/01/2018	30	7.000	$465.71	$296.39	$169.32	$51,348.63	$66,573.56
184	11/01/2018	31	7.000	$465.71	$305.30	$160.41	$51,188.22	$66,878.86
185	12/01/2018	30	7.000	$465.71	$294.50	$171.21	$51,017.00	$67,173.35
186	01/01/2019	31	7.000	$465.71	$303.32	$162.39	$50,854.61	$67,476.67
187	02/01/2019	31	7.000	$465.71	$302.36	$163.35	$50,691.26	$67,779.03
188	03/01/2019	28	7.000	$465.71	$272.14	$193.57	$50,497.69	$68,051.17
189	04/01/2019	31	7.000	$465.71	$300.24	$165.47	$50,332.22	$68,351.41
190	05/01/2019	30	7.000	$465.71	$289.57	$176.14	$50,156.08	$68,640.98
191	06/01/2019	31	7.000	$465.71	$298.20	$167.51	$49,988.58	$68,939.19
192	07/01/2019	30	7.000	$465.71	$287.59	$178.12	$49,810.46	$69,226.78
193	08/01/2019	31	7.000	$465.71	$296.15	$169.56	$49,640.90	$69,522.93
194	09/01/2019	31	7.000	$465.71	$295.14	$170.57	$49,470.33	$69,818.07
195	10/01/2019	30	7.000	$465.71	$284.61	$181.10	$49,289.24	$70,102.69
196	11/01/2019	31	7.000	$465.71	$293.05	$172.66	$49,116.58	$70,395.74
197	12/01/2019	30	7.000	$465.71	$282.58	$183.13	$48,933.44	$70,678.31
198	01/01/2020	31	7.000	$465.71	$290.94	$174.77	$48,758.67	$70,969.25
199	02/01/2020	31	7.000	$465.71	$289.90	$175.81	$48,582.86	$71,259.15
200	03/01/2020	28	7.000	$465.71	$260.82	$204.89	$48,377.97	$71,519.97
201	04/01/2020	31	7.000	$465.71	$287.63	$178.08	$48,199.89	$71,807.60
202	05/01/2020	30	7.000	$465.71	$277.30	$188.41	$48,011.48	$72,084.90
203	06/01/2020	31	7.000	$465.71	$285.45	$180.26	$47,831.23	$72,370.36
204	07/01/2020	30	7.000	$465.71	$275.18	$190.53	$47,640.70	$72,645.54
205	08/01/2020	31	7.000	$465.71	$283.25	$182.46	$47,458.24	$72,928.79
206	09/01/2020	31	7.000	$465.71	$282.16	$183.55	$47,274.70	$73,210.96
207	10/01/2020	30	7.000	$465.71	$271.98	$193.73	$47,080.97	$73,482.94
208	11/01/2020	31	7.000	$465.71	$279.92	$185.79	$46,895.18	$73,762.86
209	12/01/2020	30	7.000	$465.71	$269.80	$195.91	$46,699.26	$74,032.65
210	01/01/2021	31	7.000	$465.71	$277.65	$188.06	$46,511.21	$74,310.31
211	02/01/2021	31	7.000	$465.71	$276.53	$189.18	$46,322.03	$74,586.84
212	03/01/2021	28	7.000	$465.71	$248.69	$217.02	$46,105.01	$74,835.53
213	04/01/2021	31	7.000	$465.71	$274.12	$191.59	$45,913.42	$75,109.65
214	05/01/2021	30	7.000	$465.71	$264.15	$201.56	$45,711.85	$75,373.79
215	06/01/2021	31	7.000	$465.71	$271.78	$193.93	$45,517.93	$75,645.58
216	07/01/2021	30	7.000	$465.71	$261.87	$203.84	$45,314.09	$75,907.45
217	08/01/2021	31	7.000	$465.71	$269.42	$196.29	$45,117.80	$76,176.87
218	09/01/2021	31	7.000	$465.71	$268.25	$197.46	$44,920.34	$76,445.12
219	10/01/2021	30	7.000	$465.71	$258.44	$207.27	$44,713.06	$76,703.55
220	11/01/2021	31	7.000	$465.71	$265.84	$199.87	$44,513.19	$76,969.39
221	12/01/2021	30	7.000	$465.71	$256.09	$209.62	$44,303.58	$77,225.49
222	01/01/2022	31	7.000	$465.71	$263.41	$202.30	$44,101.28	$77,488.90
223	02/01/2022	31	7.000	$465.71	$262.21	$203.50	$43,897.77	$77,751.10
224	03/01/2022	28	7.000	$465.71	$235.67	$230.04	$43,667.73	$77,986.77
225	04/01/2022	31	7.000	$465.71	$259.63	$206.08	$43,461.65	$78,246.40
226	05/01/2022	30	7.000	$465.71	$250.04	$215.67	$43,245.98	$78,496.44
227	06/01/2022	31	7.000	$465.71	$257.12	$208.59	$43,037.39	$78,753.56
228	07/01/2022	30	7.000	$465.71	$247.60	$218.11	$42,819.29	$79,001.17
229	08/01/2022	31	7.000	$465.71	$254.58	$211.13	$42,608.16	$79,255.75

#	Date	Days	% Int.	Payment	Interest	Principal	Balance	Cum. Int.
230	09/01/2022	31	7.000	$465.71	$253.33	$212.38	$42,395.78	$79,509.08
231	10/01/2022	30	7.000	$465.71	$243.91	$221.80	$42,173.98	$79,752.99
232	11/01/2022	31	7.000	$465.71	$250.75	$214.96	$41,959.02	$80,003.74
233	12/01/2022	30	7.000	$465.71	$241.40	$224.31	$41,734.71	$80,245.14
234	01/01/2023	31	7.000	$465.71	$248.14	$217.57	$41,517.13	$80,493.27
235	02/01/2023	31	7.000	$465.71	$246.84	$218.87	$41,298.26	$80,740.11
236	03/01/2023	28	7.000	$465.71	$221.71	$244.00	$41,054.27	$80,961.83
237	04/01/2023	31	7.000	$465.71	$244.09	$221.62	$40,832.65	$81,205.92
238	05/01/2023	30	7.000	$465.71	$234.92	$230.79	$40,601.86	$81,440.84
239	06/01/2023	31	7.000	$465.71	$241.40	$224.31	$40,377.55	$81,682.24
240	07/01/2023	30	7.000	$465.71	$232.30	$233.41	$40,144.14	$81,914.54
241	08/01/2023	31	7.000	$465.71	$238.68	$227.03	$39,917.10	$82,153.21
242	09/01/2023	31	7.000	$465.71	$237.33	$228.38	$39,688.72	$82,390.54
243	10/01/2023	30	7.000	$465.71	$228.34	$237.37	$39,451.35	$82,618.88
244	11/01/2023	31	7.000	$465.71	$234.56	$231.15	$39,220.20	$82,853.44
245	12/01/2023	30	7.000	$465.71	$225.64	$240.07	$38,980.13	$83,079.08
246	01/01/2024	31	7.000	$465.71	$231.76	$233.95	$38,746.18	$83,310.84
247	02/01/2024	31	7.000	$465.71	$230.37	$235.34	$38,510.83	$83,541.20
248	03/01/2024	28	7.000	$465.71	$206.75	$258.96	$38,251.87	$83,747.95
249	04/01/2024	31	7.000	$465.71	$227.43	$238.28	$38,013.59	$83,975.38
250	05/01/2024	30	7.000	$465.71	$218.70	$247.01	$37,766.58	$84,194.08
251	06/01/2024	31	7.000	$465.71	$224.54	$241.17	$37,525.42	$84,418.63
252	07/01/2024	30	7.000	$465.71	$215.89	$249.82	$37,275.60	$84,634.52
253	08/01/2024	31	7.000	$465.71	$221.62	$244.09	$37,031.51	$84,856.14
254	09/01/2024	31	7.000	$465.71	$220.17	$245.54	$36,785.97	$85,076.31
255	10/01/2024	30	7.000	$465.71	$211.64	$254.07	$36,531.90	$85,287.95
256	11/01/2024	31	7.000	$465.71	$217.20	$248.51	$36,283.39	$85,505.15
257	12/01/2024	30	7.000	$465.71	$208.75	$256.96	$36,026.43	$85,713.90
258	01/01/2025	31	7.000	$465.71	$214.20	$251.51	$35,774.91	$85,928.09
259	02/01/2025	31	7.000	$465.71	$212.70	$253.01	$35,521.90	$86,140.79
260	03/01/2025	28	7.000	$465.71	$190.70	$275.01	$35,246.90	$86,331.50
261	04/01/2025	31	7.000	$465.71	$209.56	$256.15	$34,990.75	$86,541.06
262	05/01/2025	30	7.000	$465.71	$201.31	$264.40	$34,726.35	$86,742.37
263	06/01/2025	31	7.000	$465.71	$206.47	$259.24	$34,467.10	$86,948.83
264	07/01/2025	30	7.000	$465.71	$198.30	$267.41	$34,199.69	$87,147.13
265	08/01/2025	31	7.000	$465.71	$203.34	$262.37	$33,937.32	$87,350.47
266	09/01/2025	31	7.000	$465.71	$201.78	$263.93	$33,673.38	$87,552.24
267	10/01/2025	30	7.000	$465.71	$193.73	$271.98	$33,401.40	$87,745.97
268	11/01/2025	31	7.000	$465.71	$198.59	$267.12	$33,134.28	$87,944.56
269	12/01/2025	30	7.000	$465.71	$190.63	$275.08	$32,859.20	$88,135.19
270	01/01/2026	31	7.000	$465.71	$195.37	$270.34	$32,588.85	$88,330.55
271	02/01/2026	31	7.000	$465.71	$193.76	$271.95	$32,316.90	$88,524.31
272	03/01/2026	28	7.000	$465.71	$173.50	$292.21	$32,024.69	$88,697.81
273	04/01/2026	31	7.000	$465.71	$190.40	$275.31	$31,749.38	$88,888.21
274	05/01/2026	30	7.000	$465.71	$182.66	$283.05	$31,466.33	$89,070.87
275	06/01/2026	31	7.000	$465.71	$187.08	$278.63	$31,187.71	$89,257.96
276	07/01/2026	30	7.000	$465.71	$179.43	$286.28	$30,901.43	$89,437.39
277	08/01/2026	31	7.000	$465.71	$183.73	$281.98	$30,619.44	$89,621.11
278	09/01/2026	31	7.000	$465.71	$182.05	$283.66	$30,335.78	$89,803.16
279	10/01/2026	30	7.000	$465.71	$174.53	$291.18	$30,044.60	$89,977.69

#	Date	Days	% Int.	Payment	Interest	Principal	Balance	Cum. Int.
280	11/01/2026	31	7.000	$465.71	$178.63	$287.08	$29,757.52	$90,156.32
281	12/01/2026	30	7.000	$465.71	$171.20	$294.51	$29,463.01	$90,327.52
282	01/01/2027	31	7.000	$465.71	$175.17	$290.54	$29,172.47	$90,502.69
283	02/01/2027	31	7.000	$465.71	$173.45	$292.26	$28,880.21	$90,676.14
284	03/01/2027	28	7.000	$465.71	$155.05	$310.66	$28,569.55	$90,831.19
285	04/01/2027	31	7.000	$465.71	$169.86	$295.85	$28,273.70	$91,001.05
286	05/01/2027	30	7.000	$465.71	$162.66	$303.05	$27,970.65	$91,163.71
287	06/01/2027	31	7.000	$465.71	$166.30	$299.41	$27,671.24	$91,330.01
288	07/01/2027	30	7.000	$465.71	$159.20	$306.51	$27,364.73	$91,489.21
289	08/01/2027	31	7.000	$465.71	$162.70	$303.01	$27,061.72	$91,651.91
290	09/01/2027	31	7.000	$465.71	$160.90	$304.81	$26,756.91	$91,812.81
291	10/01/2027	30	7.000	$465.71	$153.94	$311.77	$26,445.13	$91,966.74
292	11/01/2027	31	7.000	$465.71	$157.23	$308.48	$26,136.65	$92,123.97
293	12/01/2027	30	7.000	$465.71	$150.37	$315.34	$25,821.31	$92,274.34
294	01/01/2028	31	7.000	$465.71	$153.52	$312.19	$25,509.13	$92,427.87
295	02/01/2028	31	7.000	$465.71	$151.67	$314.04	$25,195.08	$92,579.53
296	03/01/2028	28	7.000	$465.71	$135.26	$330.45	$24,864.63	$92,714.79
297	04/01/2028	31	7.000	$465.71	$147.83	$317.88	$24,546.76	$92,862.63
298	05/01/2028	30	7.000	$465.71	$141.22	$324.49	$24,222.27	$93,003.85
299	06/01/2028	31	7.000	$465.71	$144.01	$321.70	$23,900.57	$93,147.86
300	07/01/2028	30	7.000	$465.71	$137.50	$328.21	$23,572.37	$93,285.37
301	08/01/2028	31	7.000	$465.71	$140.15	$325.56	$23,246.81	$93,425.52
302	09/01/2028	31	7.000	$465.71	$138.21	$327.50	$22,919.31	$93,563.73
303	10/01/2028	30	7.000	$465.71	$131.86	$333.85	$22,585.46	$93,695.59
304	11/01/2028	31	7.000	$465.71	$134.28	$331.43	$22,254.04	$93,829.88
305	12/01/2028	30	7.000	$465.71	$128.03	$337.68	$21,916.36	$93,957.91
306	01/01/2029	31	7.000	$465.71	$130.30	$335.41	$21,580.95	$94,088.21
307	02/01/2029	31	7.000	$465.71	$128.31	$337.40	$21,243.55	$94,216.52
308	03/01/2029	28	7.000	$465.71	$114.05	$351.66	$20,891.89	$94,330.57
309	04/01/2029	31	7.000	$465.71	$124.21	$341.50	$20,550.39	$94,454.78
310	05/01/2029	30	7.000	$465.71	$118.23	$347.48	$20,202.91	$94,573.01
311	06/01/2029	31	7.000	$465.71	$120.12	$345.59	$19,857.32	$94,693.13
312	07/01/2029	30	7.000	$465.71	$114.24	$351.47	$19,505.86	$94,807.38
313	08/01/2029	31	7.000	$465.71	$115.97	$349.74	$19,156.12	$94,923.35
314	09/01/2029	31	7.000	$465.71	$113.89	$351.82	$18,804.30	$95,037.24
315	10/01/2029	30	7.000	$465.71	$108.18	$357.53	$18,446.78	$95,145.43
316	11/01/2029	31	7.000	$465.71	$109.68	$356.03	$18,090.74	$95,255.10
317	12/01/2029	30	7.000	$465.71	$104.08	$361.63	$17,729.11	$95,359.18
318	01/01/2030	31	7.000	$465.71	$105.41	$360.30	$17,368.81	$95,464.59
319	02/01/2030	31	7.000	$465.71	$103.27	$362.44	$17,006.37	$95,567.86
320	03/01/2030	28	7.000	$465.71	$91.30	$374.41	$16,631.96	$95,659.16
321	04/01/2030	31	7.000	$465.71	$98.89	$366.82	$16,265.13	$95,758.04
322	05/01/2030	30	7.000	$465.71	$93.58	$372.13	$15,893.00	$95,851.62
323	06/01/2030	31	7.000	$465.71	$94.49	$371.22	$15,521.78	$95,946.11
324	07/01/2030	30	7.000	$465.71	$89.30	$376.41	$15,145.37	$96,035.41
325	08/01/2030	31	7.000	$465.71	$90.05	$375.66	$14,769.71	$96,125.46
326	09/01/2030	31	7.000	$465.71	$87.81	$377.90	$14,391.81	$96,213.27
327	10/01/2030	30	7.000	$465.71	$82.80	$382.91	$14,008.90	$96,296.07
328	11/01/2030	31	7.000	$465.71	$83.29	$382.42	$13,626.48	$96,379.36
329	12/01/2030	30	7.000	$465.71	$78.40	$387.31	$13,239.17	$96,457.76

#	Date	Days	% Int.	Payment	Interest	Principal	Balance	Cum. Int.
330	01/01/2031	31	7.000	$465.71	$78.71	$387.00	$12,852.17	$96,536.47
331	02/01/2031	31	7.000	$465.71	$76.41	$389.30	$12,462.88	$96,612.89
332	03/01/2031	28	7.000	$465.71	$66.91	$398.80	$12,064.08	$96,679.80
333	04/01/2031	31	7.000	$465.71	$71.73	$393.98	$11,670.09	$96,751.52
334	05/01/2031	30	7.000	$465.71	$67.14	$398.57	$11,271.52	$96,818.66
335	06/01/2031	31	7.000	$465.71	$67.02	$398.69	$10,872.83	$96,885.68
336	07/01/2031	30	7.000	$465.71	$62.55	$403.16	$10,469.67	$96,948.23
337	08/01/2031	31	7.000	$465.71	$62.25	$403.46	$10,066.21	$97,010.48
338	09/01/2031	31	7.000	$465.71	$59.85	$405.86	$9,660.35	$97,070.33
339	10/01/2031	30	7.000	$465.71	$55.58	$410.13	$9,250.22	$97,125.91
340	11/01/2031	31	7.000	$465.71	$55.00	$410.71	$8,839.50	$97,180.90
341	12/01/2031	30	7.000	$465.71	$50.86	$414.85	$8,424.65	$97,231.76
342	01/01/2032	31	7.000	$465.71	$50.09	$415.62	$8,009.03	$97,281.85
343	02/01/2032	31	7.000	$465.71	$47.62	$418.09	$7,590.94	$97,329.47
344	03/01/2032	28	7.000	$465.71	$40.75	$424.96	$7,165.98	$97,370.22
345	04/01/2032	31	7.000	$465.71	$42.61	$423.10	$6,742.87	$97,412.82
346	05/01/2032	30	7.000	$465.71	$38.79	$426.92	$6,315.96	$97,451.62
347	06/01/2032	31	7.000	$465.71	$37.55	$428.16	$5,887.80	$97,489.17
348	07/01/2032	30	7.000	$465.71	$33.87	$431.84	$5,455.96	$97,523.04
349	08/01/2032	31	7.000	$465.71	$32.44	$433.27	$5,022.69	$97,555.48
350	09/01/2032	31	7.000	$465.71	$29.86	$435.85	$4,586.84	$97,585.34
351	10/01/2032	30	7.000	$465.71	$26.39	$439.32	$4,147.52	$97,611.73
352	11/01/2032	31	7.000	$465.71	$24.66	$441.05	$3,706.47	$97,636.39
353	12/01/2032	30	7.000	$465.71	$21.32	$444.39	$3,262.09	$97,657.72
354	01/01/2033	31	7.000	$465.71	$19.39	$446.32	$2,815.77	$97,677.11
355	02/01/2033	31	7.000	$465.71	$16.74	$448.97	$2,366.80	$97,693.85
356	03/01/2033	28	7.000	$465.71	$12.71	$453.00	$1,913.80	$97,706.56
357	04/01/2033	31	7.000	$465.71	$11.38	$454.33	$1,459.47	$97,717.94
358	05/01/2033	30	7.000	$465.71	$8.40	$457.31	$1,002.15	$97,726.33
359	06/01/2033	31	7.000	$465.71	$5.96	$459.75	$542.40	$97,732.29
360	07/01/2033	30	7.000	$465.71	$3.12	$462.59	$79.81	$97,735.41

Source: Calculations made with Mortgage Wizard Plus

Amortization Schedule Scenario 2
($70,000 @ 7 percent over 30 years with Extra Payments)

#	Date	Days	% Int.	Payment	Interest	Principal	Balance	Cum. Int.
1	08/01/2003	31	7.000	$565.00	$416.19	$148.81	$69,851.19	$416.19
2	09/01/2003	31	7.000	$565.00	$415.30	$149.70	$69,701.49	$831.49
3	10/01/2003	30	7.000	$565.00	$401.01	$163.99	$69,537.50	$1,232.50
4	11/01/2003	31	7.000	$565.00	$413.44	$151.56	$69,385.93	$1,645.93
5	12/01/2003	30	7.000	$565.00	$399.19	$165.81	$69,220.13	$2,045.13
6	01/01/2004	31	7.000	$565.00	$411.55	$153.45	$69,066.68	$2,456.68
7	02/01/2004	31	7.000	$565.00	$410.64	$154.36	$68,912.31	$2,867.31
8	03/01/2004	28	7.000	$565.00	$369.96	$195.04	$68,717.28	$3,237.28
9	04/01/2004	31	7.000	$565.00	$408.56	$156.44	$68,560.84	$3,645.84
10	05/01/2004	30	7.000	$565.00	$394.44	$170.56	$68,390.28	$4,040.28
11	06/01/2004	31	7.000	$565.00	$406.62	$158.38	$68,231.90	$4,446.90
12	07/01/2004	30	7.000	$565.00	$392.55	$172.45	$68,059.45	$4,839.45

#	Date	Days	% Int.	Payment	Interest	Principal	Balance	Cum. Int.
13	08/01/2004	31	7.000	$540.00	$404.65	$135.35	$67,924.10	$5,244.10
14	09/01/2004	31	7.000	$540.00	$403.85	$136.15	$67,787.95	$5,647.95
15	10/01/2004	30	7.000	$540.00	$390.00	$150.00	$67,637.94	$6,037.94
16	11/01/2004	31	7.000	$540.00	$402.14	$137.86	$67,500.09	$6,440.09
17	12/01/2004	30	7.000	$540.00	$388.34	$151.66	$67,348.43	$6,828.43
18	01/01/2005	31	7.000	$540.00	$400.42	$139.58	$67,208.85	$7,228.85
19	02/01/2005	31	7.000	$540.00	$399.59	$140.41	$67,068.45	$7,628.45
20	03/01/2005	28	7.000	$540.00	$360.07	$179.93	$66,888.51	$7,988.51
21	04/01/2005	31	7.000	$540.00	$397.69	$142.31	$66,746.20	$8,386.20
22	05/01/2005	30	7.000	$540.00	$384.00	$156.00	$66,590.20	$8,770.20
23	06/01/2005	31	7.000	$540.00	$395.91	$144.09	$66,446.12	$9,166.12
24	07/01/2005	30	7.000	$540.00	$382.28	$157.72	$66,288.39	$9,548.39
25	08/01/2005	31	7.000	$540.00	$394.12	$145.88	$66,142.51	$9,942.51
26	09/01/2005	31	7.000	$540.00	$393.25	$146.75	$65,995.77	$10,335.77
27	10/01/2005	30	7.000	$540.00	$379.69	$160.31	$65,835.45	$10,715.45
28	11/01/2005	31	7.000	$540.00	$391.43	$148.57	$65,686.88	$11,106.88
29	12/01/2005	30	7.000	$540.00	$377.91	$162.09	$65,524.79	$11,484.79
30	01/01/2006	31	7.000	$540.00	$389.58	$150.42	$65,374.37	$11,874.37
31	02/01/2006	31	7.000	$540.00	$388.69	$151.31	$65,223.06	$12,263.06
32	03/01/2006	28	7.000	$540.00	$350.16	$189.84	$65,033.21	$12,613.21
33	04/01/2006	31	7.000	$540.00	$386.66	$153.34	$64,879.87	$12,999.87
34	05/01/2006	30	7.000	$540.00	$373.27	$166.73	$64,713.14	$13,373.14
35	06/01/2006	31	7.000	$540.00	$384.75	$155.25	$64,557.89	$13,757.89
36	07/01/2006	30	7.000	$540.00	$371.41	$168.59	$64,389.31	$14,129.31
37	08/01/2006	31	7.000	$515.00	$382.83	$132.17	$64,257.14	$14,512.14
38	09/01/2006	31	7.000	$515.00	$382.04	$132.96	$64,124.18	$14,894.18
39	10/01/2006	30	7.000	$515.00	$368.92	$146.08	$63,978.10	$15,263.10
40	11/01/2006	31	7.000	$515.00	$380.38	$134.62	$63,843.48	$15,643.48
41	12/01/2006	30	7.000	$515.00	$367.30	$147.70	$63,695.79	$16,010.79
42	01/01/2007	31	7.000	$515.00	$378.71	$136.29	$63,559.49	$16,389.49
43	02/01/2007	31	7.000	$515.00	$377.90	$137.10	$63,422.39	$16,767.39
44	03/01/2007	28	7.000	$515.00	$340.49	$174.51	$63,247.88	$17,107.88
45	04/01/2007	31	7.000	$515.00	$376.04	$138.96	$63,108.92	$17,483.92
46	05/01/2007	30	7.000	$515.00	$363.08	$151.92	$62,957.00	$17,847.00
47	06/01/2007	31	7.000	$515.00	$374.31	$140.69	$62,816.31	$18,221.31
48	07/01/2007	30	7.000	$515.00	$361.39	$153.61	$62,662.71	$18,582.71
49	08/01/2007	31	7.000	$515.00	$372.56	$142.44	$62,520.27	$18,955.27
50	09/01/2007	31	7.000	$515.00	$371.72	$143.28	$62,376.99	$19,326.99
51	10/01/2007	30	7.000	$515.00	$358.87	$156.13	$62,220.85	$19,685.85
52	11/01/2007	31	7.000	$515.00	$369.94	$145.06	$62,075.79	$20,055.79
53	12/01/2007	30	7.000	$515.00	$357.13	$157.87	$61,917.92	$20,412.92
54	01/01/2008	31	7.000	$515.00	$368.14	$146.86	$61,771.06	$20,781.06
55	02/01/2008	31	7.000	$515.00	$367.26	$147.74	$61,623.32	$21,148.32
56	03/01/2008	28	7.000	$515.00	$330.83	$184.17	$61,439.15	$21,479.15
57	04/01/2008	31	7.000	$515.00	$365.29	$149.71	$61,289.44	$21,844.44
58	05/01/2008	30	7.000	$515.00	$352.61	$162.39	$61,127.05	$22,197.05
59	06/01/2008	31	7.000	$515.00	$363.43	$151.57	$60,975.49	$22,560.49
60	07/01/2008	30	7.000	$515.00	$350.80	$164.20	$60,811.29	$22,911.29
61	08/01/2008	31	7.000	$515.00	$361.56	$153.44	$60,657.85	$23,272.85
62	09/01/2008	31	7.000	$515.00	$360.64	$154.36	$60,503.49	$23,633.49

#	Date	Days	% Int.	Payment	Interest	Principal	Balance	Cum. Int.
63	10/01/2008	30	7.000	$515.00	$348.09	$166.91	$60,336.58	$23,981.58
64	11/01/2008	31	7.000	$515.00	$358.73	$156.27	$60,180.31	$24,340.31
65	12/01/2008	30	7.000	$515.00	$346.23	$168.77	$60,011.54	$24,686.54
66	01/01/2009	31	7.000	$515.00	$356.80	$158.20	$59,853.34	$25,043.34
67	02/01/2009	31	7.000	$515.00	$355.86	$159.14	$59,694.20	$25,399.20
68	03/01/2009	28	7.000	$515.00	$320.48	$194.52	$59,499.68	$25,719.68
69	04/01/2009	31	7.000	$515.00	$353.76	$161.24	$59,338.43	$26,073.43
70	05/01/2009	30	7.000	$515.00	$341.39	$173.61	$59,164.82	$26,414.82
71	06/01/2009	31	7.000	$515.00	$351.77	$163.23	$59,001.59	$26,766.59
72	07/01/2009	30	7.000	$515.00	$339.45	$175.55	$58,826.03	$27,106.03
73	08/01/2009	31	7.000	$515.00	$349.75	$165.25	$58,660.79	$27,455.79
74	09/01/2009	31	7.000	$515.00	$348.77	$166.23	$58,494.56	$27,804.56
75	10/01/2009	30	7.000	$515.00	$336.53	$178.47	$58,316.09	$28,141.09
76	11/01/2009	31	7.000	$515.00	$346.72	$168.28	$58,147.81	$28,487.81
77	12/01/2009	30	7.000	$515.00	$334.54	$180.46	$57,967.34	$28,822.34
78	01/01/2010	31	7.000	$515.00	$344.65	$170.35	$57,796.99	$29,166.99
79	02/01/2010	31	7.000	$515.00	$343.63	$171.37	$57,625.62	$29,510.62
80	03/01/2010	28	7.000	$515.00	$309.37	$205.63	$57,419.99	$29,819.99
81	04/01/2010	31	7.000	$515.00	$341.39	$173.61	$57,246.39	$30,161.39
82	05/01/2010	30	7.000	$515.00	$329.35	$185.65	$57,060.74	$30,490.74
83	06/01/2010	31	7.000	$515.00	$339.26	$175.74	$56,884.99	$30,829.99
84	07/01/2010	30	7.000	$515.00	$327.27	$187.73	$56,697.26	$31,157.26
85	08/01/2010	31	7.000	$515.00	$337.10	$177.90	$56,519.36	$31,494.36
86	09/01/2010	31	7.000	$515.00	$336.04	$178.96	$56,340.40	$31,830.40
87	10/01/2010	30	7.000	$515.00	$324.14	$190.86	$56,149.53	$32,154.53
88	11/01/2010	31	7.000	$515.00	$333.84	$181.16	$55,968.37	$32,488.37
89	12/01/2010	30	7.000	$515.00	$322.00	$193.00	$55,775.37	$32,810.37
90	01/01/2011	31	7.000	$515.00	$331.61	$183.39	$55,591.99	$33,141.99
91	02/01/2011	31	7.000	$515.00	$330.52	$184.48	$55,407.51	$33,472.51
92	03/01/2011	28	7.000	$515.00	$297.46	$217.54	$55,189.97	$33,769.97
93	04/01/2011	31	7.000	$515.00	$328.13	$186.87	$55,003.11	$34,098.11
94	05/01/2011	30	7.000	$515.00	$316.44	$198.56	$54,804.55	$34,414.55
95	06/01/2011	31	7.000	$515.00	$325.84	$189.16	$54,615.39	$34,740.39
96	07/01/2011	30	7.000	$515.00	$314.21	$200.79	$54,414.60	$35,054.60
97	08/01/2011	31	7.000	$515.00	$323.52	$191.48	$54,223.13	$35,378.13
98	09/01/2011	31	7.000	$515.00	$322.39	$192.61	$54,030.51	$35,700.51
99	10/01/2011	30	7.000	$515.00	$310.85	$204.15	$53,826.36	$36,011.36
100	11/01/2011	31	7.000	$515.00	$320.03	$194.97	$53,631.39	$36,331.39
101	12/01/2011	30	7.000	$515.00	$308.55	$206.45	$53,424.94	$36,639.94
102	01/01/2012	31	7.000	$515.00	$317.64	$197.36	$53,227.58	$36,957.58
103	02/01/2012	31	7.000	$515.00	$316.47	$198.53	$53,029.05	$37,274.05
104	03/01/2012	28	7.000	$515.00	$284.69	$230.31	$52,798.74	$37,558.74
105	04/01/2012	31	7.000	$515.00	$313.92	$201.08	$52,597.66	$37,872.66
106	05/01/2012	30	7.000	$515.00	$302.60	$212.40	$52,385.26	$38,175.26
107	06/01/2012	31	7.000	$515.00	$311.46	$203.54	$52,181.72	$38,486.72
108	07/01/2012	30	7.000	$515.00	$300.21	$214.79	$51,966.93	$38,786.93
109	08/01/2012	31	7.000	$515.00	$308.97	$206.03	$51,760.90	$39,095.90
110	09/01/2012	31	7.000	$515.00	$307.75	$207.25	$51,553.65	$39,403.65
111	10/01/2012	30	7.000	$515.00	$296.60	$218.40	$51,335.25	$39,700.25
112	11/01/2012	31	7.000	$515.00	$305.22	$209.78	$51,125.46	$40,005.46

#	Date	Days	% Int.	Payment	Interest	Principal	Balance	Cum. Int.
113	12/01/2012	30	7.000	$515.00	$294.13	$220.87	$50,904.60	$40,299.60
114	01/01/2013	31	7.000	$515.00	$302.66	$212.34	$50,692.25	$40,602.25
115	02/01/2013	31	7.000	$515.00	$301.39	$213.61	$50,478.65	$40,903.65
116	03/01/2013	28	7.000	$515.00	$271.00	$244.00	$50,234.65	$41,174.65
117	04/01/2013	31	7.000	$515.00	$298.67	$216.33	$50,018.32	$41,473.32
118	05/01/2013	30	7.000	$515.00	$287.77	$227.23	$49,791.08	$41,761.08
119	06/01/2013	31	7.000	$515.00	$296.03	$218.97	$49,572.12	$42,057.12
120	07/01/2013	30	7.000	$515.00	$285.20	$229.80	$49,342.32	$42,342.32
121	08/01/2013	31	7.000	$515.00	$293.37	$221.63	$49,120.68	$42,635.68
122	09/01/2013	31	7.000	$515.00	$292.05	$222.95	$48,897.73	$42,927.73
123	10/01/2013	30	7.000	$515.00	$281.32	$233.68	$48,664.05	$43,209.05
124	11/01/2013	31	7.000	$515.00	$289.33	$225.67	$48,438.38	$43,498.38
125	12/01/2013	30	7.000	$515.00	$278.68	$236.32	$48,202.06	$43,777.06
126	01/01/2014	31	7.000	$515.00	$286.59	$228.41	$47,973.65	$44,063.65
127	02/01/2014	31	7.000	$515.00	$285.23	$229.77	$47,743.88	$44,348.88
128	03/01/2014	28	7.000	$515.00	$256.32	$258.68	$47,485.20	$44,605.20
129	04/01/2014	31	7.000	$515.00	$282.33	$232.67	$47,252.52	$44,887.52
130	05/01/2014	30	7.000	$515.00	$271.85	$243.15	$47,009.37	$45,159.37
131	06/01/2014	31	7.000	$515.00	$279.50	$235.50	$46,773.87	$45,438.87
132	07/01/2014	30	7.000	$515.00	$269.10	$245.90	$46,527.97	$45,707.97
133	08/01/2014	31	7.000	$515.00	$276.63	$238.37	$46,289.60	$45,984.60
134	09/01/2014	31	7.000	$515.00	$275.22	$239.78	$46,049.82	$46,259.82
135	10/01/2014	30	7.000	$515.00	$264.93	$250.07	$45,799.75	$46,524.75
136	11/01/2014	31	7.000	$515.00	$272.30	$242.70	$45,557.06	$46,797.06
137	12/01/2014	30	7.000	$515.00	$262.10	$252.90	$45,304.16	$47,059.16
138	01/01/2015	31	7.000	$515.00	$269.36	$245.64	$45,058.51	$47,328.51
139	02/01/2015	31	7.000	$515.00	$267.90	$247.10	$44,811.41	$47,596.41
140	03/01/2015	28	7.000	$515.00	$240.58	$274.42	$44,536.99	$47,836.99
141	04/01/2015	31	7.000	$515.00	$264.80	$250.20	$44,286.78	$48,101.78
142	05/01/2015	30	7.000	$515.00	$254.79	$260.21	$44,026.57	$48,356.57
143	06/01/2015	31	7.000	$515.00	$261.76	$253.24	$43,773.33	$48,618.33
144	07/01/2015	30	7.000	$515.00	$251.84	$263.16	$43,510.17	$48,870.17
145	08/01/2015	31	7.000	$515.00	$258.69	$256.31	$43,253.86	$49,128.86
146	09/01/2015	31	7.000	$515.00	$257.17	$257.83	$42,996.03	$49,386.03
147	10/01/2015	30	7.000	$515.00	$247.36	$267.64	$42,728.39	$49,633.39
148	11/01/2015	31	7.000	$515.00	$254.04	$260.96	$42,467.44	$49,887.44
149	12/01/2015	30	7.000	$515.00	$244.32	$270.68	$42,196.76	$50,131.76
150	01/01/2016	31	7.000	$515.00	$250.88	$264.12	$41,932.64	$50,382.64
151	02/01/2016	31	7.000	$515.00	$249.31	$265.69	$41,666.95	$50,631.95
152	03/01/2016	28	7.000	$515.00	$223.69	$291.31	$41,375.65	$50,855.65
153	04/01/2016	31	7.000	$515.00	$246.00	$269.00	$41,106.65	$51,101.65
154	05/01/2016	30	7.000	$515.00	$236.49	$278.51	$40,828.14	$51,338.14
155	06/01/2016	31	7.000	$515.00	$242.75	$272.25	$40,555.89	$51,580.89
156	07/01/2016	30	7.000	$515.00	$233.33	$281.67	$40,274.22	$51,814.22
157	08/01/2016	31	7.000	$515.00	$239.45	$275.55	$39,998.67	$52,053.67
158	09/01/2016	31	7.000	$515.00	$237.81	$277.19	$39,721.48	$52,291.48
159	10/01/2016	30	7.000	$515.00	$228.53	$286.47	$39,435.01	$52,520.01
160	11/01/2016	31	7.000	$515.00	$234.46	$280.54	$39,154.47	$52,754.47
161	12/01/2016	30	7.000	$515.00	$225.26	$289.74	$38,864.73	$52,979.73
162	01/01/2017	31	7.000	$515.00	$231.07	$283.93	$38,580.80	$53,210.80

#	Date	Days	% Int.	Payment	Interest	Principal	Balance	Cum. Int.
163	02/01/2017	31	7.000	$515.00	$229.38	$285.62	$38,295.19	$53,440.19
164	03/01/2017	28	7.000	$515.00	$205.59	$309.41	$37,985.78	$53,645.78
165	04/01/2017	31	7.000	$515.00	$225.85	$289.15	$37,696.63	$53,871.63
166	05/01/2017	30	7.000	$515.00	$216.88	$298.12	$37,398.50	$54,088.50
167	06/01/2017	31	7.000	$515.00	$222.35	$292.65	$37,105.86	$54,310.86
168	07/01/2017	30	7.000	$515.00	$213.48	$301.52	$36,804.33	$54,524.33
169	08/01/2017	31	7.000	$515.00	$218.82	$296.18	$36,508.15	$54,743.15
170	09/01/2017	31	7.000	$515.00	$217.06	$297.94	$36,210.21	$54,960.21
171	10/01/2017	30	7.000	$515.00	$208.32	$306.68	$35,903.54	$55,168.54
172	11/01/2017	31	7.000	$515.00	$213.47	$301.53	$35,602.00	$55,382.00
173	12/01/2017	30	7.000	$515.00	$204.83	$310.17	$35,291.83	$55,586.83
174	01/01/2018	31	7.000	$515.00	$209.83	$305.17	$34,986.66	$55,796.66
175	02/01/2018	31	7.000	$515.00	$208.01	$306.99	$34,679.67	$56,004.67
176	03/01/2018	28	7.000	$515.00	$186.18	$328.82	$34,350.86	$56,190.86
177	04/01/2018	31	7.000	$515.00	$204.23	$310.77	$34,040.09	$56,395.09
178	05/01/2018	30	7.000	$515.00	$195.84	$319.16	$33,720.93	$56,590.93
179	06/01/2018	31	7.000	$515.00	$200.49	$314.51	$33,406.42	$56,791.42
180	07/01/2018	30	7.000	$515.00	$192.19	$322.81	$33,083.61	$56,983.61
181	08/01/2018	31	7.000	$515.00	$196.70	$318.30	$32,765.31	$57,180.31
182	09/01/2018	31	7.000	$515.00	$194.81	$320.19	$32,445.12	$57,375.12
183	10/01/2018	30	7.000	$515.00	$186.66	$328.34	$32,116.78	$57,561.78
184	11/01/2018	31	7.000	$515.00	$190.95	$324.05	$31,792.73	$57,752.73
185	12/01/2018	30	7.000	$515.00	$182.91	$332.09	$31,460.64	$57,935.64
186	01/01/2019	31	7.000	$515.00	$187.05	$327.95	$31,132.69	$58,122.69
187	02/01/2019	31	7.000	$515.00	$185.10	$329.90	$30,802.79	$58,307.79
188	03/01/2019	28	7.000	$515.00	$165.37	$349.63	$30,453.16	$58,473.16
189	04/01/2019	31	7.000	$515.00	$181.06	$333.94	$30,119.22	$58,654.22
190	05/01/2019	30	7.000	$515.00	$173.28	$341.72	$29,777.51	$58,827.51
191	06/01/2019	31	7.000	$515.00	$177.04	$337.96	$29,439.55	$59,004.55
192	07/01/2019	30	7.000	$515.00	$169.37	$345.63	$29,093.92	$59,173.92
193	08/01/2019	31	7.000	$515.00	$172.98	$342.02	$28,751.90	$59,346.90
194	09/01/2019	31	7.000	$515.00	$170.95	$344.05	$28,407.84	$59,517.84
195	10/01/2019	30	7.000	$515.00	$163.44	$351.56	$28,056.28	$59,681.28
196	11/01/2019	31	7.000	$515.00	$166.81	$348.19	$27,708.09	$59,848.09
197	12/01/2019	30	7.000	$515.00	$159.41	$355.59	$27,352.50	$60,007.50
198	01/01/2020	31	7.000	$515.00	$162.63	$352.37	$27,000.13	$60,170.13
199	02/01/2020	31	7.000	$515.00	$160.53	$354.47	$26,645.66	$60,330.66
200	03/01/2020	28	7.000	$515.00	$143.05	$371.95	$26,273.71	$60,473.71
201	04/01/2020	31	7.000	$515.00	$156.21	$358.79	$25,914.92	$60,629.92
202	05/01/2020	30	7.000	$515.00	$149.09	$365.91	$25,549.01	$60,779.01
203	06/01/2020	31	7.000	$515.00	$151.90	$363.10	$25,185.91	$60,930.91
204	07/01/2020	30	7.000	$515.00	$144.90	$370.10	$24,815.81	$61,075.81
205	08/01/2020	31	7.000	$515.00	$147.54	$367.46	$24,448.36	$61,223.36
206	09/01/2020	31	7.000	$515.00	$145.36	$369.64	$24,078.72	$61,368.72
207	10/01/2020	30	7.000	$515.00	$138.53	$376.47	$23,702.24	$61,507.24
208	11/01/2020	31	7.000	$515.00	$140.92	$374.08	$23,328.17	$61,648.17
209	12/01/2020	30	7.000	$515.00	$134.21	$380.79	$22,947.38	$61,782.38
210	01/01/2021	31	7.000	$515.00	$136.43	$378.57	$22,568.81	$61,918.81
211	02/01/2021	31	7.000	$515.00	$134.18	$380.82	$22,188.00	$62,053.00
212	03/01/2021	28	7.000	$515.00	$119.12	$395.88	$21,792.12	$62,172.12

#	Date	Days	% Int.	Payment	Interest	Principal	Balance	Cum. Int.
213	04/01/2021	31	7.000	$515.00	$129.57	$385.43	$21,406.68	$62,301.68
214	05/01/2021	30	7.000	$515.00	$123.16	$391.84	$21,014.84	$62,424.84
215	06/01/2021	31	7.000	$515.00	$124.94	$390.06	$20,624.78	$62,549.78
216	07/01/2021	30	7.000	$515.00	$118.66	$396.34	$20,228.44	$62,668.44
217	08/01/2021	31	7.000	$515.00	$120.27	$394.73	$19,833.71	$62,788.71
218	09/01/2021	31	7.000	$515.00	$117.92	$397.08	$19,436.63	$62,906.63
219	10/01/2021	30	7.000	$515.00	$111.82	$403.18	$19,033.46	$63,018.46
220	11/01/2021	31	7.000	$515.00	$113.16	$401.84	$18,631.62	$63,131.62
221	12/01/2021	30	7.000	$515.00	$107.19	$407.81	$18,223.81	$63,238.81
222	01/01/2022	31	7.000	$515.00	$108.35	$406.65	$17,817.16	$63,347.16
223	02/01/2022	31	7.000	$515.00	$105.93	$409.07	$17,408.09	$63,453.09
224	03/01/2022	28	7.000	$515.00	$93.46	$421.54	$16,986.55	$63,546.55
225	04/01/2022	31	7.000	$515.00	$100.99	$414.01	$16,572.55	$63,647.55
226	05/01/2022	30	7.000	$515.00	$95.35	$419.65	$16,152.89	$63,742.89
227	06/01/2022	31	7.000	$515.00	$96.04	$418.96	$15,733.93	$63,838.93
228	07/01/2022	30	7.000	$515.00	$90.52	$424.48	$15,309.45	$63,929.45
229	08/01/2022	31	7.000	$515.00	$91.02	$423.98	$14,885.47	$64,020.47
230	09/01/2022	31	7.000	$515.00	$88.50	$426.50	$14,458.97	$64,108.97
231	10/01/2022	30	7.000	$515.00	$83.19	$431.81	$14,027.16	$64,192.16
232	11/01/2022	31	7.000	$515.00	$83.40	$431.60	$13,595.56	$64,275.56
233	12/01/2022	30	7.000	$515.00	$78.22	$436.78	$13,158.78	$64,353.78
234	01/01/2023	31	7.000	$515.00	$78.24	$436.76	$12,722.01	$64,432.01
235	02/01/2023	31	7.000	$515.00	$75.64	$439.36	$12,282.65	$64,507.65
236	03/01/2023	28	7.000	$515.00	$65.94	$449.06	$11,833.59	$64,573.59
237	04/01/2023	31	7.000	$515.00	$70.36	$444.64	$11,388.95	$64,643.95
238	05/01/2023	30	7.000	$515.00	$65.52	$449.48	$10,939.47	$64,709.47
239	06/01/2023	31	7.000	$515.00	$65.04	$449.96	$10,489.51	$64,774.51
240	07/01/2023	30	7.000	$515.00	$60.35	$454.65	$10,034.86	$64,834.86
241	08/01/2023	31	7.000	$515.00	$59.66	$455.34	$9,579.52	$64,894.52
242	09/01/2023	31	7.000	$515.00	$56.96	$458.04	$9,121.48	$64,951.48
243	10/01/2023	30	7.000	$515.00	$52.48	$462.52	$8,658.96	$65,003.96
244	11/01/2023	31	7.000	$515.00	$51.48	$463.52	$8,195.44	$65,055.44
245	12/01/2023	30	7.000	$515.00	$47.15	$467.85	$7,727.59	$65,102.59
246	01/01/2024	31	7.000	$515.00	$45.94	$469.06	$7,258.53	$65,148.53
247	02/01/2024	31	7.000	$515.00	$43.16	$471.84	$6,786.69	$65,191.69
248	03/01/2024	28	7.000	$515.00	$36.44	$478.56	$6,308.12	$65,228.12
249	04/01/2024	31	7.000	$515.00	$37.51	$477.49	$5,830.63	$65,265.63
250	05/01/2024	30	7.000	$515.00	$33.54	$481.46	$5,349.17	$65,299.17
251	06/01/2024	31	7.000	$515.00	$31.80	$483.20	$4,865.98	$65,330.98
252	07/01/2024	30	7.000	$515.00	$27.99	$487.01	$4,378.97	$65,358.97
253	08/01/2024	31	7.000	$515.00	$26.04	$488.96	$3,890.01	$65,385.01
254	09/01/2024	31	7.000	$515.00	$23.13	$491.87	$3,398.14	$65,408.14
255	10/01/2024	30	7.000	$515.00	$19.55	$495.45	$2,902.69	$65,427.69
256	11/01/2024	31	7.000	$515.00	$17.26	$497.74	$2,404.94	$65,444.94
257	12/01/2024	30	7.000	$515.00	$13.84	$501.16	$1,903.78	$65,458.78
258	01/01/2025	31	7.000	$515.00	$11.32	$503.68	$1,400.10	$65,470.10
259	02/01/2025	31	7.000	$515.00	$8.32	$506.68	$893.42	$65,478.42
260	03/01/2025	28	7.000	$515.00	$4.80	$510.20	$383.22	$65,483.22
261	04/01/2025	31	7.000	$385.50	$2.28	$383.22	$0.00	$65,485.50

Source: Calculations made with Mortgage Wizard Plus.

After paying on this loan two years, your 25th payment includes $407 interest for scenario 1 versus $394 for scenario 2. This is because you've already reduced your principal — the amount you borrowed — by an extra $2,240 in the latter case, so consequently that much less interest is being compounded each month. After just ten years, you will pay $357.21 of your 121st payment toward interest alone in scenario 1, but only $293.37 in scenario 2. By now, you've paid an *extra* $10,737 more on your principal (even though you've only been paying about $50 extra per month since payment number 37). Every dollar that doesn't go to interest applies to principal, so decreasing principal early means less money goes to interest which results in even more rapid principal reduction in an interactive fashion. That's why I recommend paying as much extra early in the life of the loan as you can safely afford — it's when you get the most bang for your buck!

I have a habit of viewing loans by calculating where their "sweet spot" is. That's what I call the point when the monthly payment involves paying more principal than it does interest. If you're going to do anything special regarding a loan, you need to do it well before then. In our scenario 1, the sweet spot occurs at payment number 235 of 360 payments. In our accelerated example, principal overtakes interest by payment number 143 of 261. If you're thinking about refinancing or making lots of extra payments, it doesn't make much sense after this point. Frequently, people will try to pay off their loan near the end of its term simply because the amount they then owe seems more manageable to pay. The problem with that approach is that most of the loan's interest has long since been paid, so there's negligible savings to be gleaned.

Now that you've seen in graphic fashion how to add over $32,000 to your retirement account — or closer to $50,000 since you've bargained at least 10 percent off the price of that home — and shave years off the life of your loan (of course, your loan amount will probably vary from this example in one direction or the other), let's quickly examine two other methods to save money. Vanderbilt Mortgage wanted us to take out a 20-year mortgage but we wanted to sign a 30-year mortgage. When we insisted, the dealership and Vanderbilt relented, although they told us how much better a 20-year mortgage would be for us (even though the dealership did not offer us a lower interest rate — one of the advantages a traditional lender like a bank may have offered for a shorter term). With your choice of mortgage calculators, you can quickly punch in the numbers and reach your own conclusions in private without a high pressure salesperson or loan officer prodding you along. If we take the same loan amount and rate as in our earlier example ($70,000 at 7 percent), payments for a 20-year term would be $542.71 (or $77 more per month). The total of all your monthly payments would be $130,250.40, or *$37,405.20 less than what you would pay with the 30-year term*. Wow, so the dealership was right after all? If that's as far as you take the analysis, yes, they were correct. By now though, you realize that you can pay extra to reduce interest amounts any-way — and I know you don't want some company making $100,000 profit from you if you can avoid it. That's why you're reading this book! What if you took out the loan for the 30-year term and just made your payments as though they were for a 20-year loan (without the legal obligation, and clearly specifying extra money goes to principal)? If you pay the extra $77 a month anyway, you will pay off your loan in 241 months for a total of $130,288.89. Your 241st and final payment would be just $38.49, and that small amount would represent the total difference between the 20- and 30-year loan. *You still save well over $37,000.*

The reason I recommend the 30-year loan is that word of caution with which I prefaced the chapter. Foreclosures in general have been at record levels; manufactured housing foreclosures for various reasons already discussed have traditionally been high, and none of us knows what the future holds. If you lose your job, your spouse develops medical prob-lems, or your car drops its engine on the highway, $77 a month can sud-denly seem like a pretty big difference. If you know how a simple interest loan works (if you didn't before, you should now), you can control your own loan destiny. The only real difference there *has* to be between the different loan terms is the legal obligation if you exercise financial disci-pline. Consider opting for the longer term.

One last alternative you should know about are *accelerated biweekly* mortgages. This is just another method that some savvy consumers opt for in order to reduce interest charges and pay off their mortgage loans early. In effect, the monthly payment is divided into two smaller payments which are then due every two weeks. Because there are 52 weeks per year, the consumer then makes 26 half payments, or the equivalent of thirteen payments per year. Biweekly mortgages in and of themselves don't guar-antee that your will save money and pay off your loan early: they must be *accelerated*. If your 26 half payments add up to no more than 12 full pay-ments in total dollar amounts, then you won't yield any savings. Of course, alternatively you could just pay that amount extra each year anyway and specify that it apply toward principal.

This latter option — making an extra payment each year — will again depend on your own financial discipline to succeed, but it might be one of the easiest ways to accomplish your goal of saving money. Let's suppose that you know each year you will receive a $500 to $600 tax refund from the government, and you decide to apply that to your loan annually. If you take the $70,000 loan we did earlier at 7 percent and 30 years, you could pay $1,000 on payment number six (using your tax refund money for the extra) instead of the usual 465.71 and then do the same every following year on the same month. How would this affect your finances? With Mortgage Wizard Plus— or any of the other calculators readily available — we can see that the loan would be paid off in just 277

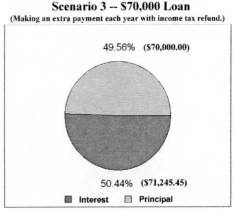

Scenario 3 -- $70,000 Loan
(Making an extra payment each year with income tax refund.)

49.56%   ($70,000.00)

50.44%   ($71,245.45)

■ Interest   □ Principal

Cumulative Payments = $141,245.45
Data Derived from Mortgage Wizard Plus

payments (almost seven years early), and we would save $26,410.15 in interest. The latter is graphically illustrated as scenario 3 (the pie chart). This is certainly less savings than in our earlier scenarios, but it still offers a great yield from your tax returns— a ready source of extra payments for many people. This last option can allow people who are normally faced with a tight budget a way to achieve the benefits of an accelerated loan, too! Of course, the tax deduction you can take for the interest you pay the mortgage company will help your tax situation as well, allowing you a bigger return to apply to your loan. Additionally, you can still pay extra with other payments as your finances allow for even greater savings. So get out that mortgage calculator and see just what your situation will allow you to save.

I haven't spent much time going over specific interest rates and the precise financial impact they have. This is in part because you are to some extent bound by the prevailing rates, although it is important to try and time your purchase to the extent possible and to demonstrate how to shop for the best available rate. As noted previously, depending on your credit rating, the

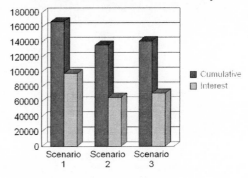

Loan Cost Comparison
Total Cumulative & Interest Payments

■ Cumulative
□ Interest

Scenario 1   Scenario 2   Scenario 3

A comparison of the first three loan scenarios.

amount you borrow, the term of your loan, and whom you are borrowing from, you can find considerable differences in rates—several point swings can be common. Keeping our loan amount and term identical, let's look at one last scenario just to have some perspective of the impact your rate can have. Let's say a consumer who hasn't read this book settles for the first or second offer a dealer proposes, or perhaps they just have a poor credit history and no one to cosign for them. Adding just 3.75 percent more brings the rate on our $70,000 loan to 10.75 percent (chosen because it's a fairly common "dealer" rate right now). What effect does this seemingly moderate (to many novice consumers) increase have? Our payments go up $188 per month (to $653.44 from $465.71, before taxes and insurance), and we pay over $235,000 for our $70,000 home (an increase of $67,582.80 beyond scenario 1), or basically enough to buy *another identical home.* Look at the visual representation of this fourth potential situation. Try to stay as close to the methods used in scenarios 2 and 3, and search high and low for the best rate you can find. For the typical manufactured home consumer, scenario 4 is somewhat akin to begging for trouble. (Remember our discussion earlier in this chapter about foreclosures/repossessions.)

Your case is also going to be unique depending on the amount of money you borrow, your credit history, the type of home you purchase, etc. You will have to look at all the available options based on the information you learn and make the right decisions for your particular situation. As a gen-

Scenario 4 -- $70,000 Loan
(Effects of a higher rate on interest / principal ratio.)

29.76% ($70,000.00)

($165,230.31) 70.24%

■ Interest   ▨ Principal

Cumulative Payments = $235,230.31
Data Derived from Mortgage Wizard Plus

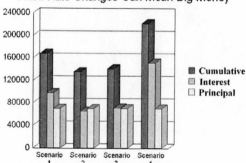

Loan Cost Comparison
Small Rate Changes Can Mean Big Money

■ Cumulative
▨ Interest
☐ Principal

Graphical analysis of all four loan scenarios.

eral guideline for the reader, I'll briefly go over the route my wife and I took to try and develop the best loan scenario we could for ourselves. We found a dealer who offered us what seemed like a competitive price on both the setup and the home we wanted. What they wouldn't do was take a letter of acceptance from a bank or other lender. This was probably part of the reason we got a competitive price — they knew they stood to make a considerable amount of money on the "back end." We could have walked away or fought them on this point and possibly won. (Another dealership with the same manufacturer had offered to take a letter of acceptance previously when we pressured the corporate offices.) Instead, we asked to see what their best financing offer would be first. The dealer offered 7.49 percent based on our good credit with six months interest free, but insisted on a 20-year term and tied the interest rate to our purchase of their insurance products. If we didn't buy their insurance, the rate would be higher. We compromised, bought the insurance, but held out and won on the 30-year rate. (The dealer said 30 years was impossible, but when we said we were leaving they called Vanderbilt Mortgage and miraculously obtained approval.) We insisted on finding out two things before signing the deal: (1) could we refinance at any time without penalty, and (2) could we change insurance carriers at any time without penalty? The answer being yes on both counts, and having already studied our sales contract and raised our concerns regarding it, we offered to give them the down payment we (my wife and I — not the dealership) had decided on. It was enough to avoid private mortgage insurance and keep our payments reasonable. The Internet certificate mentioned earlier provided $1,000 of the down payment. The dealer had no knowledge the certificate was coming; therefore, he could not have adjusted his price upward for it. At first the manager balked, but after calling the corporate offices again, he accepted the certificate.

Six months interest free meant all of our first six payments went to principal (resulting in an actual percentage rate of just over 7 percent), and to us it meant we had six months to refinance as well. Refinancing our loan meant more closing costs, but our mortgage calculator indicated it was worth it if those costs were reasonable. Before we signed the first contract, we knew we could beat the dealer's interest rate by at *least* one point elsewhere. We obtained a "good faith" estimate for 5.875 percent within three months from a major bank and faxed that to another lender across the country who advertised to beat anyone's rate by .25 percent while matching closing costs. This lender was then reluctant to actually give us that rate for that loan amount, so we responded by asking to speak to a supervisor, and finally to the owner. Before the owner became involved we had our rate of 5.625 percent, and our monthly payments were about

Finance Comparison of "Identical" Homes (2000 square feet)	Site-Built	Modular	Manufactured Homes			
	Private Land	Private Land	Private Land		Landlease Community	
			Individual Lot	Subdivision	Double-Section	Single-Section*
Construction Costs	$77,140	$65,560	$47,277	$47,277	$47,277	$26,350
Overhead/Financing	$32,274	$28,950	$15,254	$24,083	$15,554	$8,575
Land Costs	$35,314	$35,314	pre-owned	$35,314	$1,201	$1,000
Delivery & Setup	—	included	$1,500	$1,500	$1,500	$750
Total Sales Price	**$144,728**	**$129,824**	**$64,031**	**$108,173**	**$65,532**	**$36,675**
Type of Loan	Real property	Real property	Real property	Real property	Personal property	Personal property
Interest Rate	8%	8%	8%	8%	10%	10%
Term	30 Years	30 Years	20 Years	30 Years	15 Years	15 Years
% Down Payment	10%	10%	Land in Lieu	10%	10%	10%
Initial Cash Outlay	**$21,709**	**$19,474**	**$4,364**	**$17,389**	**$11,283**	**$6,389**
Down Payment $	$14,473	$12,982	— —	$10,817	$6,553	$3,668
Closing Costs	$7,236	$6,491	$3,127	$5,334	$3,142	$1,746
Sales Tax (3%)	—	—	$1,238	$1,238	$1,238	$626
Security Deposit	—	—	— —	— —	$350	$350
Loan Amount	**$130,255**	**$116,841**	**$64,031**	**$97,356**	**$58,979**	**$33,008**
Loan Payment	$956	$858	$535	$715	$634	$355
Monthly Land Rent	—	—	— —	— —	$250	$200
Total Payments	**$956**	**$858**	**$535**	**$715**	**$884**	**$555**

*Square Footage is 2,000 in all cases except that the single-section home in a land-lease community is 1,215 square feet.

From the study "Factory and Site-Built Housing, a Comparison for the 21st Century," conducted by the NAHB Research Center for HUD.

$60 lower. Again, no PMI was required, and a $250 application fee was applied toward the loan amount (in effect, not costing us any additional money). Of course, we pay a little extra each month whenever possible to pay off our loan early.

The chart on the page 126 illustrates costs connected with manufcatured homes versus modular and site-built homes. The third column represents a manufactured home placed on privately owned land and also represents the lowest monthly payment in the chart. The payment would be lower still, but it is based on a 20-year mortgage compared to 30-year mortgages for the modular and site-built examples. This example also uses the "land in lieu" of a down payment. What happens if we make a modest down payment of $5,000? Since we know that manufactured home dealers typically have about 50 percent more markup, or profit percentage, than typical site-built home sellers, it's a pretty safe bet we could also work this price down by about $2,500 more if we try. The result is that our monthly payment drops to $475 a month (saving $60 per month), and we save an *additional* $7,556.95 in interest. Now if we can just get that interest rate lowered by a point!

The final step is comparison shopping for home insurance to get the best deal there if you can't do that when you first buy your home. The ultimate lesson is that it's your money, and you should fight for it just as hard as the companies you do business with scrap over it.

Although dealer financing might be the most hazardous path you could venture down, you need to be careful no matter who provides your loan. Let's wrap this discussion up with some pointers from the Federal Trade Commission regarding how less than honest lenders operate. You probably already know to run for the door if you spot these telltale signs, but let's err on the side of caution. After all, if you're reading *The Manufactured Home Buyer's Handbook*, you're probably considering making the biggest purchase of your life. So here are the Seven Deadly Mortgage Signs:

- the lender encourages you to falsify information on your loan application
- the lender encourages you to borrow more than you need
- the lender encourages you to take out a loan with payments you don't think you can make
- the lender fails to provide full disclosure; including the APR and rescission rights (your right to back out of the loan within a certain time frame)
- the lender presents you with something different than what you agreed to at closing time

- the lender asks you to sign blank forms (often using the excuse that "it will speed things up" or "it will save you a trip")
- the lender denies you copies of any forms or documents you are asked to sign

CHAPTER 8

The Walk-Through(s)

By now, you really deserve a break! Still, you have quite a distance to go before you let your guard down. This stage can be pretty fun and exciting, though. If you custom ordered your new home, you're about to get your first look at it. You'll probably be asked to complete one or more "walk-throughs" before the home is officially delivered to your site or the keys are turned over to you. This is a formal procedure which involves written documents designed to protect the manufacturer and dealership. The purpose is to document any problems you find with the home and to provide the dealership a way of showing you have accepted any corrections. The first walk-through will most likely be on the dealer's lot, and if you find any problems (if you don't find problems, you're probably not looking hard enough), you may have to do further walk-throughs at that location after those problems are fixed so you can sign off on the repairs or changes that were made.

Look out for duplicitous stratagems at this stage as well. We were asked to go ahead and sign off on extra blank, post-dated walk-through sheets so we wouldn't have to make "additional trips" to the dealership. In effect, we were being asked by the dealership's general manager to sign a document stating any necessary corrections had been made to our satisfaction even before any repairs were made! Believe me, this tactic is not for your convenience — it is to further erode your rights and your control of the process. Make the trip as many times as required to inspect work. Go ahead and be paranoid, because they probably *are* out to get you — or at least gain an unfair advantage in the case of any disputes. If you sign off on corrections before they are made and then the repair work is improperly done, the dealer has your signature saying that on a given date you approved of the work. If you later have to tell the company-selected arbitrator (or judge and jury) that you didn't *really* approve of the work, who do you think will win?

Just as in other aspects of the entire home-buying process, preparation is crucial to your success. Both you and the dealer should keep a copy of any problems you find. You should also remember your tools from before: notepad, tape measure, stud finder, camera, and a good flashlight. Systematically go through every area of the home. Reread this chapter just before the walk-through, and if you are going with a spouse or someone else you may want to divide the home up into areas of responsibility (either literal physical areas or specific aspects such as flooring, windows, etc.) so you can cover it more efficiently. It's possible that in a multisection home, some areas may not be readily accessible because of door and room placement without cutting into the thick plastic wrap that covers exposed areas of the home. If the dealer does not want to open up and then reseal those areas to allow you access, make sure you document on the official walk-through forms that access was not allowed to those areas. In that way if there are problems in such rooms, you will be able to get them fixed later without a fight from an unscrupulous dealer.

Verify that the home is just as you ordered it if you had it custom built — check stud spacings and the locations of fixtures and doors. Is each feature you paid for there? Use your checklist from which you ordered your home (the final version of your wish list from the earlier chapters). Carefully examine the exterior as well as the interior — including the underneath and the roof of the home. In the former area, you are looking for any damage to the frame, the belly board, or anything dangling which is out of place; in the latter area you are looking for any damage to shingles or roof vents. Are there any scratches on the exterior, or is there oil anywhere from the trip from the factory (on the hitch end and sides)? If so, siding may have to be washed or replaced.

The foremost rule to remember is *thoroughness*. Don't let those who represent the dealer and accompany you rush you through the walk-through — *they* won't be living in the home. If you don't catch a problem now, you can forever lose the ability to have the dealer or manufacturer fix it — whether it's something as simple as a small scratch on a door or as major as not getting the appliances you ordered. Make sure that every problem you identify because it bothers you enough to want it fixed — whether it's cosmetic or structural — is listed on the walk-through list. Check every room and closet; look in every cabinet. Check electrical switch plates and outlets to make sure they are secure and flush against the wall (this is often a problem area for manufactured homes because they don't attach outlets to studs as they do in traditional homes). Check the shelving in every area — make sure a hurried factory worker was careful enough to get all the supporting hardware screws into wall studs and not just thin

Sheetrock (otherwise, when you put items on the shelves they will come loose from the wall.) Step on the sill at the bottom of the front door entrance — is it as solid under your foot as it's supposed to be, or does it flex down under your weight? Check the edges of every piece of wallboard — bends near the edge mean that piece is broken, and it should be replaced entirely. Look for this especially near the floor. On the outside, examine the vinyl around your electrical and water outlets — were the

This piece of wallboard is broken and needs to be replaced.

openings cut neatly, or are they jagged and exposed? The same thing goes for floodlight prewiring in the soffit: were the openings cut out neatly, or are they jagged and ugly?

You will want to check everything, but there are some specific areas you will want to examine extra carefully. One such area is your flooring, whether it's carpeted or covered in linoleum. Walk throughout the home and make sure there are no uneven places in the subflooring beneath the floor covering. You're not looking for levelness (not until after setup, anyway) but for sharp ridges that indicate one piece of flooring is not flush to another or a more gradual rise that indicates a floor joist is relatively and significantly high or low. Check for bumps under the carpet and especially under linoleum. A lot of debris settles into the home during construction, and small bumps in the floor which are hard to see at first become more visible over time as the floor covering settles. Not only is it an unsightly nuisance then, but it will cause your floor covering to wear out prematurely in that spot. Make sure all carpet edges are lying properly. With linoleum, check carefully for scratches — especially in the utility room or wherever major appliances were installed. In one after another model home, we found large scratches in utility rooms from where the water heater was pulled into place. Look carefully because the only repair for gouges is to replace the linoleum. If this has to be done before the home is delivered, make sure it's done right by having the old linoleum removed. Otherwise, the dealer will save time and money by laying the new linoleum right on top of the old material. Months later, it can then settle — clearly showing the pattern of the old vinyl underneath the top layer. It's not a pretty sight, and then you won't be able to fix it without expense because you will have signed off on it thinking it was correctly repaired.

Finally, try to locate all of your floor vents. It was one of our setup people who told us horror stories about floor registers covered over with carpet and linoleum at the factory by careless workers. Not only will your home not heat or cool properly, it can ruin your floor covering if not caught in time. In the case of one woman, purportedly this defect formed a large pocket of air under her vinyl and deformed it, and then all of it had to be replaced. This is also a safety issue in that someone's foot could drop through the carpet or linoleum into the register opening, possibly causing serious bodily injury. If you think you should have a floor register somewhere but you aren't sure, ask the factory to fax you the HVAC engineering diagrams—they will show the location of each designed outlet.

Windows can be another specific trouble spot. While they may not open or close properly until after the home is leveled and set up, you can check many things. First, make sure they are what you ordered. Then, carefully examine the installation, the sill and trim pieces, and the area around the window interior. The trim should cover the staple holes in the wallboard all the way around the window, and no gaps should be showing. Especially check underneath the lower ends of your sills for openings. *Make sure all latches and locks are secure*— meaning that none of the screws were stripped out by a careless installer. The chief symptom of this is a screw that won't tighten. If so, the window may need to be completely replaced to fix the problem. Check the carpet for any signs of broken glass—especially near large or bay windows. That's a warning sign that something may not be right (there may have been an accident in transit or at the factory), and when these windows shatter it's almost impossible to get all the glass up.

One reason factories tend to be so careless around the windows, and why so many people don't realize it until it's too late, is the installation of factory miniblinds. These are the equivalent of the plastic blinds that home improvement stores sell starting at about $2.97 each. They can suffice just fine for lesser used or less important rooms, but it is the way they are installed that covers up flaws. Instead of hanging them *in* the window casement, the factories purposely use oversized blinds and hang them *over* the window opening. Not only do the blinds protrude into the room this way and look much less attractive, they also cover up the wall for a couple of inches all the way around the window and a myriad of evils. To lazy factory workers, this spells a free pass. Raise the blinds for your inspection — and *remove the entire blind on a couple of windows at least*. To do this, you only have to slide off two pieces of plastic on the top ends to pull the blind out quickly and easily. Examine the wall just above the top of the windows. If you see a series of holes left by staples, tell the dealer that the workmanship isn't satisfactory, and it will have to be repaired. If they say it can't be seen so it's not a cosmetic defect, explain to them you might replace the $3 blinds, and then it will be visible. Be firm.

Left: Factory miniblinds not only covered up these staples, they also concealed the fact that there was an open gap between the wallboard and the window trim. *Above:* A series of staples is a common sight behind the miniblind headers. Remove at least a couple of miniblinds to examine this area.

In the picture showing the left edge of a window, you can see an opening between the wallboard and the window trim in this house. The factory miniblinds cover this gap, but with the blinds raised or even with the blinds open, the gap becomes an eyesore. You can also see a couple of exposed staples here which were not covered properly at the factory. Staples become a major problem over the windows, as seen in the photograph depicting the top of the window frame. These are normally covered by the factory blind's valance. Again, this is sloppy workmanship, and you should insist the dealership's trim workers correct it. They can bill the work to the factory if need be.

Anything that could be a safety issue in your home should be of special concern. A fireplace is one possible example. We noticed on our walk-through that the fireplace did not seem to be seated properly — as though it had shifted in transit. Looking in the bottom, I saw a considerable amount of ceiling insulation (in this case, cellulose, which looks like crumpled up brown cardboard with bits of cut up paper). Lying on my back and looking up the flu, I could see that it had an opening several feet up where it wasn't properly connected. Sparks and flame could have entered our wall cavities or roof. We took photographs and made sure the fireplace was properly repaired. A Clayton Homes/Luv Homes employee joked that it was too bad for us we caught this problem because if we had kindled a fire we could have gotten a new home for free. Since we might have lost our lives, that was not really a chance we wanted to take.

Check to make sure all trim pieces are in place and put on properly. We had a number of bathroom cabinets that had edges which appeared to be very rough. We only were able to notice them because of our flashlights. We complained about the appearance to Spanky (not his real name), the regional manager. On our next walk-through Spanky told us a crew came all the way from Tennessee and replaced the entire cabinets for us. They did look much better. However, we compared digital photographs we had taken using flashlights and the camera flash on the first walk-through to photos of the "new" cabinets. The cabinets were identical, right down to every swirl in the wood grain! The only difference was that they had added the missing trim pieces which covered the rough edges. I asked Spanky if he was positive the cabinets had been totally replaced, and he assured me with a smile he had personally supervised the change!

Also, watch for trim pieces which have so many staple holes they look like they have literally been chewed on by rats. Some of the factory work-ers get a little careless with the staple guns. Sometimes, they don't hit the wood behind the trim and just keep firing with poor aim until they do— or else there isn't wood where there should be behind the wall. If the trim looks bad, now is the time to complain and have it replaced.

One thing that almost every manufactured home brand seemed to struggle with somewhat regularly was getting breakfast-bar extensions from the kitchen counter level. Counters which often only protrude about three feet will sometimes have the far end a half inch or more higher (or lower) than where it attaches to the cabinet. Such a difference is clearly visible to most people without measuring, but use your trusty tape mea-sure to be sure. Dealer representatives will often swear to you that the counter only looks funny because the home hasn't been leveled yet. Trust me, if one end of the counter is higher or lower by that much or more com-pared to the floor on which it rests, the only thing to do is to have it fixed properly now or to be prepared to give yourself a stiff kick in the rear every time you see it for the next decade or so. Make the dealer take care of it.

Some things can really only be properly dealt with after the home is on the final site: sticking doors, windows, or drawers; cracks in the ceil-ing material; and trim pieces that don't quite sit flush. The home won't be properly leveled until the final setup (thus affecting doors and windows), more cracks may occur in the final transit, and the trim can't be completely finished until the home is permanently situated as well because manufactured homes are designed to flex as they travel. If you notice problems in these areas, make a note of them and see how the dealer wants to handle it. Just make sure they are fixed before you officially accept the keys to your home.

Don't be surprised if you find dozens of minor problems and more than a few that you would call major defects. When you do find problems, don't be afraid to propose a solution that is advantageous to you as well as the dealer. The general idea here is that horse trading never has to end. In our case, one example would be our dining room floor. We had wanted hardwood flooring initially, but we couldn't afford the $1,900 price tag the dealer wanted. We settled for linoleum with a wood-grain pattern. After we examined the home carefully, however, we found a ½" tear in the vinyl in one corner (as shown in the photo), and a bump soon showed up in another location from debris or a nail in the subfloor. (Be careful — such bumps may not show themselves until the floor has time to settle.) We knew to correctly fix both problems the dealer would have to pay someone to remove the old vinyl, which was glued down, and then lay the new linoleum and replace the trim. It was a costly, time consuming job which the dealer had no choice about doing since we had caught the flaws. Instead of making them do that, however, we gave them an option. They could pay us $500, and we would accept the floor as is. Before we had made the offer, we had gone back to our local home improvement store and found Pergo flooring on sale; therefore, we knew we could cover our dining room floor for just under $500 if we did the work ourselves. We had one more stipulation: we also wanted new floor trim from the factory to replace what we had to pull up. This meant it would match our home's other trim, and it saved us money on materials. Spanky quickly agreed, knowing this solution would save him money as well. We ended up with a floor at least as nice as the $1,900 floor we couldn't afford and probably nicer.

You may want to visit the dealer *before* you're supposed to

This tear in the vinyl cost the manufacturer $500.

meet for the walk-through. If you know your home is supposed to be delivered from the factory on a given day, drop by for an unannounced surprise inspection. Even if you can't do the walk-through until later, you can walk around the exterior of the home and peer into the windows. Don't bother stopping by the office unless you want to afterward. This trip is primarily to discover anything that may have happened to your home in transit before it can be covered up. Even the best drivers can have mishaps with these behemoths in tow. In particular, look for bends in the frame, damage to the roof or vents from hitting overpasses, gouges on the side or corners, broken windows (especially possible with protruding bay windows) or broken glass inside from an en route repair, excessive road oil and dirt, etc. If repairs have to be made to your home, you want to know about them so you can be sure that the damage was completely and properly fixed. This is just one more example where *what you don't know can hurt you*. If vents are missing or the plastic protective cover is torn, find out why, and insist the openings be covered immediately if wet weather is at all a threat. You would be surprised how negligent some dealers can be in this regard.

CHAPTER 9

Solid Foundations

It's almost time for your new home to arrive. The general manager or someone else from the dealership has probably come out to look at your property, and you may have had to have some work done in preparation for the home. In particular, you may have had the site crowned and graded both for appearance and to prevent moisture accumulation under your new home. One element of importance that cannot be underestimated is the foundation. Foundations often vary regionally: in the southeast, the use of concrete footers or pads is typical, while in the northwest and northeast solid poured slabs are common. Either can suffice nicely as long as they are done properly. You also may or may not have to have the foundation inspected by county inspectors prior to the home being placed on it — local ordinances will determine that. Local ordinances may also specify the type of foundation you use, the depth it has to reach, and the minimum size of pier supports. The home's installation manual should also have specific recommendations for the concrete footers or pads. *Make sure that your foundation meets the minimum standards of both your county code* ***and*** *the applicable manufacturer's recommendations at the very least.* While the dealership should have a setup person familiar with the code, also call your county offices and familiarize yourself with their requirements for your area. That's the only way you can verify for yourself if the work has been done properly.

The foundation is critical to a manufactured home for many of the same reasons it is in a site-built house: if the support beneath the home isn't solid and strong enough, areas of the home will begin to settle. This can cause cracks in your ceilings, make doors and windows hard or impossible to operate, and worse. If the soil-bearing capacity of the ground where you live is less than 1,000 pounds per square inch, an engineer will probably have to design your supports. Professional engineers are also required if your piers exceed a certain height, usually 80". Soil-bearing capacities

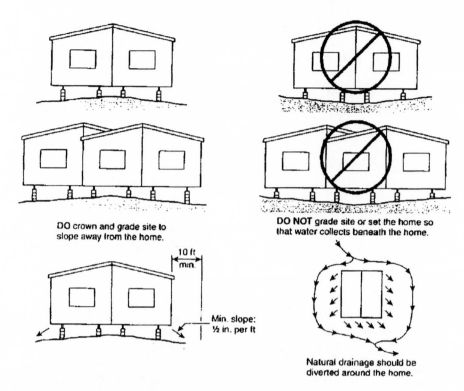

DO crown and grade site to slope away from the home.

DO NOT grade site or set the home so that water collects beneath the home.

10 ft min.

Min. slope: ½ in. per ft

Natural drainage should be diverted around the home.

"Home sites shall be prepared so that there will be no depressions in which surface water shall accumulate beneath the home. The area of the site covered by the home shall be graded, sloped, or mechanically designed so as to provide drainage from beneath the home to the property line." (*Model Manufactured Home Installation Standards*, Federal Manufactured Housing Consensus Committee, 2003.)

of 2,000 pounds per square inch and up are recommended by manufacturers. Make absolutely sure your foundation reaches to or below the frost line in your area. (You can ask a county engineer how deep that is.) *Damage from settling is commonly specifically excluded from warranty coverage.*

One of the worst mistakes to fall into at this stage is not allowing sufficient time for the foundation to dry, especially if you have a large, heavy home. Dealers are often anxious to get sold homes off their lots as soon as possible to vacate space. *Don't let anyone set the new home on concrete slabs or footers until at **least** three full days have passed.* It takes that long for concrete to achieve 50 percent strength. It can take weeks for concrete to reach 80 percent strength. Our dealer tried to set our home on our piers only 24 hours after they were poured with no advance notice to us so they could free up room on the lot. Luckily, we happened to be at

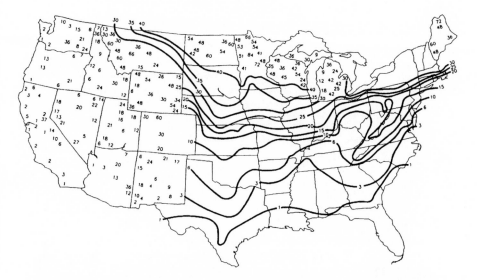

This is a "frost penetration" map of the United States. Just as you have to keep your home's support from settling, you must also protect from the effects of "heaving" in freezing weather. You do that by having your foundation poured at *least* as deep as this map indicates in your region. (Source: U.S. Department of Commerce, Weather Bureau.)

the job site and prevented it. I talked to the contractor, and he said "confidentially" that I had certainly made the right call—but that he couldn't tell that to the dealership himself because they wouldn't employ him anymore. He also made it very clear that his company would not guarantee our foundation if the concrete didn't have at least 72 hours to dry. We heard a similar refrain over and over again from the workers who were honest enough to try and help us. It

A pier support or "pad" has cracked under the weight of a home.

became extremely apparent that the dealerships put inordinate pressure on their contracted employees to bend the rules. We were also informed that our dealer routinely set homes on foundations before they were dry— sometimes putting the home on concrete footers that had been poured earlier the same day!

There are also companies now that specialize in alternative styles of manufactured home foundations. As long as they are approved by the manufacturer, local code, and your own scrutiny there's not usually too much concern about such alternatives. In upscale neighborhoods, one of the current trends is to dig into the earth farther for the foundation to set the home lower to the ground (while still providing clearance for the frame), thus making it appear more like surrounding site-built houses. In flood zones or along a beach, you can frequently find manufactured homes on specially engineered piers over ten feet high. Although it's rare, some people have even paid to have manufactured homes placed over basements. In special cases like these, ask to see references and to see other examples of the company's work.

If footers (or pads) are used, make sure that they are in the proper location. That statement may sound a little ludicrous at first — surely professional setup workers know to do this, right? Wrong. And the workers probably won't be professional. We had our home "flipped," but the setup crew went by the old plans and put several of our piers in the wrong locations! It was only after our setup crew damaged that home badly during setup that a second house had to be brought out, and the second setup crew (we insisted on different workers) noticed that a number of piers were in the wrong locations. So had it not been for this extra mishap, we could have missed the fact our home wasn't properly set up until after our setup warranty had expired and our floors and roof were sagging. Any large openings in the middle of multisection homes should have poured pads underneath the house on each side of the opening in addition to the normal supports, unless the entire home sits over a poured foundation. In short, *make sure your foundation workers have the proper engineering diagram to place pier supports with, and make sure they place them correctly — especially if the floor plan was flipped.* Finally, if you plan to place very heavy furniture like a waterbed in a certain area of the home, you may want to have an extra footer or two under that area as well, especially if your floor joists are made of the smaller 2" × 6" lumber.

Insist on footers for any brick underpinning as well if concrete pads are used instead of a poured slab so your brickwork doesn't give you problems over time because of erosion and settling of the earth. Having a few inches of concrete underneath the perimeter of your home can also aid in pest control. Most of the dealers we talked with didn't want to do this, but it's unprofessional not to do so, and you need to insist on it. Lateral supports should also be attached to any brickwork over 36" high. You may have to pay extra, but it's worth it.

Following is a rough cost comparison for different types of foundations.

Foundation Cost for a
2,000-Square-Foot, One-Story Home

Type of Foundation	Cost
Blocks (HUD Code)	$2,000
Perimeter foundation (HUD Code)	$4,500
Slab on grade	$10,990
Crawl space (concrete floor)	$12,704
Basement (unfinished)	$18,362

Source: NAHB Research Center, Inc., "Factory and Site-Built Housing: A Comparison for the 21st Century," Washington, D.C.: HUD, October 1998.

There is no easy fix subsequently if it turns out your piers are settling because they aren't properly supported. If you try to treat "hot spots" by putting jacks underneath the home, you risk causing more damage by raising isolated areas at a time, and the jacks will also settle without a proper foundation beneath them, meaning that the problem you are trying to overcome is likely to keep recurring. For isolated problem areas, you may be able to crawl underneath the home, dig out holes, and pour in concrete (after you've temporarily supported adjacent areas with jacks), but the work would be difficult at best, and if your foundation is lacking in one or two known areas, chances are it's lacking throughout. The only real solution then would be to move the home (disassembling a multisection home first and disconnecting all your utility connections), pour a proper foundation, let it dry, and put the home back. This would cost many thousands of dollars even if the home is only moved a few feet. Furthermore, all your trim would have to be reworked after the home is once more leveled and reassembled, and there is considerable potential for Sheetrock damage throughout the home in such a process, both in your walls and the ceiling. If such damage occurs when you buy a new home, the dealer or manufacturer does the work through contracted labor at discount rates. If you are hiring the workers on your own to fix a faulty foundation which your warranty doesn't cover, you won't likely get the same reduction in fees. Chances are that you will have to pay premium prices in addition to any materials which have to be purchased or replaced. The point is that you need to make absolutely sure your foundation is done right the first time. If you have any suspicions about the methods, materials used, or layout of your foundation, insist on getting proof the work is being done according to your setup manual and code (hopefully your county has codes for manufactured foundations and will assist you). Otherwise, make sure you have an iron-clad warranty provision in writing to cover any damage from settling.

The accompanying illustration is a representation of a standard industry "9-Lite" or "cottage" exterior door. The example shows just one type of the many problems that can result from a poor foundation, and this exact situation actually occurred on a manufactured home owner's door. This problem can also occur when setup crews fail to use perimeter piers around exterior home openings—all doors or large window openings should have them. The four arrows on the far left represent the fact that the home has sagged on the left (hinge) side of the door. The remaining arrows illustrate three extremely undesirable consequences: (1) air flow goes in and out of the home both summer and winter through the space between the door frame and the top of the door, running up energy costs and letting in bugs. The owner reported nothing he did could seal the 1" to 1.5" gap, and worse, the door was near the thermostat so the home temperature could never be properly regulated. (2) The door was extremely difficult to shut because it literally had to bend in the middle to do so, so the lock sets were prone to popping open unexpectedly. That happened while they were on vacation and in the middle of the night. The holes for the latches also had to be periodically adjusted for the shifting—which meant replacing part of the door frame. (3) The bottom of the door couldn't possibly shut because it was striking the door sill. This meant more air loss and bugs (ants by the hundreds). However, that was the least of the homeowner's worries. Periodically removing and shaving the door bottom helped alleviate the problem, but it kept recurring until the makeshift repair reached the hollow part of the door. (These doors apparently aren't called 9-Lite doors because they let a lot of sunshine in.) The door ended up having to be

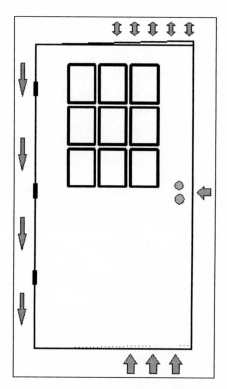

Representation of a typical industry 9-Lite door. The arrows on the far left represent "settling," while the remaining arrows represent the resulting problems. Gaps form at the top and bottom of the door and allow unwanted airflow, while the door becomes extremely difficult to shut.

replaced over and over. The owner hired someone to jack up the hinge side of the home's (and thereby the door's) frame, but the jack had to be constantly adjusted due to the settling. The reason for all of this? The dealer talked this man into setting the piers directly on the ground because the ground there was so hard that "it could never settle." This person had no warranty coverage for settling, and even if he did, it wouldn't matter. The dealer (who reportedly had a well-stocked lot with plenty of other customers) went out of business within months of the sale. The money the dealer was saving on foundations (or the lack thereof) probably helped him retire early. Don't let this happen to you!

A Consumers Union survey published in December 2002 (http://www.consumersunion.org/other/mh/paper-pr.htm) found that "Manufactured home residents are *49 percent more likely to have major door repair work* than site-built home residents, and report *broken windows at three times the rate* of site-built home residents." There are three ways to avoid adding to that statistic: (1) custom order or buy a home with better grade doors and windows, (2) make sure your foundation is rock solid, and (3) pay close attention to the chapter coming up on the setup of the home.

I've also heard horror stories from consumers who have been sold other "alternative" materials for foundations which have settled tremendously, causing a multitude of problems in their homes. If your dealer wants to insist on some alternative type of foundation material, you should ask why it doesn't want to use concrete and insist on a more comprehensive warranty. Don't be intimidated into doing anything that can ruin your home and leave you without recourse. I know it seems like I'm putting the burden for getting your home setup on you, and that may seem unfair. Unfortunately, however, doing your homework and taking on the responsibility yourself is the only way to assure it is done correctly, whether you're buying a manufactured home or a $500,000 site-built house. That theme is going to continue through the next very important chapter.

CHAPTER 10

The Setup

The setup is the last difficult stage, but again it can be an exciting one. Remember that you're paying the bills, so within reasonable limits *you* are the boss. Let the dealership know in no uncertain terms that you want to be present when the home is delivered. It is also a good idea to have a camera and video camera with you if possible so you can document potential problems as they arise. A picture is worth a thousand words, and sometimes more when disputes ensue. We were filming when our home came around our street, and the first thing the truck driver did was climb out of the cab and literally kiss the ground because he was so grateful the trip was over. This turned out to be because the "tongue" had fallen off our home in transit, and we were exceedingly glad we had the cameras to document the damage to our frame and home. Don't interfere needlessly with workers, but do watch what goes on, ask questions if you have them, and intervene when good judgment indicates you should. In effect, supervise the project. In this chapter, I'm going to point out a number of potential problem areas where you may need to intervene or make an extra careful inspection.

Before we get to the details, a few general statements about the delivery and setup crews might be appropriate. These are often good folks who are trying to make an honest living, but some do tend to come from the bottom of the barrel. They are working for employers who are often cutthroat by nature and can easily lose their jobs if someone outbids their services by a dollar or two or if they slip up and tell the customer something the dealer doesn't want the latter to know. This environment doesn't make for happy employees most of the time, and it doesn't foster quality work. It often does cultivate sniping and backstabbing. Your presence at the work site, especially if you are carrying a camera, can help alleviate that atmosphere. Let the setup folks know that you are concerned about your new home being put together properly, and be friendly. Many of them, as noted previously, are upright people who are caught up in an unfortunate employment atmosphere. These contracted workers frequently have no love lost for their employers and will often provide you with a wealth of helpful information if you treat them with respect. (Almost always they preface their remarks with the caveat, however: "You didn't hear it from me.")

You should also make sure the setup workers are properly licensed as required. South Carolina law requires setup personnel be licensed, and the Department of Manufactured Housing keeps a list of all currently licensed manufactured home setup crews/companies. Our first setup crew ruined our original home. The damage occurred because the crew underestimated the weight of the home and used only two sets of rollers and ramps to slide the two halves together when they should have used at least four sets to properly distribute the weight. When they severely bent our frame, they attempted to conceal the damage by stacking a pile of concrete blocks around the location of the bend. We found out because the company owner had his child playing at the work site, and the child mentioned something he had overheard among the workers, much to his father's consternation. When we found the damage and began to investigate, we also discovered this contractor — who the dealer said was "the best in the business"— wasn't even licensed by the state to set up manufactured homes! This child of about ten years was also allowed by his father to climb onto our roof and crawl under the home before it was properly blocked; in fact, the child ran an air gun to help remove some of the tires. *Never, ever, crawl under your home or allow anyone in your family to go under it until it is properly supported.* The likely result in the case of an accident would be a quick death. If you need to inspect something, do it from a distance, or wait until it is safe.

Your first consideration when your new home arrives is often literally at the edge of your property. The last few feet of the journey are often the most dangerous. Ditches at the roadway or some type of culvert which may cause a dip in the earth are common. Manufactured homes are designed to *flex* during delivery — the frames bend slightly, and the walls move up and down. That's why you will see gaps in the wallboard if you look behind the trim pieces: so the walls can literally move around without damaging the Sheetrock on them. There is a practical limit to how much flexing can occur without permanent damage, however, and that limit is reached rather quickly. If there is any significant ditch on your property that the home must traverse, do not let the truck driver convince you the home will be fine. Extremely heavy-duty *ramps should be used to bridge any such obstacles*, and many home delivery companies have them,

Our setup workers tried unsuccessfully to hide this damage they caused to our frame from us by stacking blocks in front of it. Fortunately, we caught the damage and the resultant bulges in our floor above. We were told this setup crew was the "best in the business." The truth was that they were negligent, irresponsible, and not even licensed to operate in the state.

although they may not want to use them because it is a chore. Likewise, don't let a driver force the wheels under the home *over* impediments like curbs or stumps. It's your home, and the alternative can include permanently twisted I-beams, leaning walls, broken wall studs, and more. The damage won't usually be obvious, either; there's little doubt that there are many thousands of manufactured homes throughout the country which aesthetically and structurally aren't what they should be, and their owners aren't even aware.

When the home arrives, you'll also want to check it again for damage sustained in transit. This means looking it over from the outside just as you did during the walk-through, searching for evidence of problems.

The vents on this home were destroyed in transit. If they aren't covered up properly, rainwater can enter the roof cavity.

Scratches on the vinyl are at one end of the spectrum of possibilities; bent frames and other major structural damage are on the other. You'll be examining it in detail later, but one place to try and get a quick look at is the roof (although 3:12 pitch roofs can be hard to see from ground level). That's a frequent problem area because of trees, power lines, and overhead passes along the roadway. *Make absolutely sure any damage to the roof or vents on the roof is covered up properly to keep out the weather if the home isn't going to be set up immediately.*

Chances are good that your new home will come in multiple sections. This affords you a unique opportunity to check on your home's construc-

Just before the home is assembled, you have the unique opportunity to examine both the roof cavity and the marriage wall studs. Most manufactured home owners never see this. Take advantage of the opportunity while you can; you might learn something important!

tion *if you act quickly* before the home is assembled. Once the protective plastic cover is removed, you can inspect both the roof cavity and the interior of the "marriage" walls. Otherwise, these areas will be permanently sealed off. (There is rarely any "attic" access in the typical manufactured home.) You are specifically looking to see if you received what you paid for and checking for structural defects. This text will focus on two aspects in particular: roof insulation and marriage wall studs.

Let's concentrate on insulation first. There are two possible ways to see into the roof cavity: using a ladder to look into openings the setup crew makes in the ends of the home and looking from the roof of one section into another one. Peering into the ends can give you an indication of problems, but you can see a lot more from the roof itself after the sections of the home are placed a few feet apart and are stable enough to walk on. If you can't climb on the roof yourself, find a family member or friend who is nimble and responsible enough to help you out. Determine if you have the R-value that you paid for in your roof. Your "Consumer Insulation

Information" sheet from the dealer will list the type and depth of insulation you are *supposed* to have. For instance, your sheet might specify 8" of cellulose insulation in the roof. For roof cavities, the number is averaged out — you may only have 5" near the outer edges of the walls because there is less space to fill there, but there should be enough insulation in the rest of your roof to make it average 8" overall. Your "Consumer Insulation Information" document gives you the amount of insulation you should have after any settling from transportation — don't let a dealer try to convince you that it is normal to have only 4" of insulation if the sheet calls for 8". Compressed insulation does not have the same R-value as thicker insulation with the proper air spaces maintained. Is it possible to be seriously defrauded here? Yes, it is — as noted in the introduction, my wife and I paid for R-28 insulation in our roof, which would have been 9.43" of rock wool insulation (our "Consumer Insulation Information" document stated the factory installed rock wool). What we actually received was *3" to 4" of cellulose insulation* on average, with some areas which had *no* insulation. The actual R-value we received was approximately a factor of 10 or less. The factory claimed it was a "fluke," but the standard R-value for this manufacturer in this region is R-11. I believe in the law of parsimony: the simplest explanation is the most likely one. We received approximately what they normally put in, and there was no bizarre coincidence. Was a factory worker just not paying attention to the order form? If so, how many other homeowners get shortchanged in the same manner? I talked with every setup employee who was willing to discuss it, and the consensus was that this is business as usual: our situation was typical rather than the exception to the rule.

The easiest way to check the roof insulation is to lie flat on your stomach (actually, the easiest way is to have someone else lie flat on his or her stomach) at various points on the ridge line of the roof and reach under it. Using a foot-long ruler, press it into the insulation until it touches the top of the ceiling. (See the accompanying photograph on page 150.) You may very well see a series of paper or cardboard rulers in the opening which factory workers have left there for the same purpose, but a rigid one works much better. Remember the insulation thickness is an average, and you are at an area which is supposed to have more than the narrow edges of the roof cavity. At this point, the number shown on the consumer insulation information sheet is a *minimum*, and you really should have more. Look deeper into the opening. Is there more or less depth on the midsection of the ceiling?

While you're examining the roof insulation, you'll also want to check for a few other potential problems. Examples include specific spots with-

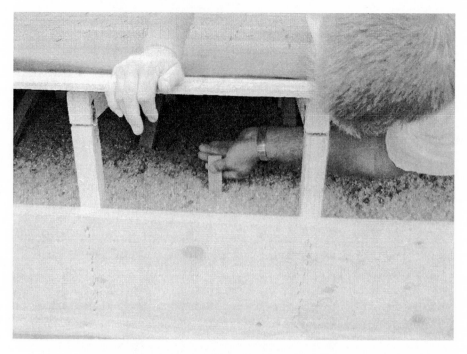

Check the insulation depth with a ruler.

out any insulation or very thin layers of insulation. This is most likely to happen near vents or the ends of the home and can be caused by air circulation under the roof during transportation. Another realm to check involves post-transit air circulation: make sure there is at least a 1" gap between the roof itself and the insulation at all points, and make sure insulation has not been blown into or shifted into your soffits (the underside of the roof overhang). The soffit has ventilation holes, and air needs to be able to travel through them and out the vents higher in the roof. Otherwise, *your insulation and your trusses can be damaged and eventually destroyed by accumulating moisture.* Because of the slope of cathedral ceilings, insulation over them can be especially prone to shifting in this manner during transit. From your vantage point on top of the roof, look under the roof on the opposite side all the way down the home, making sure you can see light toward the soffit to be sure the opening isn't blocked. Another quick and dirty check is to examine the soffit ventilation holes themselves from the ground—frequently you'll see insulation literally protruding from the ventilation holes, especially on the "hitch" end of the homes. Obviously, in areas where the soffit is clogged with insulation, your roof ventilation is going to suffer.

OK, you've been diligent and checked your roof insulation thoroughly. If it comes up lacking, what can be done? That's the good news. You can compel the company to fix it, and *while the home is still open* it's easy to have an insulation company come in and blow enough insulation to correct the problem. Most likely it will only cost the manufacturer a few hundred dollars. If this problem is not addressed now, the only way to properly fix it would be to disassemble the home, and no one would benefit. To make sure the work is done right, insist on being allowed to select the insulation company of your choice, and be sure you explain personally to that company what needs to be done. Allowing the dealer or manufacturer to hire someone of their choosing can result in corners being cut, and you'll be the one to lose. Insist that insulation baffles be installed so the minimum 1" air gap is maintained; the insulation company should know what you mean. Chances are, if you have to take the trouble to have insulation added, you can get (and should get) the manufacturer to pay for an R rating considerably higher than what you initially paid for.

The insulation in your walls is equally important, and it's quite possible that if a company will shortchange customers on roof insulation, they'll do the same in the walls. The only place to practically check this is during setup on the ends of the home — the workers will most likely have to expose some areas or can expose some areas at your request before the vinyl siding is finished. Look for markings on the fiberglass batts stating the R rating. If you paid for R-15 and the material is marked R-11, for example, insist that the rest of the home be examined at the manufacturer's expense.

If you have a home which is already assembled (or a single-section home) and suspect there is a problem because of excessive heating and cooling bills or because some rooms can't correctly be climatically adjusted, there are two possible but lamentable options. Thermal imaging can be utilized, and some engineering and contracting companies now have these infrared cameras. They work just like the cameras police and fire departments use — they detect heat (or heat loss) in buildings. These cameras are very expensive (the cheapest ones cost several thousand dollars), and companies charge quite a bit for infrared evaluations to make up for this expenditure. This won't divulge what your R-values are, but it may identify areas with missing insulation or very poorly insulated areas without being invasive. The other option is to tear into your walls and ceiling and physically look — but you can't check many locations without literally ripping the home apart. This latter option will result in destroyed Sheetrock, considerable labor, and substantial expense as well. The fact that it can be so hard to verify insulation values in manufactured homes actually might serve as an incentive for manufacturers and dealers to victimize customers in this area, so check while you can. Also, if you ever do any remodeling or Sheetrock work in the walls, take the opportunity to check the R ratings on the Fiberglas batts to see if they match what you paid for.

We haven't mentioned the third member of the insulation triad — the floor — because the way manufactured houses are constructed these areas are less likely to be shortchanged. You can test areas in the floor, however, usually without causing much damage. Look for access panels or other preexisting openings in the belly board to see what's inside. Most likely, you'll find R-11 batts between the floor joists and an insulating blanket rated R-10 laying beneath them.

Your second major consideration before the home is assembled are marriage wall studs. You might wonder what could possibly be wrong here, but you might also be unpleasantly surprised. There are two reasons why your home may be structurally defective when it comes to exterior wall supports: the use of inferior *stud grade lumber* at the factory, and the *flexing* we have talked about during delivery. The interaction of these two elements may mean that your home could have some major structural deficiencies. Walking between the two halves of our original manufactured home, we were undeniably aghast at the condition of the lumber. *Many studs had huge cracks running for several feet, extending from one edge of the board to the other.* Others looked like they had been chewed at by an army of rats or had two rounded-off corners because they came from too close to the outer edge of the tree. Still others had large knotholes near the center of them. All of these defects combine to make your house weaker in terms of roof load capacity, in the ability to withstand wind, and in resisting the effects of settling. Illustrations of some of these problems follow on page 153.

These examples and more came from the same home. Only about one third of the exterior wall studs were exposed (the ones along the marriage wall), so no one knows the condition of the remainder. You see severe splits which run completely through the boards (which render the board virtually useless from a structural point of view), and other studs are substantially weakened by other defects. In one picture, a knothole big enough to poke your finger into rests between two rounded off corners of a stud — can this board support the weight an engineer expects it to? Finally, you see a lumber grade stamp. It tells you a number of facts about the boards, including the grade and the type of tree it was cut from. In this case, the grade is "stud" grade, also often referred to as utility grade lumber. As you check the wood for defects, keep in mind what lumber experts and structural engineers do: *the most critical part of the stud is the middle third.*

The combination of inferior and stud grade lumber and flexing during transportation can result in an ugly interaction as these photographs demonstrate. These studs were all found in the marriage wall of one home; knotholes and rounded corners were common, and some 2 × 4s were literally split in two. The structural integrity of this home has been severely compromised. Examine your marriage wall studs before your home is assembled!

Defects there are especially detrimental to structural integrity. Unfortunately, that's just where we found most of the splits in this home. Could they have resulted from transportation stress on already inferior lumber? To me, that seems a likely explanation. The factory couldn't give any rationalization, but everyone agreed this lumber was unacceptable when presented with the pictures. Once again, the case for documentation is borne out. If you find problems with the lumber or the insulation, take plenty of photographs and video if at all possible. Otherwise, an unscrupulous dealer (or setup crew) can have the house quickly assembled, and then you have no visible proof of defects.

As with the roof insulation shortage, there are solutions to the stud problems. The simplest one is to have all the defective boards along the marriage wall reinforced: new 2" × 4" boards are nailed in directly next to the bad ones. This solution is quick and inexpensive. The drawback is that you have to wonder what kind of shape the other exterior walls are in, the ones which aren't exposed. There's little reason to suppose the studs in them are in better shape than the studs in the marriage wall. In our original home, we had the marriage wall problem. We also found that even after the home was properly leveled, other exterior walls had noticeable leans to them — some by as much as 1" from top to bottom. It was so bad, I could tell it with the naked eye from both inside and outside the house, although Spanky (our regional manager) swears he couldn't see it. He couldn't deny what my four-foot level indicated, however, when it was placed against the wall, although he did suggest on multiple occasions that the brand new Craftsman® level was "defective." The walls *were* leaning. There was even a discernible bulge in the exterior wall near where the tongue fell off our home in transit — as though the studs actually buckled there behind the OSB wrap when the home's frame literally hit the road-way. When our substitute home arrived, and after we had complained voraciously about the lumber, the visible studs looked fine. There were no major splits, and the lumber had obviously been much more carefully cho-sen (although it was still stud grade lumber). We also had no leaning walls or bulges elsewhere in the home. The latter fact is not likely a coinci-dence — it was a combination of better wood and more care in trans-portation. If you find that your wood is obviously split or defective, hold the dealer and factory responsible, and make them properly fix it even if you have to wait for a new home to be delivered. With evidence, you can make them fix it. You might even be able to get an upgrade for your trou-ble if you complain enough. You could try asking for grade 2 lumber in all exterior walls, an insulation upgrade, or finished drywall. Your time and sacrifice are worth something if you get a defective home and have to wait longer than necessary because of negligence. Time is money — and if you're paying for a temporary residence and storage fees for your belongings it can be quite a lot of money.

One last quick consideration before the parts of multiple-section homes are joined together involves gasket material. This gasket material is a type of Styrofoam padding which is attached to the wood around all the interior openings. It's the blue material visible in the pictures illus-trating the roof cavity earlier in this chapter. Manufacturers sometimes ship this material with their homes, and county code may or may not require it in your area. It's just good practice to use it, however, whether or not the company supplies it. If the setup crew doesn't have any, you can run down to a home improvement store yourself and purchase it for just a few dollars. Insist the crew use this material.

Another consideration at this point will be the disposition of the "tongues" or hitches which were used to tow your home to your property. The setup crew may ask you what to do with them, or they may just detach them and push them up under your new home. Unless you think you'll be

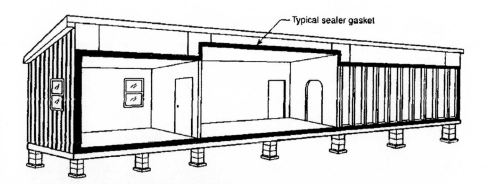

Typical sealer gasket

Above: Placement of sealer gasket (*Model Manufactured Home Installation Standards,* Manufactured Housing Consensus Committee, 2003. *Left:* Gasket material is relatively inexpensive and sold at home improvement stores.

moving your new home in the near future (thereby requiring the tongues again), they will only be a hindrance to you underneath your house. You will have to crawl around them or over them for maintenance and inspection tasks. Have the tongues set aside or carried off. If you own a large enough truck or trailer, you can carry them to a scrap metal yard yourself. They are worth a few dollars apiece. One more point here regarding access underneath the home: make sure your house is high enough off the ground for you or service workers to comfortably crawl under it at all points. Local code probably requires that your home's frame be a certain distance above the ground at its lowest point; for instance, it might be required to be 12" above ground. It can be extremely difficult to crawl through 12" openings, however; especially if you're dragging a work light, a 300mm crescent wrench, and an electric drill. You may want to tell your setup crew you need the home's frame to be at least 18" to 24" off the ground at the lowest point — especially if electrical, HVAC, and/or water hook-ups are in the most confined area under the home. Functional access doors also require a minimum height to be installed at your home's perimeter. It also makes sense to have access doors positioned where frequent service may be required (again, near electrical, water, or HVAC hook-ups) or at opposite ends of large homes so your don't have to crawl or stoop for long distances to get where you're going. If you don't choose these matters for yourself, you may not be happy with the decisions of the setup crew later.

The underside of your home is also going to be where your support piers are located. Along with your foundation, they are crucial to the integrity of your new home. The setup crews should refer to the home's setup manual, the local regulations, and their own experience in constructing these piers. You should familiarize yourself with the local codes in this regard, and you should also *ask for access to the home's setup or installation manual* prior to the setup being completed so you can determine if it is in fact being done correctly. The home's setup manual should always be given to the homeowner when the keys are. Make absolutely sure you get it because sometimes the setup crews keep them. If you need to, photocopy critical pages before you return it to the workers. You do not have to be an engineer to check the basics. Anyone with a tape measure (and a good set of kneepads will help) can tell if the home is supported properly on piers when it comes to the basics. You will check for spacing between piers, the height of piers, the size of the concrete blocks used, etc. Also keep in mind that local codes and the setup manual give the *minimum requirements*— not the ideal support. Piers are made from 8" × 8" × 16" *open-cell concrete blocks*. The openings must be oriented vertically. These should have solid *concrete cap blocks* on top of them to evenly distribute the weight. *Hardwood plates* and *shims* should then be placed over the cap blocks to both protect the cap blocks from cracking and to fill in the final void between the pier and the frame. Your manual should specify minimum thicknesses for the cap blocks and hardwood plates. In addition to piers under the steel frame, other piers are required at openings in the home's sidewalls (such as sliding glass doors or bay windows) and at the marriage walls. Make sure your piers are properly placed, properly constructed, and that they aren't loose. Perhaps most important of all, make sure no blocks are cracked or broken. A few examples of common problems follow on page 157. After all, a picture is worth a thousand words.

One last bit of advice in this regard concerns single blocking versus double blocking. *I would recommend anyone insist on double blocking— especially if they have ordered their home with construction features which increase its weight.* Some examples of such features include 6" exterior walls versus the standard 4" walls, 16" on center construction throughout versus the standard 24" on center for interior walls, using 2" × 4" construc-

Top left: The problem here is obvious. Don't let workers use broken blocks. If this block wasn't originally broken, then too much weight was placed on this pier. *Top right:* Workers didn't even bother to use wedges on this pier, and there is an unmistakable gap between the frame and hardwood plate. This pier isn't supporting anything. *Bottom left:* The setup manual for this home specifies that ¾" thick hardwood plates "*must cover the entire top of the pier.*" Obviously, this pier isn't correct. *Bottom right:* Because these piers are 32" high, the manual specifies the cap blocks must be a minimum of 4" thick — instead the crew used 2" blocks.

tion throughout instead of the standard 2" × 3" interior wall studs, or ordering heavier than standard roof trusses. Any of these features can dramatically increase weight. Single-block piers are designed to support up to 8,000 pounds, while properly constructed double-blocked piers can support up to 16,000 pounds each. Ironically, the dealers and setup crews often seem to have no concept of just how heavy these homes can be and what it takes to properly support them. The general manager of the lot where we purchased our home instructed our setup crew supervisor to single block our home, even though the house was heavy enough to rip off the tongue during transport and heavy enough to severely bend our frame during assembly because the crew didn't adequately support the

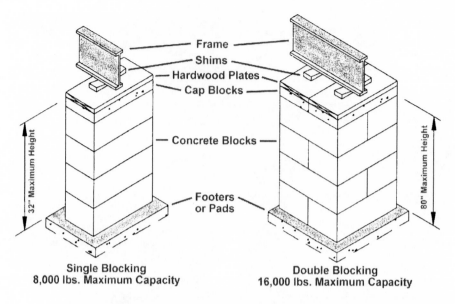

Frame
Shims
Hardwood Plates
Cap Blocks
Concrete Blocks
Footers
or Pads

32" Maximum Height

80" Maximum Height

Single Blocking
8,000 lbs. Maximum Capacity

Double Blocking
16,000 lbs. Maximum Capacity

An example of properly constructed support piers.

home's weight. Even after these catastrophes, the examples of improper piers shown in the preceding four photographs were the result of a *second crew* responsible for setting up our *substitute* home (a crew which was fully aware of our earlier tribulations). That's why I urge you not to take anything for granted — do your own homework and be your own supervisor because that's the only way to know whether or not the work is done right!

Anchoring systems are another consideration which can be equally important. Anchoring systems are used with manufactured houses to resist lift caused by strong winds, preventing your home from turning over. I've inspected homes which have been flipped on their roofs by hurricanes, and it's not a pretty sight. Fortunately, properly installed anchoring systems are extremely effective. This is, however, an area where engineering skill, local ordinances, and your particular region (in terms of both weather and soil) come strongly into play. As a general guideline, use your setup or installation manual to verify that you have the correct number and type of ground anchors and tie-down straps for your home, and ask your local building inspector to verify that your anchoring system is proper and sufficient for your region. Unless you live in a hurricane or tornado belt, most people will not have to worry about anchoring systems too much, but it's good to know you're safe when Mother Nature does decide to flex her muscles. If you live in a high-wind zone (anywhere near the beach on the east or Gulf coast, and large portions of Florida), make *absolutely sure* your home is rated for it. Look on the "Data Plate" (try the wall of the master closet) to verify your home's wind rating; it ranges from zone I to zone III with III being the best.

While you're examining the bottom of your home, don't forget the vapor barrier. The vapor barrier is nothing more than polyethylene (plastic) sheeting spread underneath your new home. It comes in three foot wide rolls at your home improvement store. Your home warranty may require the installation of a vapor barrier, but it's usually the customer's responsibility to install it unless you make other arrangements at the time of the sale. It's purpose is to help control moisture — protecting the subfloor and the home in general. You should cover the ground as completely as possible, cutting the sheets and wrapping them around the base of your piers. Use at least six mil thick polyethylene, and overlap the edges by about a foot. Try to cover at *least* 90 percent of any bare earth. To help keep things in place as you work and in the future, use pieces of duct tape to hold adjacent strips of sheeting together. Rocks or bricks can be placed on the edges around the perimeter to keep the wind from blowing it up until the home skirting is constructed around it. The easiest way to spread out the plastic is usually to roll it from one end to the other starting at either the front or back of the home, and then folding the roll open to the interior side—cutting slits to accept the piers as required. If the ground slopes, work downhill. The best time to do this is after the home is safely blocked— *never* go under the home before it's properly blocked—but before any perimeter skirting is installed. Prior to spreading the vapor barrier, make sure all organic material is removed from underneath the home—this includes any scraps of wood, vegetation, or small roots left over from site preparation. Organic material can cause problems with insects. Subfloors in manufactured homes now often come with extended warranties independent of the home manufacturer, but there's no need to risk problems needlessly. For instance, Weyerhaeuser warranties their Structurwood® OSB floors for manufactured and modular homes for 25 years.

If your property isn't properly graded, or if all the runoff from your roof ends up at your foundation, the vapor barrier won't solve all of your problems. You and your family depend on water to live, but it is your home's worst enemy. It will cause mold, mildew, condensation, and humidity in your home as well as causing real structural damage. To avoid voiding your warranty, injuring your home, and suffering respiratory and other related illnesses, you need to be vigilant and active in preventing water accumulation under the home. Ideally your site should have been crowned so that water flows away in every direction. Otherwise, there should be backfill against the perimeter to direct water away from the bottom of the home — that is, some dirt should be placed against the skirting, seeded with grass to hold it in place, and sloped away from your home. Gutters should direct rain runoff away from the home. Make sure that the gutters operate properly if your roof has a low 3:12 pitch to it. (See the section on customizing your home for more details about this potential problem, and the chapter on helpful hints for one possible solution if you do have a problem with water on a low pitched roof.) *One specific thing to watch for and prevent is having your foundation crew dig a perimeter foundation and putting the excavated dirt in a ring around your new home.* In effect, this creates a bowl in which your home will sit — literally forcing runoff water under your house. If the dirt is piled high enough, pretty soon you'll be the proud owner of an island. If this happens to you, point out to your dealer that the contracted employees are endangering your home (and the warranty) and have them take the excavated dirt to use as backfill after the skirting in complete. Local codes may also require backfill if you need some additional leverage. As a last resort, rent a small tractor or enlist the aid of friends with shovels.

One situation which can complicate getting rid of the water is sloping property. If you can't get the property sufficiently graded because of the nature of the terrain, you can try a French drain. A French drain collects the water before it gets to your foundation. Because it is placed just a foot or so from your home, it generally has to be dug by hand, and it can be nearly back-breaking labor. Expect to pay at *least* one or two thousand dollars to have this job contracted out. In a typical situation, you may have to place the drain on at least three sides of the dwelling and then run it downhill far enough to route the water safely away. Sizes vary, but 15" wide by about 12" deep is usually sufficient. The larger the drain, the more water it can redirect, so you should tailor the size according to your particular requirements.

A true "French" drain is simply a gravel-filled ditch. In practice, how-

ever, most such drains are an improved version of the original concept. You excavate the ditch to the proper size, close enough to the home to catch roof runoff if you

Creating a French drain is an extremely labor intensive project. This one kept filling up with rainwater before the work could be completed.

aren't using gutters, and then drape landscaping fabric into it. It is extremely important that the ditch have at *least* a 1 percent downward slope from its highest point near your foundation: these simple drains work on a combination of gravity and the fact water chooses the path of least resistance. If it doesn't slope away from your home, you could just be making your situation worse. The fabric should be left lying on the ground on either side of the ditch and be sufficiently wide to fold over on itself after the ditch is filled. Landscaping, weed-control fabric, or inexpensive fabric made specifically for French drains is often located in a store next to another major component in the improved version of the French drain: 4" perforated pipe. Fill the ditch with a couple of inches of gravel (¾" to 1" in diameter), then lay in your drain pipe with the holes pointed down. This seems counterintuitive to many people; common sense suggests this will cause the water to drain out of the pipe as opposed to into it. However, these drains operate using hydrostatic pressure to force the water through the bottom of the pipe — the water level in the trench is lowered because of water being forced up into the bottom of the pipe, as opposed to spilling into the top of the pipe. This makes the pipe much more effective and keeps the water level lower.

After you lay in the pipe, cover it with more gravel to within a couple of inches from the top of the ditch. Now fold the fabric over from each side, making sure it overlaps. The purpose of the fabric is to assist in keeping dirt from clogging up the rocks and the pipe. French drains tend to clog up over time, and this will help yours remain functional longer. Now you can cover the last couple of inches with gravel or topsoil. I recommend covering it with a loose, sandy soil which lets water enter freely — you can mix some sand with the dirt you previously excavated to create this — and seeding the top with grass to hold this topsoil in place. Wherever the French drain encompasses your home and you have downspouts (or plan to have downspouts in the future), cut the pipe and put in a "T" fitting so you can conduct the downspout's water output directly into the drain. Flexible perforated pipe is commonly used, but sometimes sections which lead away from the

This drain had to be carefully placed over electrical and water lines, and under phone wires. Fortunately, such hook-ups are often all in the same area.

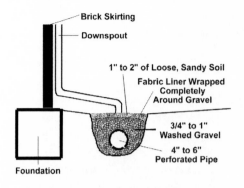

Anatomy of a French drain.

home may need more strength. For instance, if you have to direct the water runoff under a driveway, use the solid perforated pipe in that area which can withstand much greater weight without being crushed. Be careful not to pile up the excess excavated dirt in a ring around the home — put what doesn't go back into the ditch in a low area of the yard or haul it off. Finally, any time you dig in your yard, be extremely careful regarding underground lines. Striking a power or gas line can result in death, and you could also damage water or phone lines. Contact utility companies if necessary in order to locate these lines before you start.

To illustrate the possible need for a French drain, as well as to illustrate many points from the contract stage, foundation stage, and the problem-resolution chapter to come, allow me to relate the story of an Oklahoma couple. They purchased a large two-section manufactured home and financed it along with a relatively spacious tract of land. Like most manufactured home sales, it was supposed to be a turn-key deal; that is, all the buyer was supposed to do was move in and make payments. Unfortunately, the workers simply leveled a place for the home on the sloping ground. Whenever it rains, the water comes rushing down the hill and under the home — washing away the dirt which supports the couple's porch and forming standing pools of water under their home. This water will soon (if it hasn't already) begin to affect the structural integrity of the home itself and become a breeding ground for mold, mildew, and mosquitoes. The dealership's work crews also left literally tons of concrete in different piles around the lot and didn't fully fill in the septic trenches. Because of this, the owner of this turn-key deal had to break up the concrete with a sledgehammer to haul it off himself, and he had to hire earthmoving equipment at substantial expense to fill in the trenches. The dealership also failed to pay taxes they had promised to. This couple has tried in vain to have the dealership correct the problems for a year, and the dealership has done nothing as the water danger rises. Get everything in writing, and closely supervise the work or be prepared to do the work yourself! A French drain might be your best friend if you find out after the fact that "turn-key" doesn't include the grading needed to make your home site suitable!

The second area where water can present horrendous headaches brings us back to the roof once more. Water coming in from the roof will damage your home more quickly than water accumulating below it, and it doesn't take much. *As little as 5 percent decay from water damage can cause as much as 50 percent loss in wood's structural strength.* The American Society of Heating, Refrigeration and Air Conditioning reports that *90 percent of all building failures are moisture related.* Mold and mildew will also form quickly in your ceiling cavity and walls after any direct contact with water. Inspect the roof carefully after the home is set up and any sections are assembled; if you can't physically do it yourself, have someone you trust do it. Look for any signs of missing caulk around pipes or vents, and look for depressions which can represent literal holes under the shingles—especially near where pipes or other objects exit the roof. Workers sometimes cut holes in locations that won't work, and instead of repairing them, they simply cut another hole and cover the first one with shingles. I found one of these openings on our substitute or replacement house we had to have delivered. The hole was in the same area where gallons of water poured into our roof over the master bathroom the first time we had a hard rain. Workers had cut an opening in the roof for the bathroom exhaust fan vent, but it was too close to the exterior wall to connect the exhaust tube. Instead of replacing the board or otherwise patching the hole, they

Left: A roof repair is in progress to fix a leak near the bathroom vent. Notice the opening in the wood beneath the shingles to the left. *Right:* Here's a close-up of the hole. Only shingles covered it, and you can see the whitish circular area on the shingles where weight had stressed them almost to the breaking point.

simply cut a second hole for the vent and laid roofing paper and shingles over the first one! If someone had stepped on this opening, the shingles would have simply given way under foot.

If you think this is a rarity, think again. Before this ever happened to us, one member of our setup crew who used to work in a manufacturing plant told us about "Friday houses." Friday houses are a running joke among factory workers. This employee told us as he was walking on a roof in the plant one Friday, he fell all the way through up to his upper thigh because he stepped on a fireplace opening which was just covered over with nothing more than shingles. A sort of manufactured home tiger pit, as it was. The rest of the workers were so anxious to get home and start the weekend, they just said to heck with it and finished whatever they were doing as quickly as possible, even if it meant leaving off the fireplace flu and camouflaging the hole. Many workers often joked if they bought a company home, they didn't want it to be a Friday house. Given that we had already had water flood the roof of our originally ordered home and had complained voraciously about it, we never dreamed such a dereliction could have occurred in the replacement home. This defect did occur, however, because of further factory negligence. Inspect your roof carefully. It's another area dealers don't expect the customer to closely examine.

Also check for bumps or ridge lines under shingles running perpendicular to the peak of the roof. These can mean the roofing paper or felt is bunched up underneath. Your shingles need to lie flat to properly seal — this is especially important on low-pitched roofs. I've been told this ridge effect often occurs in manufactured housing plants when the roofing paper is applied one day near the end of a shift, but the shingles aren't applied until the following workday. If the condition isn't too severe, hot weather can cause the shingles to flatten out and seal, otherwise it needs to be repaired by the dealer or manufacturer by having the affected areas reshingled.

If there are no major problems found so far, the dealership should soon be turning over the keys to your new home to you. It's time for the water, power, and phone service to be turned on. Now your focus will be turning back to the interior of your home. This will be a lot like the walkthrough, but now even the finishing touches on the trim should be correct. *Make sure all trim pieces are cut to the proper length (no unsightly gaps), and that adjoining ends are flush.* Test every drawer and cabinet for proper operation. Drawers should slide smoothly without binding. After the setup is complete, *test every window and door for proper operation.* Windows should travel the length of the track without binding, doors should hang evenly and close without hitting the surrounding door jamb. Don't just test whether windows and doors open and close — make sure all locks and latches work. If you have problems with any of these, the trim crew or someone from the dealership needs to make adjustments, repairs, or replacements as needed.

Use your interior doors rigorously when you first move in — even open and close doors in rooms that you may not normally use that frequently — and then check the edges near the lock set. These doors are made inexpensively, are relatively thin, and have a minimum amount of material at the latch point combined with a maximum of stress. In short, there's not a lot of margin for error at that point in an error-prone price range. If you see any evidence of the surface laminate separating from the rest of the door, have the factory replace

The thin materials began to separate on this new door in the area of the lock set. A factory worker smeared putty into the crack and pronounced that the door was then fixed.

it. Having someone smear putty into the crack and painting over it is not a satisfactory repair for a structural defect in the door.

Check every area of the ceiling for signs of cracking. Areas around recessed fluorescent ceiling fixtures seem to be especially prone; also exercise special care in examining the ceiling for cracks at every edge next to the ceiling peak or next to exterior walls. If repairs have to be made, make sure the crew carefully matches the same pattern that the factory put on.

This ceiling crack extended for several feet out from the corner of a fluorescent light fixture in the kitchen. Ceiling cracks are common in newly transported homes. Not all of them are this obvious, so check carefully for them.

Walk barefoot over every part of where multisection homes join, making sure the floors are flush at every point underneath the carpet or linoleum. If the setup crew isn't careful, the floor of one section can be significantly higher or lower than the adjoining section, which is not only a nuisance but a precursor to premature carpet or vinyl wear. *Use a level to check for flat floors, counter tops, and straight walls.* An alternative to using a level is using the quick and easy ball test: you place a round ball on flat surfaces and see if it rolls. You can't use a ball on the walls, however, and you can obtain much more specific information using a level. A complaint that your floor rises ½" across 48"—or three floor joists—is pretty damning, whereas telling your dealer a ball rolls on your floor may not elicit much more than a smirk and a suspicious eyebrow raise. Problems in the floors or walls could indicate the home wasn't properly leveled or set up—or worse, that your home was damaged in transit. Check closet shelves again—make sure the supports are placed in wood and not just drywall.

Check every accessible water connection as soon as the water is turned on. Pull out the refrigerator/freezer on an ice-maker model to look behind them. (They should be on wheels and roll out fairly easily.) Be careful not to pull it out too far, damaging the water line. In fact, you may have to pull the refrigerator/freezer out just to turn on the water valve to it if your setup crew doesn't. Look carefully under every sink for signs of drips and also around the base of your tubs, showers, or the walls near any of these. Leaks in the walls or under the tubs may not show up for days, weeks, or until those facilities have been used—so make a point to use your guest bath just to test it. Check the washing machine connections as well, and

 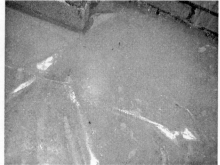

Left: Toucing this belly board underneath the master bath seemed to reveal what felt like sloshing water. Pricking it with a pen confirmed our suspicions— gallons eventually poured out. *Right:* Several inches of water are clearly visible beneath this clear plastic vapor barrier.

verify its water discharge pipe is properly in place before you use it to wash clothes. Although it's not a water-related issue, while you're in the utility room make sure your dryer exhaust tube is connected and not severely bent or pinched off. Also, *climb under the home a few days after the water is turned on to check for wet spots on the ground or water build-up in the belly board for leaks under the subfloor you can't directly see.* Actually, you or someone you can rely on should crawl under the house several times soon after moving in, because slow leaks can be more insidious than huge ones: they can cause tremendous damage but not reveal themselves for weeks or months. Check for water on the ground or under the vapor barrier, in the belly board underneath any location where you know water pipes run (under both bathrooms, the kitchen, and the utility room), and check the sewage pipe connections.

While the underside of the home is being inspected for one of the last times, *make sure your heating and air-conditioning connections are tightly sealed where they cross over in multisection homes.* In some homes, these connections run through the floor rim plates— their foam seals can only be checked before the sections of the home are assembled. Leaks here can cost you plenty in heating and cooling bills. Your duct work *should not come in contact with the ground* at any point, or be bent so severely that airflow is restricted. Your installa-

Blocks aren't the best way to hold up HVAC ducts, but this met local code and raised them off the ground— which is where the negligent setup crew left them.

tion manual or local codes should specify the maximum distance allowed between duct support straps. Also, fireplaces frequently need a vent or air intake under them —check to make sure it's not blocked by insulation if your fireplace requires one.

Before we leave setup, let's return back to water problems and the interior of your home. After you receive the keys and take possession of the home, *during the first hard rain which occurs, examine from the inside the areas around all the vents and any other openings in your roof.* This includes your bathroom vents, your range or microwave vent, your fireplace, and even any overhead light fixtures. These areas are likely to be the best early warning indicators you have of a potential leak. The harder the rain, the better your opportunity to inspect. If water's coming in, at best you'll see a fraction of it in these places if you have a cathedral ceiling because of the slope of the ceiling, so a small amount of visible water can mean big trouble. If water comes in your roof, it will find some way to flow downhill — most likely through the exterior walls and into the belly board, causing even more potential problems with wood rot, insulation damage, and mold growth. Company representatives assured us when we discovered a leak in our master bath that because the homes are built on a "jig" water cannot travel from the roof cavity to the wall cavity. However, when I placed my hand on the walls in that area I could actually feel a temperature difference. I insisted the wallboard be removed, and behind it the studs and insulation were soaking wet and black mold and green fungus were everywhere. In such a case, the factory should dispose of the wet insulation, clean the interior wood with bleach or a commercial agent designed for mold, allow the wood to completely dry, install new insulation, and then install new wallboard. Moisture meters are devices designed to detect the presence of moisture in wood. Various companies make them, including Wagner Electronics, Inc. Ideally, wood used for construction should have a moisture content less than 15 percent. If moisture content is greater than or equal to 20 percent, wood will decay, and its strength will be greatly reduced. Following the logical path of the water, I next went under the home (even though once more company workers assured me that from the wall the water would have somehow flowed out into the yard) where pressing on the belly board wrap above my head revealed it was filled with almost as many gallons as the town water tower.

Several gallons came through this opening in the ceiling during a long rainstorm, but that was only a fraction of the water that came into our roof. Even a few drops here could spell impending disaster for a homeowner.

This fiasco occurred in our substitute home. In our original home, water leaked in over the kitchen for the simple reason the dealer left damaged vents on the home. We found a pool of water in the kitchen floor, but no visible sign of where it came from. We did have a ceiling light fixture above the kitchen island, however. I removed the globe, loosened the two screws, and pulled the fixture down. Water literally poured down my arms and into my face from the opening, and the insulation was drenched. If you feel the need to check your electrical fixtures for water behind them, do make absolutely sure the power is turned off. Preventing these wet nightmare scenarios is the justification for checking out your roof yourself. Yes, the factory workers and setup crew should take care of it, but in our case we were 0 for 2 with two different homes and two different setup crews. *Without a thorough roof inspection or significant rainfall, leaks could go undetected until after your home's one year warranty has expired.*

Finally, if the dealer offers to or needs to pressure wash your home after delivery because of dirt or oil from either setup or transportation, *do not let anyone spray water into your soffit*— it will quite probably ruin your insulation (cellulose will never completely regain its R-Value) and once again create a breeding ground for mold and mildew. Enough water will quickly cause substantial damage to your ceilings. Some insulation was poking out through the holes in our soffit after our home was delivered (the air flow during travel moves the insulation around) and the "trim" man said he would clean it up for us that way — by shooting high pressure water at it! If your home needs road dirt or engine grime from the delivery truck removed, watch the workers and make sure they do it carefully.

As you supervise the setup, remember that dealers and manufacturers rely on your ignorance — just as they did during the sales and finance processes. When we first complained about our shortage of insulation and our broken studs, I took it as a tell tale sign that the factory representative's response was an incredulous "How do you know that?" It was as if we had performed a magic trick. That is, it didn't surprise them that we had these particular defects, it surprised the company that we discovered them. Furthermore, once I discovered these problems, I told our setup crew supervisor to immediately stop assembling the home as I began calling the dealership's general manager on a cell phone to solve the problems. Instead, our setup crew literally began to race to join the sections of the home faster — thereby forever entombing the incriminating evidence. I actually had to physically stand between the sections to stop the work until I could reach someone on the telephone. The moral of the tale is that along with a watchful eye, you must also be prepared to be as forceful as the situation dictates to protect your interests. So watch the movie *Rocky* or whatever you need to do to steel yourself, and stand your ground when you know you're right. Don't let anyone intimidate you into accepting a defective home!

CHAPTER 11

Final Analysis

After all these tales of problems, I hope you haven't changed your mind about buying a manufactured home! Truthfully, many people are satisfied customers, and many others wind up disgruntled. From my research, a fairly large percentage of the discontented customers have more problems with the way dealerships treat them and their complaints than they do with the home itself. The purpose of this book has been to help you select a good home, avoid quality problems or identify and correct problems properly when they do occur; and to help you negotiate with the dealerships on equal footing. After reading this text, you are much more likely to save yourself headaches and money because it shares the learning curve with you without the associated first-timer risk. So remember that any home choice comes with risks, and feel confident that you can make a good deal on a good home. You simply need to comprehend the oftentimes unsavory nature of the business as well as possess a thorough understanding of the way manufactured homes are constructed and set up.

If you're still unsure, consider what *Consumer Reports* found in its 1998 nationwide survey of over 1,000 manufactured home customers. *Eighty-two percent of respondents were largely satisfied with their homes*, although most still had at least one problem they considered major — but then they didn't have this book! That finding is fairly consistent with a 2002 survey of 21,314 manufactured home owners by Foremost Insurance which reported 88 percent of home owners were either "very satisfied" (53 percent) or "somewhat satisfied" (35 percent). *Consumer Reports* also found that manufactured homes can last just as long as site-built homes and that there was a correlation between the purchase price and the number of problems customers have. The cheaper the home, the more likely problems will arise. Survey respondents identified the following six problem areas:

1. **Floors**— 25 percent had problems with *particle board flooring* which had gotten wet. When particle board gets wet, it swells considerably and loses its strength. You can fall right through it. Currently, tongue-and-groove oriented strand board (OSB) is more common and much more resistant to water damage. Do not believe salespeople who tell you OSB is anything more than *resistant* to water. Avoid water, and avoid particle board floors.

2. **Central Heating and Air Conditioning**— 20 percent reported problems with *uneven heating and cooling* because of incorrect placement of registers. Ordering *perimeter heat ducts* can help this situation as well as buying a home with *graduated heat ducts.* Graduated heat ducts taper as needed so that they achieve the same volume of air in different areas of the home, but not all companies offer them.

3. **Plumbing**— 36 percent of respondents had problems with leaky plumbing. The primary culprit was *polybutylene water pipes,* but these are seldom used now. In fact, a huge class-action lawsuit was successfully brought against the manufacturer of polybutylene pipes, so they won't be making a comeback anytime soon. Just to be sure, inquire about the type of pipes in the homes you look at, and make sure there is a main water cut-off and individual water cut-offs in case you do have a problem (leak). In older homes you often had no cut-offs and had to run to the street valve or run to the electrical box to shut off your well. By then the ducks were usually circling.

4. **Roof**— 31 percent had problems with *metal roofs leaking at the seams.* Metal roofs are typically found on single-wide models and are becoming more and more rare. The main problem with the metal roofs (besides wind noise) was that they really required annual maintenance. Sealants like Cool Seal were supposed to be applied after the home was set up and applied regularly thereafter. These roofs were much more likely to leak without such treatment.

5. **Windows and Doors**— 32 percent reported problems with *leaking windows.* These problems can occur with cheap windows without continuous welds in the corners or from broken seals around doors and windows resulting from delivery. The newer, vinyl energy efficient windows should not have this problem nearly as often. Also, make sure your door sills are caulked as required *after* the setup of your home. In older homes, the combination of window air-conditioner units and particle board flooring were an almost sure-fire recipe for disaster.

6. **Installation**— homes not set on a proper concrete foundation were found to be prone to Sheetrock cracks and to binding doors and windows because of settling. You, however, know the importance of your foundation, so you won't let this happen to you!

Notice that 4 out of 6 problems listed are water-related! Most of these problems either aren't concerns for today's manufactured home shopper or can be appropriately avoided with wisely chosen upgrades and supervision of the setup crew. The standards set by the Department of Housing and Urban Development (HUD) is one reason for this improved consumer environment, and the expanding list of options for customers is another. Chances are excellent — better than 82 percent — that you can avoid any long-term major problems (or correct them at setup time) and be quite content in your new manufactured home if you exercise diligence.

Because it used to be a major concern in the past, I would like to address one more issue along these lines. Manufactured homes used to be widely regarded as "fire traps." Burning mobile homes once showed up almost as regularly on nightly news programs in winter as video footage of my brethren Southerners saying really stupid things (TV news crews seem to love both). Despite the fact that many of these fires were caused by some combination of kerosene heaters and lack of mental acuity (whether self-induced and temporary, or God-given and permanent), the reputation of manufactured homes being fire traps stuck. Personally, I don't think the United States Capitol building could stand for more than a week if someone introduced a kerosene heater in the mix. Even today, many people will raise their eyebrows if you say you're planning to buy a manufactured home with a fireplace. Foremost Insurance, one of the leading insurance companies for manufactured homes, undertook a study that compared these structures to their site-built counterparts since the 1976 HUD code went into effect. Foremost found than while site-built homes experienced fires at a rate of 17 per 1,000 homes, the rate for manufactured homes was only 8 per 1,000. If fire safety is a major concern, the finding that site-built homes are twice as likely to catch fire should be a compelling one for you. Richard Wettergreen, a Foremost Insurance Company assistant vice president, stated, "When construction methods and standards are considered, it appears to be a distinct and safe advantage to live in a factory-built home. It's time for the myth of high fire potential in manufactured housing to be laid to rest."

According to the National Fire Protection Association's 11th Edition of "Fire in the United States," the HUD standards have had a positive impact, and the rate of manufactured home fires did fall by about 20 percent from 1987 to 1996 (sadly, the figures for loss of life in manufactured home fires have not fallen as precipitously). While the decrease in fires is to be applauded, there is still definitely room for improvement. In site-built homes the usual source of fire is cooking, but in manufactured homes the more likely culprit is a *defect in the electrical or heating system*. There-fore, it is a problem with the home itself more often than homeowner care-lessness. Thus, to save more manufactured homeowner lives, we need a higher quality product and more careful inspection at the factory and at the time of setup.

## CHAPTER 12

When Things Go Wrong

If there is a legitimate problem or concern that you can't get the dealer to address, you may need help. When you've done all your homework and things still go wrong, where do you turn? First, consider the nature of the problem: if it's something that the factory is responsible for directly or indirectly, you can bypass the dealer and complain to the manufacturer. In the early chapters, you learned how to get contact information. If the problem is strictly dealer related, or if the factory refuses to help you, you still should have some recourse. There are three typical avenues, with the third possibility depending on the wording of your sales agreement or contract: (1) contact the Manufactured Housing Board (or your state's equivalent); (2) complain to local or regional "consumer action lines" or something similar; or (3) go to arbitration or court.

First, if you have structural concerns, you may want to consult your Yellow Pages for the name of a *structural engineer*. This might be the case if you suspect the frame is damaged or bent or if you have found numerous broken studs which the dealer or manufacturer won't fix. As noted previously, bulges in walls or leaning walls can be an indication of serious problems with the structure. A qualified engineer can also determine if your foundation is properly done. Most large cities should have several structural engineering firms to choose from; you may want to look for one with experience in manufactured housing if possible. (If it comes to a contentious disagreement with the factory, manufacturers are apt to try to discredit an engineer without specific experience in the manufactured housing field; whether or not an arbitrator or court would agree with such a dismissal is another matter.) Depending on your particular problems, you may also want to ask if they have access to specific equipment such as moisture meters to test wood structural members which have been exposed to water or infrared cameras to check for missing insulation without tearing open walls and ceilings.

A preliminary assessment may be all you need, and be sure to get a *written report*. Such a report will likely cost you several hundred dollars, but in the event of a serious dispute that investment may pay for itself many times over. In fact, if you have enough evidence to warrant a structural analysis, you may be able to persuade the dealer or manufacturer to foot the bill for an engineer — but make absolutely sure that the engineering firm is reporting to *you*. If necessary, pay for the engineer out of your own pocket and have the company reimburse you if they have agreed to pay the bill. As often happens in courts of law, the expert testimony tends to favor the person who is paying the bill. Make sure the engineer is working for you and not the dealer or manufacturer.

If you've followed this text so far, you've probably documented any concerns or problems with photographs or videos. You may feel the need, again depending on your particular circumstances, to hire a structural engineer before contacting the Manufactured Housing Board, but most likely you will want to see if the housing board can solve your problems first without going to that expense. A list of the various housing board agencies (state administrative agencies or SSAs) for the United States and more information about the complaint process is included in appendix C. The procedure usually involves requesting a complaint form. When you fill out the details of the problems you have with your home, the Manufactured Housing Board will contact the dealer or manufacturer for their side of the story. If the latter doesn't offer a satisfactory solution at this point (sometimes a complaint is all it takes to get action), then the housing board should set up a time to meet with you and company representatives at the home to personally inspect the situation. If your claims have obvious merit, at this point the dealer or manufacturer will likely offer some sort of compromise or fix. If there is doubt about your assertions of problems, or for that matter even if there isn't, the Manufactured Housing Board often has little real authority (or volition) to force the company to fix anything unless it's a safety-related defect. If a company in question continually makes egregious errors or is totally negligent, the state board could theoretically prevent it from doing business in the state, but that's not likely to happen.

Some state administrative agencies are better than others. The Consumers Union found, for example, that the Texas Manufactured Housing Division acted "more as a service agency for the industry than a protector of home buyers." It rejected more than a third of consumer warranty complaints without even investigating and audited retailers at a rate of once per 37 years (http://www.consumersunion.org/other/mh/paper-pr.htm). Even though the Manufactured Housing Board can't automatically solve every problem, it does give you one recourse which owners of site-built homes don't have. *Your best bet when problems arise at this stage and at any stage is to be able to prove your case.* Have documentation and expert opinions readily available. Just seeing that you mean business and that you know what you're talking about (more homework) is the best way to make a stubborn dealer or manufacturer more cooperative.

The second option resides somewhere between the Manufactured Housing Board and going to arbitration (or court) in terms of seriousness—although it can also be used as a weapon of last resort. Using consumer "action" lines—complaining to local television stations and newspapers—is pretty much a hit-or-miss proposition. If you can convince the media to contact the dealer or especially the manufacturer, with the implicit understanding that a story is forthcoming about your plight, then chances are good that something will be done to correct any problems. This hits the company where they like it the least: in their pocketbook. A story about how they provided a shoddy home or left a customer in the lurch will impact future sales, and if even the local dealer isn't smart enough to care, the corporate headquarters almost certainly will. The problem is that such consumer lines receive a lot of complaints, and yours may not get considered. Try multiple outlets, as many as you can find. A second problem is the media outlet may consider the complaint unjustified after a cursory explanation from the manufacturer. If that's the case, ask the media to come to your home or look at your documentation of the problems. (Never send originals, only duplicates.) Consumer complaint reporters like simple situations (where they can't possibly end up looking like they were wrong) and are sometimes afraid to take on large companies that have lawyers on the payroll. Sometimes, just sending a copy (cc:) of your consumer complaint letters to the manufacturer's corporate headquarters can get results—even if the newspaper or television station never responds.

The final option may be limited by the contract you signed: *arbitration or judicial relief.* As noted earlier, many contracts now stipulate that you cannot seek judicial relief—that is, you can't sue the dealer or manufacturer in court. If things reach this stage, chances are you will need the services of an attorney. While you can represent yourself in either case, you most likely will be at a severe disadvantage when you go up against corporate attorneys who are specifically trained to fight this kind of case as well as being much more familiar with legal procedures in general. Choose attorneys wisely; all men may be created equal, but there is considerable qualitative variation in regard to attorneys. Word of mouth is often the best advertisement. You will probably have to pay several hundred dollars for a retainer fee in advance, although if judicial relief is an option and you have a good case an attorney may take the case on a contingency basis. Arbitration is a simpler procedure than a formal court case, and it is less likely to result in any substantial judgment against the company you are fighting. Don't expect any punitive damages or reimbursement for your attorney fees if you have to go this route, even if you have a complaint which has obvious merit. You should have this in mind *before* you sign a contract which forces you to accept arbitration.

Finally, some problems can be avoided altogether if they involve local ordinances. If your setup has been done incorrectly and you know it, be present when the local inspector comes out to perform the inspection. You may have to wait around for a while because the county office can't usually give you an exact time of day for the inspection, but it's worth it. Point out any mistakes— broken or missing piers, improper anchoring, missing septic clean-outs, etc. *Have the home's installation manual with you, and be prepared to show why the setup is wrong.* Code inspectors aren't usually experts in manufactured housing, but they will generally insist the setup is completed to the manufacturer's recommendations if they know what those requirements are. If the home doesn't pass inspection, the setup crew will have to fix any problems the inspector cites.

CHAPTER 13

Indoor Air Quality

By now you've hopefully learned a lot about mistakes the factory or the setup crew could make on your home, and you've learned how to spot and correct the various problems. There's another aspect of ownership that every prospective homeowner should be cognizant of as well which doesn't necessarily involve a mistake on the seller's part: indoor air quality. We've looked at a number of factors so far that indirectly affect this topic, but let's focus specifically on the important overall area of indoor air quality for a bit. Manufactured homes were once known for environmental problems because of materials like pressed boards which emitted high levels of formaldehyde and urea-formaldehyde foam insulation. There are still concerns in this area, and not just in manufactured homes: any new home is likely to have relatively high levels of potentially toxic chemicals in it. They come from the wood used in construction, the new carpets, any paint and caulk used, etc. The levels produced generally subside over time, but new homes invariably come with lots of new material and can quickly make many people uncomfortable or even unhealthy. The Environmental Protection Agency (EPA) states the immediate effects can include irritation of the eyes, nose, and throat, headaches, dizziness, and fatigue. Now factor in the reality that modern homes have much tighter construction and improved insulation, and you have a potential recipe for disaster. Little wonder that some scientific research shows *indoor air quality is up to five times more polluted than outside air*!

We can't cover everything about indoor air quality in this text, but we can discuss its importance to your health, look at a couple of the most worrisome concerns for the fledgling home owner, and discuss some possible solutions to the problems. Mostly, we'll be looking at the practicality of various solutions because this book's main focus is practical answers to what can be very difficult questions. Some are simply common sense — if you are one of the 33 percent of families who has at least one member

178

with a respiratory ailment (according to Venmar ventilation), you probably already know that having pets indoors (dander) or smoking indoors can exacerbate the problem.

The effects of poor indoor air quality can be immediate, or it can take years for them to fully manifest themselves. The EPA points out that individual sensitivity, age, and preexisting medical conditions all affect how indoor irritants impact you. The symptoms can also be quite insidious in that they can mimic other conditions—confusing both you and your doctor and confounding the treatment. *Recurring cases of the flu, persistent allergies, regular headaches, or a chronic cough can all be symptoms of toxic indoor air.* Immediate effects can sometimes show up after a single exposure to irritants or after repeated exposures. As we've seen, these include irritation of the eyes, nose, and throat, headaches, dizziness, and fatigue. Immediate effects are frequently short-term and treatable. If it can be identified, eliminating the person's exposure to the source of the pollution might be sufficient treatment. The EPA also observes that symptoms of some illnesses, including asthma, hypersensitivity pneumonitis, and humidifier fever, may also show up shortly after exposure to indoor air pollutants. If symptoms subside or dissipate completely when the person leaves the home for extended periods, chances are good that something in the home is causing or exacerbating the illness. These problems are little league in nature compared to what can happen to you or your loved ones, however:

> Other health effects may show up either years after exposure has occurred or only after long or repeated periods of exposure. These effects, which include some respiratory diseases, heart disease, and cancer, can be severely debilitating or fatal. It is prudent to try to improve the indoor air quality in your home even if symptoms are not noticeable. [Source: http://www.epa.gov/iaq/pubs/]

One of the first things you will notice in a new manufactured home is the pungent odor. It comes from an invisible gas and is related to the HUD required warning label you'll most likely find somewhere in or near the kitchen. (See the graphic on page 180.)

Formaldehyde — the very name sounds scary, doesn't it? This chemical is critical in the building materials industry and even in many household products. It's a by-product of combustion (thus cigarette smoking and fuel burning products like kerosene heaters also create formaldehyde in the home) and other natural processes and is found both indoors and out. The EPA points out it's a component of many glues and a preservative in some paints and coating products and is even used to give a per-

IMPORTANT HEALTH NOTICE

Some of the building materials used in this home emit formaldehyde. Eye, nose, and throat irritation, headache, nausea, and a variety of asthma-like symptoms, including shortness of breath, have been reported as a result of formaldehyde exposure. Elderly persons and young children, as well as anyone with a history of asthma, allergies, or lung problems, may be at greater risk. Research is continuing on the possible long-term effects of exposure to formaldehyde.

Reduced ventilation resulting from energy efficiency standards may allow formaldehyde and other contaminants to accumulate in the indoor air. Additional ventilation to dilute the indoor air may be obtained from a passive or mechanical ventilation system offered by the manufacturer. Consult your retailer for information about the ventilation options offered with this home.

High indoor temperatures and humidity raise formaldehyde levels. When a home is to be located in areas subject to extreme summer temperatures, an air-conditioning system can be used to control indoor temperature levels. Check the comfort cooling certificate to determine if this home has been equipped or designed for the installation of an air-conditioning system.

If you have any questions regarding the health effects of formaldehyde, consult your doctor or local health department.

This Notice is required by the DEPARTMENT OF HOUSING AND URBAN DEVELOPMENT and shall not be removed by any party until the entire sales transaction has been completed.

This formaldehyde warning is required in all new manufactured homes by the Department of Housing and Urban Development (HUD).

manent-press quality to clothing and draperies. Let's see what else the EPA has to say:

> In homes, the most significant sources of formaldehyde are likely to be pressed wood products made using adhesives that contain urea-formaldehyde (UF) resins. Pressed wood products made for indoor use include: particleboard (used as subflooring and shelving and in cabinetry and furniture); hardwood plywood paneling (used for decorative wall covering and used in cabinets and furniture); and medium density fiberboard (used for drawer fronts, cabinets, and furniture tops). Medium density fiberboard contains a higher resin-to-wood ratio than any other UF pressed wood product and is generally recognized as being the highest formaldehyde-emitting pressed wood product.
>
> Other pressed wood products, such as softwood plywood and flake or oriented strand board, are produced for exterior construction use and contain the dark, or red/black-colored phenol-formaldehyde (PF) resin. Although formaldehyde is present in both types of resins, pressed woods that contain PF resin generally emit formaldehyde at considerably lower rates than those containing UF resin. [Source: http://www.epi.gov/iaq/pubs/]

Oriented strand board is OSB — the same type flooring and exterior wrap I recommended earlier — and as you can see, it's not only more water resistant, it also emits less formaldehyde. Beginning in 1985, the Department of Housing and Urban Development has set specific limits on formaldehyde emissions resulting from plywood and particle board in manufactured homes, helping to alleviate the problem somewhat. The government-mandated formaldehyde warning also helps bring attention to the remaining danger. (The Council of American Building Officials' [CABO] code for site-built homes features no formaldehyde limits.) As the home ages, emissions from these wood products will also decrease. The same applies to the urea-formaldehyde foam insulation (UFFI) which was frequently installed in wall cavities in the 1970s — as time goes by, the emissions decrease steadily.

Some factors can intensify formaldehyde emissions as well, particularly in new homes. Some known factors are high heat, high humidity, and confined spaces with limited fresh ventilation. Formaldehyde can cause watering eyes as well as burning eyes and throat. It can also cause difficulty breathing and trigger asthma attacks. Anything over 0.1 parts per million is considered to be an elevated and dangerous level. People can also develop a particular sensitivity to formaldehyde — just as they can to many toxins. Formaldehyde also causes cancer in lab rats, so the odds are pretty good that it can do the same in larger, bipedal critters.

All right, now that we know it's bad, what do we do? If you're choosing materials for a new home, *use OSB wherever possible*. If you're adding on, remodeling, or building a new entertainment center, choose solid wood or OSB over products with urea-formaldehyde resins, or consider coating particle board material with a thick coating of *polyurethane*. Cover all exposed areas of the wood. If you know you're sensitive to formaldehyde, be extra careful to have excellent ventilation while applying the polyurethane (do it outside if at all possible) because *many such products emit substantial formaldehyde fumes before they are completely dry*. You don't want the cure to cause the illness. In a new home, *ventilate as much as possible*. When weather permits, open windows throughout new homes and turn on those ceiling fans. It will help to also have a couple of strategically placed window fans drawing in fresh air from the outside. While the home is airing out, spend a few hours in the garden or sipping tea under a shade tree. Keep newer homes from getting too hot inside by liberal use of air-conditioning when you aren't pumping fresh air through them, and if need be keep your humidity controlled by a home *dehumidifier*. If you do use a dehumidifier, make absolutely sure you drain and clean its collection tray frequently — or it will become a breeding ground for microorganisms that may make formaldehyde's curses seem relatively Pollyannaish. The EPA recommends keeping your home humidity level below 60 percent. You can buy an inconspicuous humidity gauge (or a large ornate one, if you prefer) at almost any store which carries a selection of thermometers. Put it in a central area of the home for best results.

By now, you probably also know I have a "thing" about water. It ruins the home structurally, it voids your warranty (even if the damage results from an improper dealer setup), and it can make you and your loved ones sick while you ponder what the problem is. Water damage in its various forms is always among the most common complaints in every survey done with manufactured home owners. As briefly noted previously in this book, water quickly results in the wicked stepchildren known as mold and mildew. Whereas formaldehyde is a gaseous chemical, mold and mildew are biological contaminants. Mold spores exist practically everywhere, both inside and outside your home. They are Lilliputian fiends that drift through the air effortlessly, and there is no practical way to eliminate them from your home. When these mold spores find excessive moisture or an accumulation of water, they begin to grow. They can undergo maturation on and actually digest food, paper, carpet, or wood.

The only realistic way to control mold is to control moisture. Fix leaky plumbing or any other water leaks in your home *immediately*. Dry wet areas within twenty-four hours if possible, within forty-eight hours at the most. Clean hard surfaces, like wood, which show mold growth with strong detergent or bleach, and make sure they dry completely. Use fans or small heaters to assist in drying. Absorbent materials, like carpet or insulation, which show any sign of mold growth are usually best replaced. It is virtually impossible to properly clean them.

The health effects from biological contaminants like mold are serious. Such pollutants may initiate allergic reactions, including hypersensitivity pneumonitis, allergic rhinitis, and asthma. Infectious illnesses (including influenza, measles, and chicken pox) are transmitted through the air. Mold and mildews also release disease-causing toxins. The EPA lists some possible symptoms of biological contaminants as sneezing, watery eyes, coughing, shortness of breath, dizziness, lethargy, fever, and digestive problems. Just as with formaldehyde, people can easily develop sensitivities to such biological toxins. While these pollutants may produce little or no visible symptoms in any given person over a period of time, the same person could quickly become very sensitive to the toxin, having severe allergic reactions to it. Other diseases, such as humidifier fever, result from exposure to microorganisms that are best known for growing in the ventilation systems of large buildings like schools but which can also be found in home heating and air conditioning systems, and even in home humidifiers (hence the name). As with other home contaminants, the young, the old, and those with preexisting medical conditions are most vulnerable to their effects.

The Environmental Protection Agency lists these ten things you should know about mold on their Web site:

1. Potential health effects and symptoms associated with mold exposures include allergic reactions, asthma, and other respiratory complaints.

2. There is no practical way to eliminate all mold and mold spores in the indoor environment; the way to control indoor mold growth is to control moisture.

3. If mold is a problem in your home or school, you must clean up the mold and eliminate sources of moisture.

4. Fix the source of the water problem or leak to prevent mold growth.

5. Reduce indoor humidity (to 30–60 percent) to decrease mold growth by: venting bathrooms, dryers, and other moisture-generating sources to the outside; using air conditioners and dehumidifiers; increasing ventilation; and using exhaust fans whenever cooking, dishwashing, and cleaning.

6. Clean and dry any damp or wet building materials and furnishings within twenty-four to forty-eight hours to prevent mold growth.

7. Clean mold off hard surfaces with water and detergent, and dry completely. Absorbent materials, such as ceiling tiles, that are moldy may need to be replaced.

8. Prevent condensation: Reduce the potential for condensation on cold surfaces (i.e., windows, piping, exterior walls, roof, or floors) by adding insulation.

9. In areas where there is a perpetual moisture problem, do not install carpeting (i.e., by drinking fountains, by classroom sinks, or on concrete floors with leaks or frequent condensation).

10. Molds can be found almost anywhere; they can grow on virtually any substance, provided moisture is present. There are molds that can grow on wood, paper, carpet, and foods.

Another handbill/warning is apt to be applied to the new home's interior as well. This one regards moisture. Do not expect a mea culpa, however; this flyer seems to blame any moisture problems on the government regulations or the usual and normal activities of the homeowner (breathing, cooking, showering, and laundry — if we could only cut back on *breathing* just a bit). Their recommendation? Ventilation. As we've noted, ventilation is indeed a healthy thing to have in your home, but your parents probably pointed out to you that leaving windows open both summer and winter tends to drain the proverbial pocketbook. So we're going to look at some more financially feasible solutions to indoor air quality shortly. There are answers available to the manufacturers and home owner that stop short of holding your breath and going about dirty. Some solutions have probably already come to mind regarding moisture, however. First, use a dehumidifier if necessary to keep home moisture under control. You should also make liberal use of the exhaust fans/vents which came with your home — when bathing or cooking turn on the exhaust fans. If you have a heated Jacuzzi in a large master bathroom, consider upgrading to a more powerful exhaust fan from a home improvement store. Make sure your dryer vent is properly connected to an outside vent, and make sure your home's skirting is adequately vented as well for control of moisture beneath the home.

I've described what I would consider to be the two major indoor air quality issues (formaldehyde and moisture control) in this field since 1985 when the new HUD standards took effect, and these would be potential issues in any home whether manufactured or not. One last specific issue I would like to quickly revisit involves that fireplace I recommended to you for ambience. Such fireplaces (and certainly kerosene heaters) emit a number of potentially dangerous products in addition to formaldehyde:

ATTENTION HOMEOWNER
EXTREMELY IMPORTANT
MOISTURE CONTROL

THE DEPARTMENT OF HOUSING AND URBAN DEVELOPMENT (HUD) ESTABLISHED HIGH INSULATION AND AIR INFILTRATION STANDARDS IN 1976. THE MANUFACTURER OF YOUR NEW HOME CONFORMS TO THESE STANDARDS, WHICH REQUIRE TIGHT CONSTRUCTION, LIMITING AIR INFILTRATION. THIS NATURALLY REDUCES AIR CIRCULATION AND INCREASES THE CHANCES OF CONDENSATION DAMAGE.

DURING HEATING SEASON, YOUR HOME MAY SHOW EVIDENCE OF EXCESSIVE MOISTURE BUILDUP. IT WILL BY YOUR RESPONSIBILITY TO PROVIDE FRESH AIR TO PREVENT CONDENSATION WHICH IS CAUSED BY BREATHING, LAUNDRY, COOKING, SHOWERS, ETC., PLUS THE HEATING OF PRE-HEATED AIR. A SLIGHTLY OPENED WINDOW SHOULD HELP REDUCE MOISTURE PROBLEMS.

DOCTORS LONG HAVE RECOMMENDED THAT FRESH AIR BE INTRODUCED INTO A HOME, EVEN IN COLD WEATHER. THIS IMPROVES AIR QUALITY, MAKING FOR A HEALTHIER ENVIRONMENT, AS WELL AS PREVENTING DAMAGING CONDENSATION.

TO BE REMOVED ONLY BY RETAIL PURCHASER

This HUD warning pertains to moisture control.

carbon dioxide, nitrogen dioxide, and particles. Remember that I recommended you make sure that the setup crew open any vents required by your fireplace? This vent is usually under the home and often arrives covered up from the factory. This dedicated exterior air supply is designed to help prevent "back-drafts" from the fireplace into your den or living room, meaning the contaminants largely go up the chimney and out of your home the way they should. Of course, portable kerosene heaters don't have any dedicated intake or exhaust vent, and they can also produce acid aerosols.

The Environmental Protection Agency recommends three strategies to reduce indoor pollutants and improve your indoor air quality: source control, ventilation improvements, and air cleaners. The EPA believes that the first, source control, is the most effective way for an individual home owner to improve indoor air quality. It involves eliminating or reducing the source of the pollutant. If the source is particle board with formalde-hyde or asbestos, the source might be completely sealed off or enclosed (as in our example with the polyurethane coating). Gas stoves can be adjusted so they produce fewer emissions. You can clean up water quickly to help discourage biological contaminants, keep pets outside, and strongly dis-courage or prevent smoking inside the home. Not only can source control be effective, it is probably the most cost-efficient solution.

Ventilation improvements are also important. Most home owners are more concerned with air temperature than with air quality for obvious financial reasons, and the vast majority of home heating and cooling sys-tems don't bring in much fresh outside air. As mentioned previously, lib-eral use of your bathroom and kitchen exhaust fans can help some. Fortunately for the owners of manufactured housing, this is another area where code actually favors them. According to the 1998 study *Factory and Site-Built Housing, A Comparison for the 21st Century*, which was prepared for HUD by the NAHB Research Center, Inc., HUD code requires mechan-ical ventilation to the outside of the home in both kitchens and bathrooms. The CABO code does not require venting to the exterior in kitchens, and in the bathrooms the presence of windows in a site-built home is consid-ered acceptable in lieu of a mechanical exhaust system. Open your win-dows up when weather permits, and use fans (especially window fans) to circulate the fresh air through the home — particularly if you're engaged in activities which produce lots of contaminants like painting or cooking. (Did the latter surprise you?) If you use window air conditioners, running them with the vent control open is somewhat less efficient, but it will force in fresh outside air. When possible, perform air-polluting activities out-side rather than inside. There are some better solutions starting to be implemented as well, but the initial cost is a critical factor for many home owners: energy-efficient heat recovery ventilators (or air-to-air heat exchangers). For more information about air-to-air heat exchangers, the EPA recommends contacting the Conservation and Renewable Energy Inquiry and Referral Service (CAREIRS), PO Box 3048, Merrifield, VA

22116. These systems can not only provide a constant supply of fresh air, but they can expel excess humidity and filter many indoor pollutants back to the outside.

The last strategy involves air cleaners. The EPA has this to say:

> There are many types and sizes of air cleaners on the market, ranging from relatively inexpensive table-top models to sophisticated and expensive whole-house systems. Some air cleaners are highly effective at particle removal, while others, including most table-top models, are much less so. Air cleaners are generally not designed to remove gaseous pollutants.
>
> The effectiveness of an air cleaner depends on how well it collects pollutants from indoor air (expressed as a percentage efficiency rate) and how much air it draws through the cleaning or filtering element (expressed in cubic feet per minute). A very efficient collector with a low air-circulation rate will not be effective, nor will a cleaner with a high air-circulation rate but a less efficient collector. The long-term performance of any air cleaner depends on maintaining it according to the manufacturer's directions. [Source: http://www.epa.gov/iaq/pubs/]

Since the small air cleaners are relatively ineffective (with the possible exception of modest areas), I'd like to focus on a broader potential solution: furnace filters or solutions built around the heating and air conditioning system. I've examined a plethora of filters and filtering equipment for the furnace, ranging from the simple spun fiberglass filters which can be bought for about 50 cents each (about $2 for a pack of 4), to whole-house, high efficiency particulate air filters (HEPA) which can easily cost $1,500 or more. To properly examine this field, we need to define some terms, including HEPA. A standard efficiency test for air filters is the DOP, or Di-octyl Phthalate efficiency test. It measures a filter's effectiveness against minute particles, which makes the HEPA standard a good measure of high efficiency filters. For HEPA certification, a filter has to trap more than 99.97 percent of 0.3-μm (micrometer) particles during a given DOP experiment. For reference, *respirable particles are smaller than 2.5 μm, or one millionth of a meter.* Larger particles than this are typically trapped in the nose or throat before they reach the lungs (*"Is It Worth Putting in a Better Furnace Filter?,"* Don Fugler, Home Energy Magazine Online May/June 2000). In late 1999, a new filter standard was adopted, ASHRAE 52.2 (ASHRAE: American Society of Heating, Refrigerating, and Air Conditioning Engineers). This latter standard specifies filter performance over various particle sizes and results in a *minimum efficiency reporting value,* or MERV score. Good filters will often display MERV scores now; the higher the number, the more efficient they are. There are also other filter standards which are less important now, such as the weight arrestance and the dust spot efficiency. The former simply measures how well a filter removes particles from the air by weight, but filters which score high on this value often do a poor job of filtering out respirable particles. Dust spot efficiency measures a filter's effectiveness on some respirable particles, but not accurately on those in the submicron range (less than one submicrometer as expressed in <1 µm). The following chart shows these various standards and should help you to evaluate filters more effectively. Note that MERV scores of 5–8 are shown for better residential filtration, and scores of 9–12 represent excellent residential filtration.

MERV Std. 52.2	Average Dust Spot Efficiency	Average Arrestance	Particle Size Ranges	Typical Applications	Typical Filter Type
17–20	99.97–99.999%	N/A	≤0.30 µm	International Standards Organization clean rooms	HEPA
				High-risk surgery	ULPA (ultra low penetration air)
				Hazardous materials	
13–16	80–95%	>98–99%	0.30–1.0 µm	Smoke removal General surgery Hospitals and health care Superior commercial	Rigid cell Rigid box Bag
9–12	40–75%	>95–98%	1–3 µm	**Superior residential** Better commercial Better industrial Pleated filter	Rigid cell Rigid box Bag
5–8	<20–35%	80–95%	3–10 µm	**Better residential** Commercial Industrial Paint booth	Pleated filter Pocket filter Cube filter Media panel filter
1-4	<20%	60–80%	>10 µm	**Residential** Light commercial Minimum standard	Spun fiberglass Washable

The more effective filters (especially the pleated ones) often have passive electrostatically charged fibers to help trap contaminants; more expensive solutions may feature active electric charging, that is, you literally plug the filter unit into an electrical outlet.

As you can see, unless you're doing home surgery, you're probably going to be looking for filters that range in effectiveness from 1 to 12 MERVs. One of the most common brands you'll encounter is likely to be Flanders—which makes many cheap fiberglass filters as well as their own line of pleated filters. They also make pleated furnace filters for other companies, including Arm & Hammer and Lysol. Other popular brands include 3M (who claim that their pleated filters outperform all other 1" filters) and Dupont (which features Oguard Odor Reduction). There's not much way to know whether or not the odor protection helps other than to try them in your home. Arm & Hammer filters (made with real baking soda) and Lysol filters (featuring a layer of antimicrobial protection) also promise help with household odors. There are a host of other filters on the market as well, including store brands and specialty filters. The Web Absorber Three Phase Electrostatic Control (and odor control) filter seems to be marketed at pet owners, and the HEPA-Pure pleated filter seems to be marketed at folks who, frankly, have a lot of money. (These cost around $50 to $60 each but claim they last up to a year or more.) This latter filter, which I found on a number of Internet sites, didn't list a MERV rating at all. The name also bothered me a bit—was this really a HEPA filter, or does the name only imply it? Judging by the ad at Exactair.com and other sites, the claim was made that this was the "most efficient filter you can use in your system." The ad also indicated it traps up to a "whopping 99.97 percent of particles over 1.3 microns in size." That sounds right, doesn't it? Didn't we say the HEPA standard was 99.97 percent? Actually, the real HEPA standard means a filter *has to trap more than 99.97 percent of 0.3 μm particles.* By my calculations, that means that numerous filters which cost only a fraction of that amount would do a better job of removing contaminants from your home's air. Neither would I recommend leaving any pleated filter in place for more than three months, unless you like paying higher utility bills and reduced efficiency. Filters which become overloaded with particles also create back-pressure on your HVAC system, which can strain your blower motor and cause premature failure. Pleated filters do clog less quickly than some other filter types because the pleated design gives them more surface area, but three months is the limit that almost every reputable manufacturer recommends.

Let's take two more examples, this time of specialty filters. The BoAir 5-Stage Electrostatic Filter is a permanent filter with a lifetime guarantee. I found it on sale for $79.95. The ad for this filter stressed that it had been performance tested at an independent laboratory, but it didn't list any MERV rating. Instead, it claimed that "up to 90 percent of contaminants were trapped during testing." This sounds like the old ASHRAE 52.1 weight arrestance standard. Looking at the previous chart, that would translate into a likely MERV score of approximately 7, lower than most of the disposable filters I found but adequate if it's accurate (arrestance is the worst way to judge a filter, nonetheless). This filter has to be washed regularly, however, and I would be more than reluctant to keep introducing substantial moisture in my home's heating and cooling system, even if the manufacturer claimed the product had antimicrobial protection. You could start breeding mold, mildew, and bacteria throughout your air system — which would then be blown throughout your home. To be fair let's examine one more filter: the EnviroSept Electronic Filter. These filters cost $365 each and plug into an AC outlet. No MERV score is listed for this filter either, but an arrestance of 99 percent and an efficiency of 70 percent is listed. That means it's probably more effective than the BoAir, but we don't know how effective the EnviroSept really is on submicron particles. Plus, this permanent filter requires "inexpensive disposable collector pads." They cost over $4.58 each (bought in sets of 12) and are replaced every one to two months. That comes to $36.64 a year (or $73.28 if you have a larger heating and air system which uses two filters). For under $16 per year, you could install, as frequently as the manufacturer recommends, Arm & Hammer MERV 8 filters, or Arm & Hammer MERV 10s for under $32 per year. The latter solutions don't require a large initial cash outlay and a drain on your electric bill, either. (Many electronic furnace filters, although reportedly not the EnviroSept, also produce ozone as a by-product.)

There are still other air-cleaning solutions for those who can afford them or who may literally need them because of health concerns. One example is the Pure Air HEPA Shield, a self-contained unit that attaches to your forced air heating/cooling system. The 600H model comes with its own 600 cubic feet per minute blower, and is rated for homes up to 2,500 square feet in size. According to the literature, it is a true HEPA filter, removing 99.97 percent of all allergy-causing particulates as well as odors and gases (including formaldehyde) using a granular filter. (See www.envirodoc.com/hepa-air-filter-600h.htm.) By-pass filters (these systems usually are by-pass systems; although the diagrams on the Web site wouldn't enlarge, so I can't determine exactly how this particular model works), though, by definition don't treat all the air as it travels through the ducts. If 50 percent of the air doesn't pass through the HEPA filter, for instance, you would cut the 99.97 percent efficiency rate in half. Following is a comparison of readily available filters at major stores. I've highlighted in bold what I believe are the best three bargains in terms of performance and cost.

Comparison of Readily Available Filters at Major Stores

MERV Rating	Brand	Life Span	Cost Each	Yearly Cost (assuming 2 filters required)
12	Dupont	90 days	$15.97	$127.76
12	3M Filtrete	90 days	$15.99	$127.92
11	**3M Filtrete**	**90 days**	**$9.99**	**$79.92**
11	Dupont	90 days	$10.99	$87.92
10	**Arm & Hammer**	**90 days**	**$7.96**	**$63.68**
10	Lysol	90 days	$7.99	$63.92
9	Web Absorber	90 days	$7.99	$63.92
8	**Arm & Hammer**	**90 days**	**$3.88**	**$31.04**
8	Dupont	90 days	$8.47	$67.76
7	Enviroflow	90 days	$5.96	$47.68
?	Flanders Pleated	60 days	$1.88	$22.56
?	Flanders EZ Flow	30 to 60 days	$0.56	$8.96

The stores I used for my small furnace filter survey were Lowes, Wal-Mart, and Target. This list in no way is meant to be a comprehensive listing of the various manufacturers' offerings. Both the Arm & Hammer filters seemed like relative bargains and, for a high performance filter, $9.99 seemed like a good price for the MERV 11 3M Filtrete. As with everything thing else, however, it pays to shop around. One of the stores I went to had the same 3M filter but was charging $12.88 for it — in this comparison that would add up to $23.12 more per year, easily making the Dupont MERV 11 the best value in its class. The better filters listed here should be fairly effective against particles as small as 1 micron which make their way into your heating and air-conditioning intake: mold spores, microscopic allergens, pollen (ragweed, tree, and grass), household fibers, dust mite debris, pet dander, and smoke from cooking or smoking. Their effectiveness would be very limited on bacteria, allergenic molds, lead dust, insecticide dust, and disintegrated feces (from litter boxes or mice).

Before the thought of microscopic monsters sends you out to your nearest store, however, and before we leave this chapter, let's take a brief step back. Don Fugler of *Home Energy Magazine* wrote an article in May/June of 2000 entitled, "Is It Worth Putting in a Better Furnace Filter?" The truth is, while specifications like MERV do simplify comparing individual filters, there isn't much data on real homes and real occupants. The Canada Mortgage and Housing Corporation (or CMHC, which is actually a department of the Canadian government) funded research into this very question, and Mr. Fugler's article reveals the results. This study tested filters ranging from $2 disposable filters to $700 electrostatic precipitator filters, as well as bypass filters which utilized the extremely efficient HEPA filters. Among the findings, filters do generally meet their rated specifications, and none of the filters tested appreciably reduced air flow rates (with the exception of a 4" thick commercial filter). In fact, some HEPA by-pass filters with their own fans may actually increase overall air flow, albeit at the price of more electricity. Despite the fact that most furnace filters do a good job of cleaning duct air, the results indicated that a *"furnace filter many meters away down a duct will not make a difference to the 'personal cloud' that occupants are creating just by getting out of bed, walking across the carpet, or making toast."* (Picture Pigpen from *Peanuts!*) Furnace filters have the most effect on particulates in your home's air when the fan is left on constantly. Since furnace fans typically consume 400 to 800 watts, that in itself could add a couple of hundred dollars per year to your energy bill, aside from the possible noise irritation of having your fan run constantly. If the extra air scrubbing ability is important to you, the study suggests installing a high-efficiency fan (an electronically commutated motor, or ECM fan, which only uses an average of 100 to 200 watts). The Canada Mortgage and Housing Corporation study concluded that to significantly reduce indoor particulate exposure, one should:

- remove footwear on entry;
- keep major dust generators out of the house (smoking, pets, etc.);
- keep dust collecting surfaces to a minimum (open shelves, carpets, upholstered furniture);
- frequently and thoroughly vacuum (using a vacuum with a HEPA filter or a central vacuum if possible);
- reduce particulate laden exterior air by closing windows, improving home "tightness," and using an intake filter on air supply;
- *use the most effective furnace filter your budget permits.*

CHAPTER 14

Making Your House a Home

At this point, you should congratulate yourself! You've done a lot of hard work, but hopefully it's going to be rewarding you for many years to come. Making a house a home is a very personal process, but there are some tips or hints I would like to suggest from experience which can make the overall process easier or otherwise enhance your new home. Some of these suggestions are specific to manufactured housing, and others are more generic, but many should be helpful to the new home owner.

First, set up a couple of trash cans in convenient locations for the workers and insist they use them. Otherwise, you will likely spend many hours picking up bottles, food wrappers, and cigarette butts in your yard. We had to go through setup twice, and the amount of trash was unbelievable. We even had to deal with discarded clothing and found socks in our back yard smeared with excrement. If the workers won't cooperate, talk to their supervisor or the home dealer. You might also want to buy an inexpensive "retrieving" magnet — the sort often found in discount tool catalogs. There were literally thousands of dropped/discarded nails and bolts in our yard all around the home. Tying a strong string to the eye bolt on the top of the powerful magnet makes cleanup of these dangerous items much easier — rather than bending down constantly, you simply drag it over the ground. Nails will quickly ruin your pneumatic lawn mower tires (or worse, your car tires), can be struck by lawn mower blades and injure others, or easily poke through soft-soled shoes and pets' pads. Pick up as many as you can.

"Pass" keys can be an issue as well. Setup people and salespeople frequently have master keys for your home (even if you custom order it). Master keyed locks are locks which open with more than one key. They are used for convenience, so employees don't have to carry a lot of keys. It's also common for work crews to leave the keys to your new home where anyone who might work on the setup can get to them for convenience —

taping them to the inside of the electrical panel is a common practice, for instance. That means that any worker who might want to get into your home at any time in the future for nefarious reasons has only to come back at night and steal or copy the key. Even workers who didn't personally work on your home, but who have worked for the dealership in the past, will know the location they use to store the keys on-site. There are a lot of disgruntled employees who work in this industry already, and if you keep a watchful eye on them as they work on your home, some of them probably won't be very pleased with you to start with. Theft (or worse) is a real possibility. (Don't forget our multiple-felony burglar salesman from the chapter on cases.) *Change or re-key your locks soon after moving in.*

If you re-key, have all the locks keyed alike so one key will fit all your locks, and have deep cuts placed next to shallow cuts (which makes the lock much harder to pick). While you're checking out those manufacturer lock sets, closely examine each key-way to make sure all your lock sets were installed right-side up. Manufacturers frequently install them with the lock pins on the bottom — which causes dust, grit, and moisture to slip into the pin chambers and quickly affects the smooth operation of the lock and, in time, frequently causes complete failure of the lock set (this includes dead-bolts). If the cuts on your key don't face upward when you insert it into the lock, either make the dealer fix them properly or have a locksmith do it when you either re-key or upgrade your locks as described. If the dealer balks at this, offer to have a locksmith explain the reasoning for it. Just showing that you know what you're talking about and that you can back it up usually works. If you're fairly handy with tools, you may be able to do the work yourself. You'll need a Phillips screwdriver and a hammer for the most basic lock upgrade situations, but you

The top key here was an actual example of a key used in a new 2003 manufactured home — and could be picked open by the average elementary school kid in many neighborhoods. There were only two depths of cut used, and a straight piece of metal inserted into the lock could have lined up the pins well enough to open it. Worse, it was a master keyed lock, so other key combinations could open it as well. The second key has been re-cut for a new combination. This five-pin lock now uses five different depths, and shallow cuts are next to deep ones. This lock would now be very difficult to open without the proper key.

may need a wood chisel or more specialized tools for some installations (for example, if you're working with a metal covered door). Kwikset lock-sets are sold in multipacks at home improvement stores and major chains like Wal-Mart. You can buy a package of two entryway lock sets and two matching deadbolt locks all for only $39. They are superior in quality to the ones that come on a home as standard equipment, and they come keyed alike. Look at the keys in the blister pack before you buy it, and make sure the key cuts vary enough to make them resistant to lock-picking as described previously.

This security bar (in the center of the picture) is no eyesore.

You might want to pick up a security bar for your patio door while you're at the home improvement store, too. They are inexpensive, and easy to install. Security bars are most effective near the center of the door, and consider placing it parallel to one of the sliding door's internal supports. The result is that the security bar does little to detract from the appearance of the door — in fact, it's nearly invisible to the casual observer. Also for security and convenience, don't forget to pick up some motion detector floodlights for those eaves if you had them prewired when you custom ordered your home. Floodlights come with both round and rectangular bases. If possible, match the base of the security lights to the shape of the electrical box the factory installed under your eaves.

Pests like mice can quickly become a problem even in a new home. Before the skirting is installed, buy some mouse bait and place it on top of some strategically spaced support piers. This will help intercept mice before they can slip inside. Even if you do this, there's no guarantee you won't receive some free mice with your new home — they are fairly common in factories. Keep an eye out for droppings in your kitchen and near water sources. Rodents spread disease, they can damage your new home, and dead rodents in hidden spaces can make you wish you lived somewhere else (the smell can be atrocious). For the latter reason, if mice do get inside or come with the house, use traps rather than poison. Another tremen-

This little fellow rode all the way from Tennessee to South Carolina in a new home. The telltale droppings revealed the presence of unwanted tenants.

dous help with pests of all kinds (as well as insulation) is Great Stuff or some generic equivalent. This is self-expanding foam sealant in a can, and you can use it to close up any holes where pipes or wires enter either your subfloor or your perimeter skirting.

Save any leftover brick, shingles, and vinyl siding. The factory usually includes more shingles and siding than required to finish the home's setup, and the mason is also likely to have brick left over. You've already paid for these items, so you should be allowed to keep them. All can come in very handy if you need to make repairs in the future or if you plan to add a covered porch. They'll save you money and will match your existing materials perfectly — something that's sometimes hard to do five or ten years later. If you stay on good terms with the trim crew, you can also get some matching wall putty and ceiling repair material. They probably have these items in bulk and will be glad to provide you with enough to meet your needs. Again, not only will this save you money when you need to make repairs, it should match without a trial-and-error process. As soon as you start decorating, holes are going in that new wallboard, and some are almost certainly going in the wrong place. You are also going to find some staples that you missed during the walk-through that need to be covered up.

You might want to (or need to if money's tight) run telephone wires yourself instead of paying the phone company. It's easily accomplished before any skirting is put up. Most likely the manufacturer will just have the wires hanging down about a foot beneath the home at the exterior walls in the vicinity of any rooms with phone jacks. You can get weatherproof phone line connectors at Radio Shack, and phone line is available at many stores including Wal-Mart and home improvement stores. It requires only basic skills, and any good Radio Shack employee should be able to answer most uncertainties you might encounter. Running the line yourself to the phone company's outside box can save you considerable money — a call to your telephone service provider can tell you exactly how much. You'll need pliers for the weatherproof connectors and a screwdriver for the phone company box. We had three phone jacks, and we saved about $200 by doing the external wiring ourselves. It only took about an hour to run all three lines. Keep the wire away from the ground, and don't let it dangle loosely under the home — it's usually easy to run it between the belly board and the metal frame.

One thing you want to test early is your thermostat to make sure it's accurate. Standard mechanical thermostats from the factory are usually very cheap, but most heating/AC companies will replace them for free with a better one if you have any trouble with it when you first move in. If your thermostat seems to be inaccurate or unreliable, call the heating and air-conditioning vender as soon as possible. A digital thermostat detects temperature electronically and is better than standard thermostats; a programmable digital thermostat is best and can help you reduce your heating and cooling bills. In fact, *Energy Star programmable thermostats can reduce your utility bill by up to 33 percent*. If you notice any unusual spike in your utility bill, check underneath the home again to make sure your crossover HVAC connections are still air tight. Also, changing your air filter regularly will save money.

Most people who find themselves buying a new home also find themselves buying a lot of light bulbs. Consider buying compact fluorescent light bulbs (CFLs) if you can afford them initially. Prices for these have declined considerably over recent years, and they will more than pay for themselves because of their increased efficiency. Expect to save *about $25 for each one you install* over the life of the bulb, which typically lasts anywhere from five to seven years. Many fluorescent bulbs now can be safely used in totally enclosed fixtures, although they can't be used with dimmer switches. Ceiling fans can make attractive room additions and can also save substantial amounts of energy. One fan manufacturer (Hunter) contends the wind-chill effect from a ceiling fan can make a room feel eight degrees cooler in summer. *Ceiling fans can save up to 40 percent on summer cooling costs*, and by reversing them to push down and disperse warm air trapped near the ceiling in winter they can *save up to 10 percent off heating bills in wintertime*. While you're shopping, keep in mind that flush mount ceiling fans will not work on cathedral ceilings. Whether you're installing thermostats, light bulbs, or fans, look for the government's Energy Star label. It will save you money, and it will help save energy resources while simultaneously reducing pollution. It's a win-win situation. While we're on the subject of lighting, replace the inexpensive factory exterior porch lights with better ones from a home improvement store. It will really help the appearance of your new home. Better porch lights also offer options like motion detection and automatic dusk-to-dawn operation.

If you like your water very hot, you may need to open the water heater compartment and turn up the thermostat. The manual included with your home should provide instructions if you need them. The default factory setting is limited for safety reasons, although for many people it's entirely sufficient. The Environmental Protection Agency recommends a setting of 120 degrees, unless you use a dishwasher that does not have a preheater, in which case you may need hotter water to properly clean your dishes. While you're there in the water heater compartment, you may want to wrap it in an insulation blanket — an economical item which, once again, you can obtain at your local home improvement store. Also insulate the first five feet of pipe (both hot and cold). A programmable thermostat is another possible option for your water heater. Water heaters can consume between 15 percent to 25 percent of your total utility bill, or about $200 per year. The EPA estimates high-efficiency units can save homeowners anywhere from $20 to $100 of this amount.

Aesthetically speaking, windows and window treatments are among the important elements in the home. Most manufactured homes include plastic miniblinds. As mentioned previously, these are blinds of the same quality as those that sell for about $3 at home improvement stores. Metal miniblinds cost considerably more but look many times more attractive and are far easier to properly clean. The cheaper plastic blinds are prone to quickly taking on a mottled or blotchy appearance. They also are merely light filtering as opposed to room-darkening. Buy metal blinds for any rooms which are to be used for entertaining, and purchase room-darkening blinds for any bedrooms. (A better grade of plastic room-darkening blinds can be purchased for about half the price of metal blinds.) Measure the width of your windows before you go shopping so you can put the new blinds *inside* the window casements as opposed to over them. Carefully putty over any exposed hardware and staple holes which are left (with the putty you entreated from your trim person, or else you'll need to pick that up also while you're at the store). Patio door blinds can also be replaced for as little as $25 with much better vinyl ones. The fabric ones factories typically use break extremely easily and typically block very little light.

While on the subject of window treatments, drapes may be a problem area. The factory drapes are, of course, cheap and often poorly placed. (Our curtain rods attached near the ceiling, well over a foot above the windows.) You probably will want to replace the factory drapes anyway, so you might want to see how much credit you can get for them if you leave them off your home. Alternatively, you could replace them gradually, starting in the most important rooms, as recommended earlier with the carpet. Also with carpet, don't forget to use vinyl runners or throw rugs in high traffic areas with factory carpet — and if you have a rolling office chair to use with a home computer, be sure to put a heavy duty vinyl chair mat under the chair. The chair will roll much easier and, otherwise, the carpet under the chair will be quickly destroyed.

If you are willing to shop around, there are a lot of items you can pick up for your new home that will add considerably to both its functionality and attractiveness for a relatively small amount of money. Here are three handy examples which cost $100 altogether. (See the accompanying photographs.) First is an oak wall unit which was placed in a bathroom. The top shelf provides a good location for decorative items; it includes a handy towel bar, and it provides plenty of enclosed storage space for personal items. It also matches the home's existing molding, and it only costs $40 at K-Mart. Second, a Hampton Bay fan from Home Depot costs about $45. This was placed in a kitchen. Not only does it provide air circulation to displace the kitchen heat and provide extra light over the kitchen island but its stylish black blades and wire mesh light covers blend with the kitchen decor perfectly. Finally, we added a dimmer switch to the dining room light fixture which came with the home. The light fixture is identical to one which was featured on The Learning Channel's *Trading Spaces* show (where neighbors redecorate rooms in each other's homes). Although the fixture really looks great, as one of the show's designers noted it produces enough light to illuminate a ballpark. The dimmer switch lets you go from floodlight bright to subdued romantic overtones or anywhere in between. All of these items can be installed by the average do-it-yourself handyperson with minimal hassle. The fan we installed is small and lightweight; however, some of the larger fans can take a little muscle to hold them up until they are secured.

This solid oak wall cabinet matches this home's trim perfectly and only costs $40 at K-mart.

Remember, however, to always *double-check that the power is turned off* whenever you work with electricity, and follow local codes as required. Home improvement stores offer regular free classes if you need a little help with the ins and outs.

Left: The wire mesh and black blades on this small but stylish fan blend well with kitchen decor while providing extra light and air circulation for ony $45. *Right:* This faux antique light fixture came with the home, but the lumens generated overwhelmed the dining room. The solution was a dimmer switch for under $15.

We've talked about finished drywall or wallboard before, and it's frequently the major issue for people who are buying a manufactured home because it looks better and isn't always an option (or is too expensive to consider). Manufactured homes typically come with thin trim strips covering the gap between the four-foot sections of wallboard. As pointed out previously, you may be able to find independent contractors who will do this work for much less than the manufacturer or your setup crew would charge. (Our setup crew quoted $6,000 versus $1,800 for an independent contractor for three rooms.) Another option for those on a budget is to do the majority of drywall work themselves. It's not too hard to put up the drywall or to paint it — the skill is involved in doing the tape and texture, or getting the seams properly covered. If you hire an expert just for that aspect of the work you can save a great deal of money. While you're inside the walls, you may want to go a step further. Let's say you have a 15' × 15' master bedroom in one corner of your home (the usual location for the master bedroom) that you want to redo in finished drywall. If you have R-11 insulation in your exterior walls, when you pull off the wallboard to expose the inside of the exterior walls, you might want to replace the insulation with superior R-15 — it fits in the same width wall. Then what should you do with the leftover R-11? Place it in the bedroom's two interior walls! (Interior walls are normally hollow.) The result is that your bedroom has much better insulation all around, and has added soundproofing. That way your spouse can sleep soundly when you're staying up late to catch that movie you've been wanting to see. Merely replacing the standard wallboard with thicker material will also help considerably with sound insulation.

If you couldn't get a roof steeper than a 3:12 pitch (and some models simply aren't available with any other roof pitch), then you may find that water flows back against your eaves rather than dripping off the edge of your gutters. I've heard various suggestions on the best solution to this, but most of them are either cost prohibitive or could possibly cause problems in their own right. My suggestion would be to buy a high grade of clear silicone caulk and run about a ¼" bead all the way along the bottom of the shingles about ¼" to ½" from the edge. The principle is rather like that of a drip loop in an electrical line — theoretically, when the water reaches the raised bead, it will fall straight down rather than continuing along the bottom of the shingle to the house. If you've already put up gutters (and discovered the 3:12 pitch renders them virtually useless), do you need to remove them to apply the caulk? Maybe not. Instead, attach a piece of clear flexible tubing about 6" long over the tip of the tube of caulk (slide it on until it's very tight). That way, you can bend the tubing over the gutters and up to the shingles without removing the former. If the caulk is going to show, try to apply it as neatly as possible. Gutters will usually obscure the caulk completely, so tidiness in that case is not as much of a concern as effectiveness against water is.

While you're up there around the soffit, you may notice that the white perforated metal sheeting that covers and ventilates the eaves often isn't flush — where the pieces join, one may hang an inch or two below the other. It looks unsightly, and you can easily fix it by screwing in a couple of #8 ½" white gutter screws wherever you see the gaps. Just screw them into a hole in the lower sheet until they go into a hole in the upper piece. It leaves a very professional appearance. Whenever you are using an extension ladder to do this type of work, put a couple of rubber boots (available at hardware or home improvement stores) over the ladder ends so you don't damage your siding. Alternatively, you can duct tape a couple of old towels over them. Make sure any setup workers use care when using ladders on the home as well.

Before you're done, you're probably going to be adding a larger rear or side deck (your setup crew will usually provide a small landing only, or just basic steps if your local codes permit that), and you may want to build a front porch and extend that dormer you ordered out over it so that you have an attractive sitting area out of the rain. It will break up the boxy lines of your home and enhance the appearance considerably. If you forgot to order a dormer, then your front porch cover will look less natural, or you'll have to add one at considerable expense. Foresight pays, so from the very beginning of the home-buying process you need to be thinking about what you want your home to be like in the end.

Conclusion

Buying a home is a huge investment, whether it's site-built or factory-built. I've tried to stress the importance of doing research — or homework — in this book because that's the only safe way to make such a consequential decision. The bulk of consumer information for purchasing a manufactured home is condensed here in this text for you, but you will still need to take stock of your particular requirements. *Knowledge is power, so don't be caught short of it regarding what may be the largest single purchase of your life.* Manufactured home dealers count on customer ignorance to make the majority of their sales and their profit.

This book also strived to exemplify ways to *save money.* That's the single most important reason people turn to manufactured housing. A relatively inexpensive home in and of itself does not automatically translate into savings, however. You have to first make sure the home you purchase will be properly built and set up and energy efficient enough so that you can afford the utility bills. Then you have to be careful the dealer doesn't take financial advantage of you, and finally you have to fight to make sure your loan is competitive. Through all of this, the burden weighs solely on the consumer. The sheer number of repossessions in this industry illustrates that no one else has been looking out for the consumer — the dealers or the finance companies certainly haven't been. Then there are a hundred other ways to save money, from wisely choosing home options to making extra payments when you can to adding extra insulation or doing some of the work yourself.

Having gone through the process, I've learned the importance of being proactive and assuming the responsibility for making sure I got a good home and had it set up properly. We've looked at *Consumer Reports* and Foremost Insurance surveys earlier, but my firsthand experience has taught me not to discount Consumers Union's December 2002 findings: (1) one third of respondents were more dissatisfied than satisfied with their new manufactured home, (2) 17 percent were *completely* dissatisfied, and (3) a whopping 79 percent had experienced significant problems. What's more, Consumers Union found 30 percent of home owners were *completely* dissatisfied with warranty work on their new homes and "largely ineffective regulation of the manufactured housing industry" (see http://www.consumersunion.org/other/mh/paper-pr.htm). This study is bolstered by a survey taken by the American Association of Retired Persons (AARP) of manufactured home owners of *all* ages; in fact, the parallel findings between them are almost uncanny at times. AARP found 77 percent of manufactured home owners reported at least one major problem, and 57 percent reported multiple problems. Even though 95 percent of homeowners in the AARP reported having warranties, only 35 percent of major problems referenced above were fixed under warranty — the rest were either fixed at the homeowner's expense (31 percent) or not at all (30 percent). As Dirty Harry might say, "Are you feeling lucky?" You don't have to gamble on the biggest financial decision of your life if you've done your homework and you *take charge of the process* as opposed to being conducted through it like a sacrificial lamb.

If the manufactured housing industry ever hopes to shake the inferiority complex it has fought for decades now, it has a simple solution at hand. They *can* make a quality product, and it is possible to set them up properly. We've seen a manufactured home serve as a governor's mansion, and we've seen that they can last just as long as site-built homes. A more thorough commitment to quality might raise the price of the average home by a few thousand dollars but would be well worth the added cost to the consumer. (This book has also taught that even now for a few hundred extra dollars, you can enjoy options that will add tremendous value to your investment and your enjoyment of it.) Everyone in the industry from the salespeople to the company presidents also needs a new *attitude*— they ironically and quite literally treat their customers like proverbial "trailer park trash." They lie to customers; they bully them; they assume customers are ignorant and trick them in the worst ways. It is an undeserved attitude in most instances, and it only limits the manufactured housing companies' market share. The industry negates its inherent competitive advantages by alienating many educated consumers. Many disgusted customers give up considering manufactured homes when they discover how the system operates. If, as our dealer said, the legion of defects and problems with his service and quality were due to "bad karma," perhaps he should consider that karma is the direct result of our own past actions (or that you reap what you sow). If manufacturers and dealers were to treat their customers and their employees with more respect, I suspect they themselves would be surprised by the rewards that might engender for themselves as well as their customers.

Because the industry is unlikely to change without more outside influence (and why should it change what has been such a profitable way of business), I would make several recommendations for legislators and consumers at large to pursue. First, *every* state should have a state administrative agency — not just 37 states— and they each should have a stronger mandate, more active involvement in the process, and more of a consumer-protection orientation. Not just safety complaints should be followed up on, and heavier fines need to be levied. (A search of South Carolina records found that $500 fines are typical for a wide range of offenses. Why should a dealer or manufacturer care about the law if so much more money is to be made by breaking it?) Product defects and negligence should have serious repercussions. Salespersons and dealership managers should be held to a much higher ethical standard than they currently are. All homes should be examined by *independent* inspectors for safety and quality, both in the factory and on-site — using the money levied from violations to subsidize the inspections. Under the current system, HUD allows either state governments or third party inspectors to check quality at the plants. We've seen how lax the state agencies have been, and the third party inspectors frequently "serve at the pleasure of the manufacturer, are paid by them, and can be fired by them" ("Paper Tiger, Missing Dragon," Consumers Union Southwest Regional Office, November 2002). Second, because many structural problems are hidden in manufactured homes and because of the industry's past record, longer warranties need to be mandated. Covering only 90 days for setup and one year for the home is really outrageous. Would you buy a new car with a 90-day warranty? Many problems, like settling caused by a second-rate setup, may not manifest themselves for months or even years. A setup warranty for one year and a five-year structural warranty would be much more equitable, and the trend for a few companies moving in this direction already is encouraging. Third, because frame flex is so detrimental to the structure of manufactured homes, HUD needs to mandate that the minimum lumber grade manufacturers can use is grade #2; utility or stud grade lumber should be banned. For the same reason, it should be a violation punishable by a fine to traverse obstacles like ditches without proper support (heavy duty ramps). Fourth, retailers should be forced to accept payments in installments rather than having 100 percent of the financing up front. If they refuse to take a letter of acceptance from an independent bank (as discussed in "Who Owns the Bank?"), then they should accept one-third of the funds as a down-payment, one-third after the keys are turned over, and one-third when an independent agent verifies any needed repairs are complete. This change in the incentive system alone would make a tremendous difference in the way dealers operate, while causing extremely little bona fide hardship on the dealers. The sooner a dealership has the home properly set up, the sooner it will get paid in full. Fifth, manufacturers should not be allowed to force arbitration or insurance on consumers—especially not in the deceptive manner they do now. If a manufacturer wants to reduce liability in this way, then it should offer customers a discount for accepting such a contract. As James Madison said, "In suits at common law, between man and man, the trial by jury, as one of the best securities to the rights of the people, ought to remain inviolate." Finally, given the long history of problems within this industry, HUD needs to maintain detailed records of complaints and violations broken down by manufacturer and dealerships which are *open to public scrutiny*. Preferably, it should be provided in an easily accessible manner, such as an Internet database so consumers will have broad access to it. This would serve a dual purpose; not only would it make consumers more aware of problematic companies, but it would also be an incentive for manufactured home companies to work to keep their reputation clean. "Customer satisfaction" might become a meaningful term to the dealerships and factories, as opposed to meaningless advertising doggerel like "dream home." The ultimate purpose of all of these proposals is to impel *honesty* on an industry that is reluctant to voluntarily embrace it.

Moreover, if a groundswell of support can be mustered to bring about these needed changes, that movement should then be directed at the insurance industry, which currently charges considerably higher premiums on manufactured homes than for equivalent coverage on site-built homes. The industry gets away with this because of structural concerns which would be eliminated with better regulation and inspection of manufactured home setups. This excuse needs to be taken away from the insurance companies. The long-overdue changes which have finally begun to open up competitive financing options for manufactured homes need to migrate to the insurance industry, and then finally manufactured housing can present an economical alternative in every sense of the word.

Until such changes are wrought, however, all is not lost. You can defeat the industry at its own game even though the deck seems stacked against you *if* you know what to ask for, what to look for, and how to deal with the system. With current interest rates and pricing, it's quite possible to get a $100,000 manufactured home for around $500 a month (before insurance and taxes). For that amount of money, if you carefully do your homework, you can buy an exceedingly nicely equipped, well constructed, and spacious home. In the case of my family, everyone who has visited always comments how beautiful our home is, and we have the added satisfaction of knowing that the construction is 16" on center and that we have extra insulation. It's a custom home built to our requirements. You can win against the odds as well if you follow these guidelines. On our replacement home, the trim person we had requested to finish out our home commented to us that he had never seen anyone "get so much" out of a manufactured home dealer/factory. We had gotten things fixed properly that other customers weren't able to and had company officials jumping through the hoops rather than smirking at us. If you are willing to exercise due diligence, purchasing a manufactured home is a splendid way to get a lot more home for considerably less money. *The knowledge you need is here, if you provide the required tenacity you too can swim with the sharks and end up feasting on shark steaks!*

Sample Requirements List

This appendix contains a sample requirements list for prospective manufactured home buyers as discussed in "Doing Your Homework." This list will differ from yours, but it is meant to give you an example of how a well-made home might be optioned out. You can easily draw up your own form on a computer or by hand on a legal pad. Remember to *make a notation whenever an option you really want is not available*— don't assume you'll remember. After a few visits to dealerships, things can get pretty confusing. Make copies of your version of the form, and then fill it out for every model you're interested in at every dealership. *Never let anyone from any dealership see your notes from any other dealership.*

Home Requirements

Model # :_____ Lot: _____

Salesperson: _____ Base Price: _____

	Standard Feature?	Cost?
Tongue & groove OSB flooring (length of warranty?)	Y / N	
Full OSB wrap around home exterior	Y / N	
All wall studs must be 16" on center	Y / N	
Roof trusses placed 16" on center	Y / N	
2" × 8" floor joists	Y / N	
30 PSF roof load	Y / N	
Shingled roof (roofing paper used? length of warranty?)	Y / N	
Wire & brace for fans in every bedroom, den, & living room	Y / N	
Wire & brace for floodlights on all four exterior home corners	Y / N	
40-gallon hot water heater (energy efficient?)	Y / N	
Insulation: R-28 (roof), R-13 (wall), R-21 (floor)	Y / N	
Perimeter heat ducts	Y / N	
Thermopane Low-E windows	Y / N	

	Standard Feature?	Cost?
All exterior doors 36"	Y / N	
Large dormer over front door	Y / N	
Residential 3" crown molding	Y / N	
6-panel interior doors	Y / N	
Carpet upgrade	Y / N	
Main water cut-off & water cut-offs at all wet locations	Y / N	
Porcelain sinks & toilets	Y / N	
Fiberglass tubs	Y / N	
Raised-panel solid oak kitchen cabinets	Y / N	
Basic kitchen appliance package	Y / N	
Sliding patio door placed off dining room	Y / N	
Fireplace (full stone hearth)	Y / N	
Water & electrical outlets on both sides of house (4 total)	Y / N	

Setup (including brick underpinning, brick color _____,
   2 access doors & skirting vents as needed, poured perimeter
   foundation, 3.5 ton AC/heat pump, 4' × 4' landings with
   railings at each door, set up to county code)   NA

Amount to Add to Base Price: $ _____
Total price of home with setup & necessary options: $ _____

APPENDIX B

Sample Wish List

A wish list consists of things you'd like to have in your new home if you can afford them. Even if you can afford them and you know it, it makes sense to itemize in some way because otherwise you have no way of knowing whether or not you're being overcharged. Chances are, you'll end up choosing some of these and eliminating others. It should logically build on the requirements list (Appendix A) in some ways. For instance, you may decide you *require* a minimum 30 PSF roof load rating, but you would *like* to have a 40 PSF roof load if it's affordable. If the standard roof load rating is 20 PSF, and you put 30 PSF on your requirements list, then make sure on the wish list you only put the difference in cost of a 40 PSF versus a 30 PSF (as opposed to the standard 20 PSF)—otherwise you'll think these options are more expensive than they really are. Many other items on this second list will be totally independent, such as the addition of a garbage disposal. It doesn't hurt here to get jiggy with it, you're only window shopping. So ask about everything you're interested in, and then pick the items that you find you can afford and that you like the most. *Once again, never let anyone from any dealership see your notes from any other dealership.*

Home Wish List

Model # :_____ Lot: _____
Salesperson: _____ Base Price: _____

	Standard Feature?	Cost?
Minimum stud size 2" × 4" in all walls (interior & exterior)	Y / N	
40 PSF roof load	Y / N	
R-15 insulation in walls—if not an option, see next item	Y / N	
6" thick exterior walls with R-19 insulation (R-28, R-19, R-21)	Y / N	
4:12 roof pitch	Y / N	

	Standard Feature?	Cost?
Baseboard molding	Y / N	
Full-length interior doors (consider return air)	Y / N	
Den, living room, & master bedroom done in finished drywall	Y / N	
Upgraded kitchen appliance package	Y / N	
Garbage disposal installed	Y / N	
Washer & dryer	Y / N	
50-gallon hot water heater (energy efficient?)	Y / N	
Graduated heating ducts	Y / N	
Enlarge closet in one bedroom to full length of wall	Y / N	
Bay window in living room	Y / N	
Fan-shaped windows added over den windows	Y / N	
Hardwood flooring in foyer & dining room	Y / N	
Raised dining room floor	Y / N	
Jacuzzi tub in master bath	Y / N	
Glass skylight over master bath	Y / N	

Amount to add to base/setup/required options price: $ _____

State Administrative Agencies for Manufactured Housing

Thirty-seven states have state administrative agencies (SAAs) to assist consumers with complaints regarding manufactured housing. State administrative agencies are more commonly referred to as manufactured housing boards or commissions. These agencies are the result of a partnership between state and federal government. While the federal government, or specifically the U.S. Department of Housing and Urban Development (HUD), only regulates problems specifically originating during the home's manufacture, these various state agencies may also regulate retailers, transporters, and installers (setup crews). Therefore, you will need to communicate with your state's contact to find out what problems are covered in your area if you live in one of the thirty-seven states. If your state doesn't provide a SAA, or if your SAA fails to address your concerns, you may contact HUD directly. (See the last entry for HUD contact information.) This is what HUD states about the complaint process:

> The extent to which HUD can help a homeowner resolve a complaint depends on the seriousness of the problem. In cases where safety-related defects in homes create an unreasonable risk of injury or death to the occupants, manufacturers must correct the defect in a short period. HUD cannot require correction unless the defects were introduced into the home during the manufacturing process. The on-site installation of a manufactured home is not regulated by HUD.
>
> If a problem arises with a manufactured home, the first contact should be the retailer. Most problems can be eliminated quickly. If the retailer cannot help, the second contact should be the manufacturer. Manufacturers, for the most part, are quick to respond to consumers.
>
> It is important to put a complaint in writing. Also, make a copy

to keep with your records. The letter should include the serial number of the home with a list of the problems. List any known factors that contributed to the problem. Also list any secondary issues related to the problem.

Source: http://www.hud.gov:80/offices/hsg/sfh/mhs/mhssaa.cfm

State	State Administrative Agency
Alabama	Mr. Jim Sloan, Administrator Alabama Manufactured Housing Commission 350 S. Decatur Street Montgomery, AL 36104-4306 PH: (334) 242-4036 ext. 22 or 25 FAX: (334) 240-3178
Alaska	Use HUD address following.
Arizona	Mr. N. Eric Borg, Director Arizona Dept. of Building & Fire Safety Office of Manufactured Housing 1100 West Washington, Suite #100 Phoenix, AZ 85007 PH: (602) 364-1028 FAX: (602) 364-1052
Arkansas	Mr. Whit Waller, Director Arkansas Manufactured Home Commission 523 S. Louisiana Street, Suite 500 Lafayette Building, AR 72201-5705 PH: (501) 324-9032 FAX: (501) 374-7874
California	Mr. Richard Weinert, SAA Administrator Dept. of Housing & Community Development Manufactured Housing Section P.O. Box 31 Sacramento, CA 95812-0031 PH: (916) 445-3338 FAX: (916) 327-4712
Colorado	Mr. Tom Hart, Director Housing Division, Dept. of Local Affairs 1313 Sherman Street, #518 Denver, CO 80203-2244 PH: (303) 866-2033 FAX: (303) 866-4077
Connecticut	Use HUD address following.
Delaware	Use HUD address following.
District of Columbia (Washington, D.C.)	Use HUD address following.

State	State Administrative Agency
Florida	Mr. Edward D. Broyles, Bureau Chief Bureau of Mobile Homes & RV Division of Motor Vehicles 2900 Apalachee Parkway, Room A-129 Tallahassee, FL 32399-0640 PH: (850) 488-8600 FAX: (850) 488-7053 Designee: Chuck Smith, Program Manager
Georgia	Mr. Chris Stephens, Asst. State Fire Marshal Manufactured Housing Division State Fire Marshal's Office #2 Martin Luther King Jr. Dr., #620 West Tower Atlanta, GA 30334 PH: (404) 656-3687 or (404) 656-9498 FAX: (404) 657-6971 Designee: Joe Hall (IPIA)
Hawaii	Use HUD address following.
Idaho	Mr. Dave Munroe, Administrator Division of Building Safety — Building Bureau 1090 E. Watertower Street Meridian, ID 83642 PH: (208) 334-3896 FAX: (208) 855-9399 Designee: Tom Rodgers
Illinois	Mr. John D. Reilly Jr., P.E. Illinois Department of Public Health Division of Environmental Health General Engineering Section 525 W. Jefferson Street Springfield, IL 62761 PH: (217) 782-5830 FAX: (217) 785-0253
Indiana	Ms. Richelle (Shelly) Wakefield, CBO Director Codes Enforcement Division Office of the State Building Commissioner 302 Washington Street, Room W246 Indianapolis, IN 46204 PH: (317) 232-1407 FAX: (317) 232-0146
Iowa	Mr. Ronald Humphrey Manufactured Housing Coordinator Iowa State Building Code Bureau 215 E. 7th Street Des Moines, IA 50319-0001

State	State Administrative Agency

State   *State Administrative Agency*

PH: (515) 281-5821
FAX: (515) 242-6299

Kansas   Use HUD address following.

Kentucky   Mr. Harry J. Rucker, Chief
Manufactured Housing Division
State Fire Marshal's Office
101 Sea Hero Road, Suite 100
Frankfort, KY 40601-4322
PH: (502) 573-0365
FAX: (502) 573-1004

Louisiana   Sammy J. Hoover, SAA Agent
Manufactured Housing State Administrative Agency
Louisiana Manufactured Housing Commission
P.O. Box 4249
Baton Rouge, LA 70821
PH: (225) 342-5919
FAX: (225) 342-2999

Maine   Mr. Robert V. LeClair, Executive Director
Manufactured Housing Board
Office of Licensing and Registration
35 State House Station
Augusta, ME 04333-0035
PH: (207) 624-8678
FAX: (207) 624-8637

Maryland   Mr. James Hanna, Director
Dept. of Housing & Community Development
Maryland Code Administration
100 Community Place
Crownsville, MD 21032-2023
PH: (410) 514-7220
FAX: (410) 987-8902

Massachusetts   Use HUD address following.

Michigan   Mr. Kevin DeGroat
Office of Local Government and Consumer Services
6546 Mercantile Way
Lansing, MI 48909-8203
PH: (517) 241-9347
FAX: (517) 241-6301

Minnesota   Mr. Randy E. Vogt
Minnesota Dept. of Administration
Building Codes & Standards Division
121 E. 7th Place, Suite 408
St. Paul, MN 55101-2181

State	*State Administrative Agency*
	PH: (651) 296-9927
	FAX: (651) 297-1973
Mississippi	Mr. Eugene Humphrey
	State Fire Marshal's Office
	P.O. Box 79
	Jackson, MS 39205-0079
	PH: (601) 359-1061
	FAX: (601) 359-1076
Missouri	Mr. Ronald Pleus, Manager
	Manufactured Housing Dept.
	200 Madison Street, Suite 500
	P.O. Box 360
	Jefferson City, MO 65102
	PH: (573) 751-7119 or (800) 819-3180
	FAX: (573) 522-2509
Montana	Use HUD address following.
Nebraska	Mr. Mark Luttich, Dept. Director
	Housing & Recreational Vehicle Dept.
	Nebraska Public Service Commission
	P.O. Box 94927
	300 The Atrium; 1200 "N" Street
	Lincoln, NE 68509-4927
	PH: (402) 471-0518
	FAX: (402) 471-7709
Nevada	Ms. Renee Diamond, Administrator
	Dept. of Business & Industry
	Manufactured Housing Division
	2501 E. Sahara Avenue, Suite 204
	Las Vegas, NV 89104-4137
	PH: (702) 486-4135
	FAX: (702) 486-4309
	Designee: Gary Childers
New Hampshire	Use HUD address following.
New Jersey	Mr. Paul Sachdeva, Manager
	New Jersey Division of Codes and Standards
	Dept. of Community Affairs
	P.O. Box 816101
	S. Broad Street
	Trenton, NJ 08625-0816
	PH: (609) 984-7974
	FAX: (609) 984-7952
New Mexico	Mr. John Alejandro, Director
	Manufactured Housing Division
	Regulation & Licensing Dept.

State *State Administrative Agency*

725 St. Michael's Drive
Santa Fe, NM 87504-7605
PH: (505) 827-7070
FAX: (505) 827-7074

New York

Mr. Tim King, Code Compliance Specialist
Division of Code Enforcement and Administration
Department of State
1530 Jefferson Road
Rochester, NY 14623
PH: (585) 427-9231
FAX: (585) 424-3658

North Carolina

Mr. C. Patrick Walker, Deputy Commissioner
Manufactured Building Division
Office of State Fire Marshal
P.O. Box 26387
Raleigh, NC 27611
PH: (919) 661-5880
FAX: (919) 662-4414
Designee: David Goins, Administrator
PH: (252) 753-3260

North Dakota

Mr. Paul Govig, Manager
North Dakota Dept. of Commerce
Division of Community Services
P.O. Box 2057
Bismarck, ND 58502
PH: (701) 328-5300
FAX: (701) 328-5320
Designee: Richard Gray, SAA Manager

Ohio

Use HUD address following.

Oklahoma

Use HUD address following.

Oregon

Mr. Mark S. Long, Administrator
Dept. of Consumer & Business Services
Building Codes Division
P.O. Box 14470
1535 Edgewater Drive, NW
Salem, OR 97309-0404
PH: (503) 378-4150
FAX: (503) 378-2322
Designee: Dana Roberts

Pennsylvania

Mr. John F. Boyer, Jr., Division Chief
Manufactured Housing
Office of Community Development
Center for Community Development
4th Floor, Commonwealth Keystone Building

State	*State Administrative Agency*
	Harrisburg, PA 17120-0225
	PH: (717) 720-7413
	FAX: (717) 783-4663
	Alternate: Mark Conte
	PH: (717) 720-7416
Rhode Island	Mr. Daniel R. DeDentro, State Building Commissioner
	State Building Code Commission
	One Capitol Hill
	Providence, RI 02908-5859
	PH: (401) 222-3032
	FAX: (401) 222-2599
	Designee: Richard A. Mancini
South Carolina	Mr. David Bennett, Administrator
	SC Dept. of Labor, Licensing & Regulation
	Real Estate & Building Code Professions
	P.O. Box 11329
	Columbia, SC 29211-1329
	PH: (803) 896-4682 or (803) 896-4688
	FAX: (803) 896-4814
South Dakota	Mr. Paul Merriman
	Office of State Fire Marshal
	118 W. Capitol Avenue
	Pierre, SD 57501-5070
	PH: (605) 773-3562
	FAX: (605) 773-6631
Tennessee	Mr. Randy Safer, Codes Enforcement Director
	Dept. of Commerce & Insurance
	Division of Fire Protection
	Davy Crockett Tower — Third Floor
	500 James Robertson Parkway
	Nashville, TN 37243-1162
	PH: (615) 741-7190
	FAX: (615) 253-3267
Texas	Ms. Cindy Bocz, Administrator
	Manufactured Housing
	Texas Dept. of Housing & Community Affairs
	P.O. Box 12489
	Austin, TX 78711-2489
	PH: (512) 475-2884 or (800) 500-7074
	FAX: (512) 475-4250
	Designee: Tim Irvine
	PH: (512) 475-1174
Utah	Mr. Daniel S. Jones, Director
	Construction Trades Bureau
	Division of Occupational & Professional Licensing

State	*State Administrative Agency*
	Dept. of Commerce
	P.O. Box 146741
	160 E. 300 South
	Salt Lake City, UT 84111-6741
	PH: (801) 530-6720
	FAX: (801) 530-6511
	Designee: Ed Short
	PH: (801) 530-6365
	FAX: (801) 580-3029
Vermont	Use HUD address following.
Virginia	Mr. Curtis McIver, Associate Director
	State Building Code Administration Office
	Dept. of Housing & Community Development, Jackson Center
	501 N. 2nd Street
	Richmond, VA 23219-1321
	PH: (804) 371-7160
	FAX: (804) 371-7092
	Designee: Lorenzo Dyer
Washington	Ms. Teri Ramsauer, Manager
	Office of Manufactured Housing
	Washington State Office of Community Development
	906 Columbia Street SW
	Olympia, WA 98504-8350
	PH: (360) 725-2960 or (800) 964-0852
	FAX: (360) 586-5880
West Virginia	Ms. Mitch Woodrum, Director
	Manufactured Housing
	West Virginia Division of Labor
	Building 6, Room B-749
	State Capitol Complex
	Charleston, WV 25305
	PH: (304) 558-7890
	FAX: (304) 558-2447
Wisconsin	Larry Swaziek, MH Program Manager
	Dept. of Commerce, Safety and Buildings Division
	MH Program Development Bureau, Thompson Commerce Center
	PO Box 2689
	201 W. Washington Avenue
	Madison, WI 53701-2689
	Telephone: (608) 267-7701
	FAX: (608) 283-7401
	E-mail: lswaziek@commerce.state.wi.us

State	*State Administrative Agency*
Wyoming	Use HUD address following.
HUD	Office of Manufactured Housing Programs Office of Regulatory Affairs and Manufactured Housing Dept. of Housing and Urban Development 451 Seventh Street SW, Room 9152 Washington, DC 20410-8000 Telephone: (202) 708-6423 or (800) 927-2891 FAX: (202) 708-4213 E-mail: MHS@hud.gov

Index